WILLIAM DWIGHT WHITNEY
LINGUISTIC SERIES

EDITED BY
FRANKLIN EDGERTON EDWARD SAPIR
EDUARD PROKOSCH EDGAR H. STURTEVANT
of the Department of Linguistics in Yale University

A HITTITE CHRESTOMATHY

BY

EDGAR H. STURTEVANT

AND

GEORGE BECHTEL

A HITTITE CHRESTOMATHY

BY

EDGAR H. STURTEVANT
Professor of Linguistics in Yale University

AND

GEORGE BECHTEL
Research Assistant in Linguistics in Yale University

WILLIAM DWIGHT WHITNEY
LINGUISTIC SERIES

WIPF & STOCK · Eugene, Oregon

Wipf and Stock Publishers
199 W 8th Ave, Suite 3
Eugene, OR 97401

A Hittite Chrestomathy
By Sturtevant, Edgar H. and Bechtel, George
Softcover ISBN-13: 978-1-7252-8015-1
Hardcover ISBN-13: 978-1-7252-8017-5
eBook ISBN-13: 978-1-7252-8016-8
Publication date 5/6/2020
Previously published by Linguistic Society of America,

PREFACE

This book is intended for beginners; it assumes no preliminary acquaintance either with cuneiform writing or with the Hittite language. It does not, however, contain all the material that a beginner will need. He must consult a grammar for a systematic account of the language, and he should also use a dictionary. The book is designed to go with Sturtevant's Comparative Grammar of the Hittite Language (Philadelphia, 1933) and Hittite Glossary (Baltimore, 1931). The latter book is out of date; but it will serve until a new edition can be prepared.

Although several lists of the cuneiform signs employed in Hittite texts have been published, none of them could readily be used with this book, since we frequently disagree with them in the method of transcribing the signs, especially the ideographic signs. Consequently it was necessary to include a sign-list. We have adopted Forrer's (Die Boghazköi-Texte in Umschrift 1.25–37) device of arranging this alphabetically rather than according to the shapes of the signs, since that arrangement is more convenient for the learner. One who is actually deciphering cuneiform texts needs a list of signs arranged according to shape; but our list is not intended for that purpose. Similarly we have restricted the list to signs that occur in our texts and a few others that are more or less closely related to them. The sign list may be used as a dictionary to the ideograms, many of which the present edition of the Glossary does not include in the transcription employed in this book.

Some scholars will be shocked at the amount of help we have given the learner. One advantage of such a book as ours is that it can easily be used without the aid of a teacher. But in any case it is, in our opinion, a mere waste of time to confront the student with riddles to solve. We believe that the quickest way to learn the cuneiform system of writing is to compare a cuneiform text with its transliteration, and so we set the two on opposite pages at the beginning. There follows ample cuneiform material for the student to test his competence without having the key before his eyes. Similarly we hope that much time will be saved by confronting the transliterated text with the translation.

The texts here included have all been published in transliteration elsewhere, and we have not repeated textual discussions except where necessary. All except the Anniwiyanis ritual are based upon more than one cuneiform tablet, and we enclose in square brackets only those parts of our text that do not appear on any of the tablets. We have indicated supplements in this way only in the transliterated text; the cuneiform text and the translation, therefore, should be used only with reference to that.

The commentary serves three purposes. First and most important, it provides information that the beginner is likely to need in order to understand the meaning and grammatical structure of the texts. Secondly, our readings and supplements are explained and justified where that seems necessary, and previously published critical apparatus are sometimes supplemented. Finally, new interpretations of words and passages are discussed as fully as seems desirable. No attempt is made to discuss the many historical, geographic, religious, and cultural questions raised by the texts. When it seems advisable to write a Hittite word in broad transcription, the system employed in the Glossary is followed; that is, only a minimum of phonetic interpretation is introduced. The more ambitious system used in HG can be defended only if constantly accompanied by syllabic transcription.

Bechtel prepared the sign list and autographed all the cuneiform texts except the Instructions for Temple Officials. Sturtevant is primarily responsible for the rest of the book. Both authors, however, have conferred about the work at all stages of its progress; it would be quite impossible to separate their contributions.

We are under obligations to the previous editors of the texts here included, and to other scholars whose names will be found in the commentary.

Eva Fiesel of Yale University has read the manuscript on the Hattusilis, the Telipinus, and the Code. E. Adelaide Hahn of Hunter College and Albrecht Götze of Yale University have read all the manuscript except the sign list and the cuneiform text. All three have made many valuable suggestions for which we express our thanks. Our obligation to Götze is particularly heavy; many of his contributions are acknowledged in the commentary, but the record is far from complete. Nevertheless we have not adopted all of his suggestions, and so he cannot be held responsible for any of our errors.

TABLE OF CONTENTS

ABBREVIATIONS

1. BOOKS AND PERIODICALS

All references are to pages, except cross references and references to HG.

AJP = American Journal of Philology, founded by B. L. Gildersleeve. Baltimore.

AO = Der Alte Orient, gemeinverständliche Darstellungen herausgegeben von der Vorderasiatisch-Aegyptischen Gesellschaft. Leipzig.

AOF = Archiv für Orientforschung, internationale Zeitschrift für die Wissenschaft vom vorderen Orient. Berlin. (The first two volumes are entitled: Archiv für Keilschriftforschung.)

AOr. = Archiv Orientální, Journal of the Czechoslovak Oriental Institute. Prague.

BoSt. = Boghazköi-Studien, herausgegeben von Otto Weber. 10 parts. Leipzig. 1917–24.

BoTU = Die Boghazköi-Texte in Umschrift, von Emil Forrer. 2 vols. = 41 and 42 Wissenschaftliche Veröffentlichung der Deutschen Orient-Gesellschaft. Leipzig. 1922–6.

BSL = Bulletin de la Société de Linguistique de Paris. Paris.

Congr. 1 = Actes du Premier Congrès International de Linguistes. The Hague. 1928.

Congr. 2 = Actes du Second Congrès International de Linguistes. Geneva. 1931.

Deimel = P. Anton Deimel, Šumerisches Lexikon. Rome. 1928—.

Delaporte = L. Delaporte, Syllabaire Hittite Cunéiforme = Manuel de la Langue Hittite I. Paris. 1929.

Forrer = E. Forrer, Die Keilschrift von Boghazköi = BoTU 1.

Forrer, Forsch. = E. Forrer, Forschungen. Berlin. 1926—.

Friedrich, Vert. = J. Friedrich, Staatsverträge des Ḫatti-Reiches in Hethitischer Sprache. 2 parts = Hethitische Texte in Umschrift mit Uebersetzung und Erläuterungen. Heft II, IV = MVAG 31.1, 34.1. Leipzig. 1926–30.

Glossary = E. H. Sturtevant, Hittite Glossary, Words of Known or Conjectured Meaning with Sumerian Ideograms and Akkadian Words Common in Hittite Texts = Language Monographs, published by the Linguistic Society of America, No. 9. Baltimore. 1931.

Glotta = Glotta, Zeitschrift für griechische und lateinische Sprache. Göttingen.

Götze, AM = A. Götze, Die Annalen des Muršiliš = Hethitische Texte in Umschrift. Heft VI. = MVAG 38. Leipzig. 1933.

Götze, Hatt. = A. Götze, Ḫattušiliš, der Bericht über seine Thronbesteigung nebst den Paralleltexten = Hethitische Texte in Umschrift. Heft I = MVAG 29.3. Leipzig. 1925.

Götze, KlH = A. Götze, Kleinasien zur Hethiterzeit, eine geographische Untersuchung = Orient und Antike 1. Heidelberg. 1924.

Götze, Kulturgeschichte = Kulturgeschichte des alten Orients 3.1. A. Götze, Kleinasien = W. Otto, Handbuch der Altertumswissenschaft. Dritte Abteilung. Erster Teil. Dritter Band. Dritter Abschnitt. Erste Lieferung. Munich. 1933.

Götze, Madd. = A. Götze, Madduwattaš = Hethitische Texte in Umschrift. Heft III. = MVAG 32.1. Leipzig. 1928.

Götze, NBr. = A. Götze, Neue Bruchstücke zum Grossen Text des Ḫattušiliš und den Paralleltexten = Hethitische Texte in Umschrift. Heft V = MVAG 34.2. Leipzig. 1930.

Götze-Pedersen, MS = A. Götze and H. Pedersen, Muršilis Sprachlähmung, ein hethitischer Text mit philologischen und linguistischen Erörterungen = Det Kgl. Danske Videnskabernes Selskab, Historisk-filologiske Meddelelser 21.2. Copenhagen. 1934.

HG = E. H. Sturtevant. A Comparative Grammar of the Hittite Language. Philadelphia. 1933. [References to this book are to paragraphs. They are enclosed in square brackets.]

Hrozný, CH = F. Hrozný, Code Hittite Provenant de l'Asie Mineure. Première Partie = Hethitica, collection de travaux relatifs à la philologie, l'histoire, et l'archéologie hittites 1.1. Paris. 1922.

Hrozný, SH = F. Hrozný, Die Sprache der Hethiter, ihr Bau und ihre Zugehörigkeit zum indogermanischen Sprachstamm, ein Entzifferungsversuch = BoSt. 1, 2. Leipzig. 1917.

HT = Hittite Texts in the Cuneiform Character from Tablets in the British Museum. London. 1920.

IF = Indogermanische Forschungen. Berlin and Leipzig.

JA = Journal Asiatique, recueil trimestrielle de mémoires et de notices relatifs aux études orientales, publié par la Société Asiatique. Paris.

JAOS = Journal of the American Oriental Society. New Haven.

JSOR = Journal of the Society of Oriental Research. Chicago.
KBo. = Keilschrifttexte aus Boghazköi. 6 parts = 30, 36 Wissenschaftliche Veröffentlichung der Deutschen Orient-Gesellschaft. Leipzig. 1921–3.
KlF = Kleinasiatische Forschungen. Weimar.
Korošec, Vert. = V. Korošec, Hethitische Staatsverträge = Leipziger Rechtswissenschaftliche Studien 60. Leipzig. 1931.
KUB = Staatliche Museen zu Berlin, Vorderasiatische Abteilung, Keilschrift-Urkunden aus Boghazköi. Berlin. (27 Hefte have been issued. 1921–34.)
Lang. = Language, journal of the Linguistic Society of America. Baltimore.
MDOG = Mitteilungen der Deutschen Orient-Gesellschaft. Berlin.
MSL = Mémoires de la Société de Linguistique de Paris. Paris.
MVAG = Mitteilungen der Vorderasiatisch-Aegyptischen Gesellschaft. Leipzig.
RHA = Revue Hittite et Asianique, organe de la Société des Études Hittites et Asianiques. Paris.
Sommer, AU = F. Sommer, Die Aḫḫijavā-Urkunden = Abhandlungen der Bayerischen Akademie der Wissenschaften, phil.-hist. Abteilung, NF 6. Munich. 1932.
TAPA = Transactions of the American Philological Association. Middletown, Conn.
VBoT = A. Götze, Verstreute Boghazköi-Texte. Marburg a.d. Lahn. 1930.
Weidner, Stud. = E. Weidner, Studien zur Hethitischen Sprachwissenschaft 1 = Leipziger Semitistische Studien 7.1,2. Leipzig. 1917.
Witzel, HKU = F. Witzel, Hethitische Keilschrift-Urkunden in Transcription und Uebersetzung mit Kommentar 1 = Keilinschriftliche Studien 4. Fulda. 1924.

2. OTHER ABBREVIATIONS

A = The Ritual of Anniwiyanis (below, pp. 100–26).
abl. = ablative
acc. = accusative
act. = active
adv. = adverb
aor. = aorist
Bo. = Boghazköitexte (unpublished)
C = Selections from the Code (below, pp. 202–28).

cf. = compare
dat. = dative
determ. = determinative
e.g. = for example
f. = following page
ff. = following pages
fn. = footnote
gen. = genitive
H = The Apology of Hattusilis (below, pp. 42–99).
I = Instructions for Temple Officials (below, pp. 127–74).
ib. = ibidem
imper. = imperative
ind. = indicative
infin. = infinitive
inst. = instrumental
loc. = locative
masc. = masculine
midd. = medio-passive
neut. = neuter.
NF = Neue Folge
nom. = nominative
obl. = oblique
part. = participle
perf. = perfect
pl. = plural
pres. = present
pret. = preterit
sg. = singular
s.v. = sub voce
subj. = subjunctive
Sum. = Sumerian
T = The Proclamation of Telipinus (below, pp. 175–200)
VAT = Vorderasiatische Abteilung Tontafel (unpublished)
verb. n. = verbal noun
w. = with
[ ] In transliterated text square brackets enclose material not preserved on a tablet but supplied by conjecture. In a note they enclose references to paragraphs of HG.
<> In transliterated text angular brackets enclose material erroneously omitted by the scribe.

( ) In transliterated text and translation line numbers are enclosed in parentheses. Bits of transliterated text enclosed in parentheses are to be disregarded; they were erroneously written by the scribe. In translation words in parentheses do not represent any specific word or words in the text, but have been inserted for clearness or for the sake of better English style. In the first column of the sign list relatively rare phonetic values are enclosed in parentheses. In the second column of the sign list words enclosed in parentheses are determinatives. Parts of Hittite, Akkadian, or Sumerian words are sometimes enclosed in parentheses to indicate that they were sometimes omitted either in writing or in pronunciation.

Sumerian words are printed in capitals and Akkadian words and sounds in Italic capitals. Hittite words and all cited words are in Italics.

Hittite nouns, adjectives, and pronouns are generally cited in the nominative, and a form not receiving a case label is nominative. If the number is not designated, it is singular. Verbs are cited either in the stem form (with following hyphen) or in the pres. 3 sg.

INTRODUCTION TO THE CUNEIFORM SYSTEM OF WRITING.

Since this book is intended chiefly for Indo-Europeanists who have had no previous experience with cuneiform writing, and who are likely to be working without the aid of an instructor, the following paragraphs contain information which would be taken for granted by an Assyriologist but which it is hoped will save the beginner a good deal of confusion. The student should read also the chapter in HG on Writing and Pronunciation, especially pp.34-50. We shall discuss the signs from the twofold point of view of how they are made, and how they are to be interpreted.

Form of the Signs. The Hittites borrowed their form of writing from the Babylonians, who got it from the Sumerians, who in turn got it possibly from a still earlier people. We can trace the varying shapes of the signs back through two millenia, but even the earliest Sumerian records that have been found show the system at a considerable stage of advancement. The signs must have been originally pictographic, as were the Egyptian hieroglyphs or the most archaic Chinese, but after becoming conventionalized they tended to lose their original shapes, and only in the case of a relatively small number can we be sure what the original picture was. Thus the sign for 'hand' , archaic , is obviously a picture of a hand, though in the usual Hittite form it has lost a finger. On the other hand, the sign for 'sky' or 'god' gives no indication of its original picture, which is, however, shown by earlier forms (, very early) to have been that of a star.

It is characteristic of any system of writing that it is affected in its external form by the nature of the writing material most commonly used, and the cuneiform is one of the best examples of this. The characters on the very earliest Mesopotamian documents are drawn with lines. The peculiar wedge-shaped symbols came in as a result of the use of clay tablets; the scribe held in his left hand the tablet moulded of soft clay, and in his right a stylus with rectangular cross-section, with which he impressed the characters. Now if such a stylus is held horizontal with its edge against the tablet, it produces a groove in the clay; it is natural, however, to hold the stylus at more or less of an angle, with the result that the groove is deeper at one end and tapers out at the other; this gives the wedge-shaped impression which very early became conventional. A wedge thus corresponds to a straight line of the original picture-character. A wedge looks on the tablet something like this: In modern copying of the signs, however, it is customary to omit part of the outline of the wedge, and make a drawing like this: If the student will remember that three or four strokes of the pen represent a single impression of the ancient stylus, and that in turn the most complicated signs are built up out of single wedges, the characters will appear much less formidable. It is suggested that, as reproducing the signs is the best way to fix them in the memory, the learner should devote considerable time to this, and as a necessary preliminary should practice drawing single wedges until he is fairly proficient. The best way to draw a wedge is to make two sides of the head in separate strokes of the pen, thus: , and the rest in a single stroke, thus: So for a vertical wedge:

According to the position in which the stylus was held, we distinguish five types of wedge: 1) horizontal 2 & 3) oblique , 4) vertical and 5) a wedge which the Germans call *Winkelhaken,* formed by reversing the stylus and holding it almost perpendicular to the tablet, so that the impression was made by the end rather than the side-edge. Theoretically there might be other wedges, but none actually occur. *These five elements alone, singly or in various combinations, serve to make up the entire cuneiform syllabary.* Thus the student will note that a few signs consist each of but a single wedge: *aš,* numeral 1, *u* or 10. Others consist of two wedges, of like or unlike type, as *bal,* *tap,* *pár,* *me,* *ni,* *nu,* *be;* etc., etc. Note that the relative position of the wedges is also important. Signs containing three wedges are: *iz,* *pa,* *hat,* GAG, *a,* *an,* SAL, KUR, *tin;* etc., etc. So others contain four, five, or any number of wedges. Some of the more complicated signs may be more easily remembered by noting that they contain certain groups of wedges which occur also in other signs; thus the group , which alone is the sign *hi,* appears also in *am,* *ne,* *gi, im*, and *it*; the group , which alone is *a*, forms also part of the signs *e*, *kal*, *kar*, DUG. The student will discover other such groups for himself. Other signs differ only slightly from one another, and may be learned together: Compare *pí*, GUD, *ul*, *ša*, *ga*, *ta*, DUG, AMAR, SISKUR; or *ki* versus *di*. An extreme case of this may be noted in *ku* and *ma*, which differ only in the length of the horizontal wedges. Other signs may be considered as combinations of two or more simpler signs; while in many cases this is merely a mnemonic device it often has an actual historical basis; thus a comparatively recent one is *ya*, made up of *i* and *a*; and ideograms of the type of KÚ 'eat', which is composed of KA 'mouth' and NINDA 'bread', are shown to be combinations by both their form and their meaning.

Variants. The long historical development of the cuneiform signs led to modifications of them at various times and places and frequently to the use of more than one variety at the same time and place. The Hittite documents show a considerable number of such variants, a sign even assuming several forms in the course of a single tablet. This circumstance contrasts with classical Assyrian, where variants are rare.

In the texts in this book, we have not followed the original tablets slavishly in the matter of particular forms of signs, but have attempted to introduce the student to the variants gradually, by using one form until he has a chance to become familiar with it, then shifting to another, and so on. As it happens, the variants are by no means so troublesome as they might at first appear. In only a few cases (for example *li* and), does a sign assume forms that are radically different from one another, though several do show a considerable number of variations. There are certain well defined types which may be noted. 1) Variation in the number of the wedges: This may be due to the omission of a wedge or more that belong to the sign in an earlier form, as for *qa*, for *šu* —in both these cases the simpler variant is more common in the Hittite texts, and *šu* is even modified occasionally to the form . Variation in number is most frequent in the case of groups of three or more parallel wedges, where the number may usually be three, four, five or even more indiscriminately; so or URU, or *tàk*, or MEŠ, or É. On the other hand, in some cases such variants are avoided by the scribes when they would confuse two signs nearly alike; thus *ku* and TÚG are always carefully distinguished. 2) Variation in the position of the wedges: for example or *uš* (similarly *iš* etc.), or *ša* (similarly *ta* and other signs of the same sort); etc. Groups of parallel wedges are likely to be varied, as or *ku*, or URU—but on the other hand note that *at* and *la* are kept distinct. 3) Substitution of one type of wedge for another: for a good example, note the forms of *al* (most typically) in the sign list. A horizontal wedge is likely to be substituted for an oblique one, though the converse is rare; and a short oblique is often not to be distinguished from a small *Winkelhaken*. The student will further note that in a given group of wedges, the same set of variations is likely to occur in whatever combination the group occurs: thus the group mentioned above, may have the variant form whether it occurs alone as *ḫi*, or as part of the signs *am*, *ne*, *gi*, *im* or *it*.

Interpretation of the Signs. In regard to meaning, we may notice three stages in the development of any system of writing. First are signs (pictographs) which in form are crude pictures, intended to convey a meaning, but without any special connection with the spoken language. In the second stage, the signs attach themselves to particular words, first words of concrete meaning and later also abstract ones and even derivational or grammatical elements; and there is thus a connection with the spoken language, insofar as its concepts, but not its actual sounds, are concerned. Such word signs are called *ideograms*. The third stage comes when a sign that denotes a particular word comes to be associated with the sound of that word rather than its meaning, and then may be used to indicate other words or parts of words which have nothing in common as far as meaning goes, but which have a similar sound. As such phonetic signs are likely to stand for single syllables, we have a *syllabic* system of writing. The cuneiform script had already progressed as far as this at the time of the very earliest Sumerian documents known. It still preserved abundant ideograms, however, and never reached a fourth stage which would have dispensed with these altogether and relied entirely on phonetic signs. In fact, even today we still employ a certain number of ideographic signs in addition to our alphabetic writing, because of their convenience: such characters as &, $, %, the Arabic numerals, and various symbols used in chemistry, astronomy, or other technical subjects, are of this nature.

A survival of the earliest stage, when a sign conveyed a general meaning without standing for a particular word, may be noted in the fact that in the writing as we have it many single signs have more than one ideographic meaning; some, in fact, have a great many: for example, the sign means either 'sky' or 'god', similar concepts, but expressed in Sumerian by quite different words, AN and DINGIR respectively. In other cases a multiplicity of meanings for a sign resulted from the falling together into one form of two or more originally different pictures. Two methods were developed for a partial avoidance of ambiguity in the meaning of a sign. In the first place, other ideograms, called *determinatives,* were appended (usually prefixed, in certain cases suffixed), without being pronounced; these denoted the general class to which the word in question belonged. Thus the sign used alone, means 'omen', Sumerian IZKIM; with the sign LÚ 'man' prefixed, it is read AGRIG and denotes a certain kind of official. The determinative is customarily transcribed by writing it above the line: ^{LÚ}AGRIG. The use of determinatives came to be standard not only with ideograms, but also with words spelled phonetically; thus LÚ is prefixed to all nouns denoting masculine occupations or professions, GIŠ, which alone means 'tree' or 'wood', to names of trees or wooden objects, and so forth. The second method of avoiding ambiguity was in the use of phonetic signs, known as *phonetic complements,* appended to ideograms, and representing the last portion of the word in question. Thus the sign 'god' is regularly followed in Akkadian texts by some such sign as *LUM,* showing that the combination is to be read *ILUM,* the Akkadian word for 'god'. Hittite complements are also frequent. A parallel in modern usage is such a writing as 1*st* for 'first', the phonetic complement indicating that the ordinal instead of the cardinal is intended.

The development of phonetic values out of ideographic was assisted by the fact that the majority of simple Sumerian words were either monosyllables or nearly so; thus the sign mentioned above, which was pronounced AN when it meant 'sky', came readily to be used with the value of the syllable AN regardless of meaning. This sort of thing is similar to the rebuses which children today sometimes play with, where for example a picture of the insect known as a bee is used also for the verb 'be', or for the same syllable in some longer word. The multiplicity of ideographic values led naturally to a multiplicity of phonetic values. The taking over of the system by the Akkadians from the Sumerians resulted in further complications; for as the ideograms were taken over and pronounced with Akkadian readings, new phonetic values often became attached to the signs from these. Thus the sign as an ideogram meant 'hand', Sumerian ŠU, and had also acquired the phonetic value ŠU; now the Akkadian word for 'hand' was *qātu*, whence the sign came to have also the phonetic value *qat*. The development of polyphones, as the variant readings are called, went so far that they form one of the greatest difficulties for modern scholars in reading Akkadian texts.

Fortunately the Hittites in taking over the syllabary simplified it greatly. Many signs still have ideographic as well as phonetic values, but only a few maintain more than one phonetic value, at least in Hittite words. In a few cases, the Hittites added new phonetic values to the syllabary, in particular the value *wi* for the sign 'wine' (Sum. GEŠTIN), and some others which are not very common.

Beside the employment of the same sign in more than one value, we find also the converse of this, namely the occurrence of more than one sign in the same value. In the case of ideograms, this was due partly to the fact thar Sumerian had a great many homonyms, words which though pronounced alike were represented originally by different pictures—for example, GIR was the pronunciation of three words meaning 'foot', 'sword', and 'asphalt', represented respectively by the signs , and . Further the same word might often be designated by more than one sign, as NITA 'male' by or . In a similar manner, phonetic values were often duplicated. When we add together both ideographic and phonetic values, the number of readings for a given sign is sometimes extreme: Thus Thureau-Dangin, in *Les Homophones Sumériens,* lists twelve signs in the value *gar,* sixteen in the value *du,* most of these signs having of course other values also. In order to avoid confusion, Assyriologists have adopted the practice of marking homophones by means of diacritical marks or subscript numerals. Unfortunately, there have been almost as many systems of marking as there have been scholars in the field; but within recent years the system of Thureau-Dangin, which we also follow in this book, has been widely accepted; by this system, the commonest sign in any given value is left unmarked, the next commonest is marked with an acute accent, the next with a grave accent, and after that subscript numerals are used. Thus we write GÍR 'sword', GÌR 'foot', GIR_4 'asphalt'; or *šu* and *šú.* *The student should not be misled into thinking that these accents have any phonetic signification; they serve merely to indicate to the reader of a transcription which sign was employed in the original.* Though the Hittites eliminated most of the homophones, we necessarily employ the same accentuation that is used in Akkadian and Sumerian.

Method of Transcribing Hittite. Obviously there are several possible ways of transcribing in Latin letters a language written in cuneiform. One method is to ignore the exact form of the original altogether and spell as the users of the language might have spelled had they employed the Latin alphabet. This, which we call the "broad" transcription, involves more or less phonetic interpretation, particularly in a language like Hittite whose phonetics are so much in doubt, but it is useful in lists of words and other places where the particular spelling is not important. Thus the Hittite word could be read *dāi, dai, tāi, tai,* according to our opinion of the quality of the consonant and the quantity of the vowel. The alternative is to transcribe the original sign for sign and leave the reader his choice of interpretation; thus we write *da-a-i,* representing each sign by its normal value, and separating the signs by hyphens. This is the "syllabic" transcription, which is generally used, for texts and elsewhere. The simplest form of such transcription would be to use one reading for each sign, and only one, but this would be actually misleading in cases where a sign has more than one phonetic value, and it is further desirable to give a certain amount of interpretation particularly for those words which are not spelled out as Hittite. Hence scholars employ as many readings for a sign as may be required, and use such devices as writing determinatives above the line, and different kinds of type (Roman capitals for Sumerian, Italic capitals for Akkadian, lower-case letters being reserved for spelled-out Hittite words); but always keep distinct the individual signs so that the original cuneiform can always be reconstructed from the transcription. In other words, the aim is *the maximum interpretation possible without destroying the actual picture of the text.*

The transcription of a Hittite text is complicated by the great amount of material which was written ideographically—not only ideograms proper, that is single signs standing for words, but also the numerous Sumerian and Akkadian phrases which were spelled as such, though the Hittite equivalents must have been substituted for them in reading the tablets. Obviously, if we were to try and transcribe such phrases by the corresponding Hittite, we should destroy the actual picture of the text. In the case of single ideograms in Akkadian texts, scholars regularly transcribe with the Akkadian words, the lack of hyphens showing that the word in question is represented by a single sign and not spelled out. This is impossible in Hittite in the numerous cases where the Hittite readings for ideograms are either uncertain or quite unknown; hence the custom has become established of using the Sumerian values even in those cases where we know the Hittite equivalents. The choice of the Sumerian readings is not meant to imply that the scribes knew Sumerian; it simply provides the best means of identifying the signs. Unfortunately, there is often difficulty in determining what the correct Sumerian reading for a given sign is, and there has been a good deal of variation on the part of editors of published texts. In this book we have, except in a few cases, followed the readings of Deimel, *Šumerisches Lexikon*, the latest standard work on the subject. A few ideograms are read as Akkadian, for example *ŠUM* 'name', which is the construct form of Akk. *šumu*, and apparently developed into an ideogram because in forms like *šum-šu* 'his name', the first syllable was spelled with a single phonetic sign.

We may illustrate the treatment of more complex groups of signs by the common group 𒀭𒅆𒉌, which denotes the dative case of the word for 'god', in Hittite probably *karimni*. Sign for sign we might read *an-ši-ni,* taking the commonest values of the three signs in question, but the result is obviously not the Hittite word. As a matter of fact, the first sign is the ideogram for 'god', Sumerian DINGIR, Akkadian (in this case-form) *ilim*. The second sign, 𒅆, has in Akkadian the additional phonetic value *lim,* and is here used as an Akkadian phonetic complement to identify more clearly the word intended by the ideogram. Assyriologists would transcribe the combination 𒀭𒅆 by *ilim*^{lim}, placing the complement above the line to show that it is not to be repeated in the pronunciation. In Hittite the two signs were taken over as a group and a further phonetic complement added, the *ni* which represents the last syllable of the Hittite word. We transcribe the entire combination DINGIR-*LIM-ni,* a mixed mode of representation which nevertheless shows exactly what we are dealing with in the text.

The Sign List. A list of cuneiform signs can be arranged in either of two ways, according to the shape of the signs or alphabetically according to the readings. The former arrangement is obviously preferable for one working directly from the cuneiform, and Assyriologists regularly choose it for the added reason that the numerous polyphones in Akkadian would make an alphabetical list awkward, while in classical Assyrian, which is taken as a standard, there are practically no formal variants. In Hittite, on the other hand, variants in form are numerous, and a list by readings is more practicable. The list in this book is therefore arranged in this way, following the usual alphabetical order for Hittite (*b* listed under *p, d* under *t, g* and *q* under *k,* and, further, *s* and *š* together), with cross-references for those polyphones that occur. Since all the cuneiform texts in this book are accompanied by transliteration, we have not felt it necessary to include an index of signs arranged by form.

In the sign list, phonetic and ideographic values are listed in separate columns; the list is fairly complete for the former, but we have not attempted to include more ideograms than are needed in using this book. Ideograms are given in the form used in transcription, and meanings are given for reference, though by no means fully. For compound ideograms and for spelled out Sumerian words, the student should consult a dictionary; except in certain cases where a combination was treated as a single sign even in Sumerian—for example, the combination KU(G).UD is read KUBABBAR 'silver' and listed separately. Where an ideogram is generally used with a determinative, we have indicated that fact in the column of meanings by adding the determinative in parentheses. In the column of phonetic values, no attempt has been made to distinguish between Hittite, Akkadian and Sumerian, since in most cases the values given are valid for all three. For example, the sign *ra* has this value in Hittite in a word like *a-ra-an-zi* 'they arrive', in Akkadian in a word like *RA-BU-Ú* 'great', and in Sumerian in a word like ANŠU.KUR.RA 'horse', literally 'mountain ass', where the first two signs are ideograms and RA a Sumerian combination of phonetic complement and genitive ending. However, in the Hittite texts, a considerable number of phonetic values occur only in Akkadian words, and others in Hittite only in proper names, and these, together with a few others which occur in Hittite words only to a very limited extent, we enclose in parentheses, the purpose being to guide the learner in distinguishing common from less common signs.

One other point should be noted, namely that in the cuneiform writing those phonetic signs which end in a stop consonant never distinguish whether that consonant is voiced, voiceless, or (in Akkadian) emphatic. Thus the sign is read *ad* or *at*, or in Akkadian also *aṭ*, according to the following consonant; in the list we give only *at*, the other readings being implied. The same rule applies to the sibilants *s*, *ṣ* and *z*, but of these Hittite words have only *z*; *š* is everywhere kept distinct.

We have included also references to Forrer's sign list, and to Delaporte where his readings differ from ours, and have also given the standard Assyrian forms of the signs for those students who wish to inquire farther into the cuneiform.

LIST OF CUNEIFORM SIGNS.

For the convenience of the learner we have selected and listed below 75 of the most common Hittite signs for preliminary practice. For variant forms, and for additional values, some of which are not infrequent, one should consult the main list on the following pages.

a	*ḫi*	*la*	*pí*	*du*
aḫ	ḪI.A	*li* or	*ra*	*tu*
al	*ḫu*	*lu*	*ri*	DUMU
an	*i*	LÚ	*ru*	*u*
ar	*in*	*ma*	*ša*	*ú*
aš	*ir*	*me*	SAL	*ul*
at	*iš*	MEŠ	*šar*	*un*
az	*it*	*mi*	*še*	URU
e	*iz*	*mu*	*ši*	*uš*
É	*ka*	*na*	*šu*	*ut*
EGIR	GAL	*ni*	*da*	*wa*
en	*kán*	*nu*	*ta*	*ya*
eš	*ki*	*pa*	*tar*	*za*
ḫa	*ku*	*pár*	*te*	*zi*
ḫar	KUR	*be*	*ti*	1

Phonetic Values	Ideograms	Signs	Forrer	Assyrian Forms
a	A *water*		1	
aḫ, iḫ, uḫ	—		10	
ak	—		6	
—	1. AGRIG (LÚ) *an official.* 2. IZKIM *omen.*		3 (ABRIG)	
al	—		11	
am	—		13	
—	AMA *mother.*		14	
—	AMAR *calf, young animal.*		326 (ZUR)	
an	1. AN *sky.* 2. DINGIR *god; as determ. read* D.		16	
—	ANŠU *ass*		17	
ap	AB (GIŠ) *window.*		2	
—	ÁB *cow.*		159 (LID)	
—	APIN (GIŠ) *plow.*		18	
ar	—		19	
aš, (rum)	—		21	
at	—		4	
az	—		22	
e	—		58	
—	É *house; temple.*		59	

Phonetic Values	Ideograms	Signs	Forrer	Assyrian Forms
—	EGIR *back; again*		61	
el	—		62	
—	EME *tongue*		64	
—	EMÈ *she-ass*	(=ANŠU.SAL)	—	
en	EN *master, lord*		65	
—	EBUR *harvest*		60	
—	ERÍN *troops, soldiers*		318 (ZAB) (Delaporte ERÍM)	
—	1. ERUM *slave* 2. NITÁ *male*		20 (ARAD) (usually transcribed IR	
eš	1. numeral 30 2. *SIN* (D) *moon*		67	
—	EZEN × ŠE *festival*		68 (EZEN)	
ḫa	-KU$_6$ *fish*		99	
ḫal	ḪAL (LÚ) *seer*		100	
(*ḫap*) see under KUR$_4$				
ḫar, ḫur, (*mur*)	—		101	
(*ḫaš*) see under *tar*				
—	ḪAŠḪUR (GIŠ) *date-palm*		102	
(*ḫat*) see under *pa*				
ḫé	—		103	
ḫi	—		104	
—	ḪI.A *plural sign*		105 (Delaporte ḪÁ, ZUN)	
ḫu	MUŠEN *bird; also post-determ.*		107	
—	ḪUL *bad, evil*		110	

Phonetic Values	Ideograms	Signs	Forrer	Assyrian Forms
ḫur see under *ḫar*				
i	—		111	
—	I (determ., really Roman numeral, see under *diš*			
iḫ see under *aḫ*				
ik	1. IG (GIŠ) *door* 2. GÁL		117	
—	IGI see under *ši*			
il	—		118	
—	ILDÁG (GIŠ) *a kind of tree or wood.*	(=A-AM)	—	
im	1. IM *clay* 2. IM *storm, wind;* ^{D}IŠKUR *storm-god* 3. NÍ (NÍ.TE *self*)		119	
in	—		120	
—	INIM see under *ka*			
ip	—		113	
ir	—		122	
iš	IŠ (LÚ) *charioteer*		123	
—	*IŠTAR* (D) *Goddess Ishtar.*		124	
it	—		114	
—	ÍD *river; determ. w. names of rivers*		115	
—	ITU *month*		125	
is	GIŠ *tree; wood; also determ.*		126	

Phonetic Values	Ideograms	Signs	Forrer	Assyrian Forms
—	IZI see under *ne*			
—	IZKIM see under AGRIG			
ga	GA *milk*	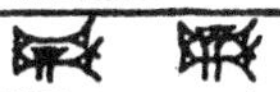	69	
ka	1. KA *mouth, face* 2. INIM *word*	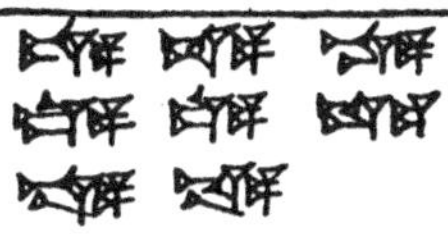	127	
—	KÁ *door, gate*	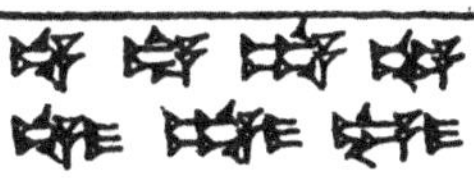	128	
qa	—	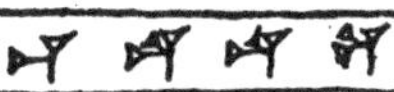	219	
—	KA × IM *thunder*		131	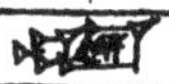
—	KA × GAG *nose*		129	
—	KA × U *mouth*		134	
—	1. KA × UD *tooth* 2. KA × KÁR Götze ZA 6.70-3		135	1)  2) 
—	KA × A read NAG; KA × ME read EME; KA × NINDA read KÚ.			
—	1. GAG (GIŠ) *peg, stick of wood* 2. DÙ *build, make*		73	
(*gal*)	GAL *large, great; chief*		74	
—	GÁL see under *ik*			
—	GÀL see under URU			
kal, dan	KAL *strong;* ^{D}KAL	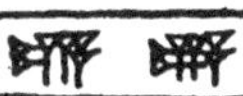	137	
—	GAM *down; with*		75	
(*kam*)	1. KAM *suffix with expressions of time* 2. UTÚL *pot; pot of food*		138	
kán	GÁN *field*		76	
—	GAB see under DU_8			
kap	GÙB *left hand; left*		136	

Phonetic Values	Ideograms	Signs	Forrer	Assyrian Forms
(gar)	1. GAR *to place* 2. NINDA *food, bread* 3. NÍG *Sum. noun-forming prefix*		77	*šá*
kar	KAR 1) *find;* 2) cf. An. 1.4		139	
—	QAR		220	
—	KARAŠ *army*	(=KI.KAL.BAD)	—	
—	KAŠ see under *pí*			
—	$KAŠ_4$ *run*		141	
—	GAŠAN *mistress, lady*		78	
—	KASKAL *road, campaign*		140 (KAS)	
kat, kit_9	GAD *cloth; napkin*		72	
(gaz)	—		79	
—	GEŠTIN see under *wi*			
—	GEŠTU(G) see under *wa*			
gi	GI *reed; also determ.*		80 (GE)	
ki	KI *earth*		142	
—	GIG *ill, illness*		83	
—	GIGIR (GIŠ) *chariot*		84	
—	GIM *as, when*		87	
—	GÌM *female slave*		15 (AMAT)	
—	KIN *work, serve; service*		144	

Phonetic Values	*Ideograms*	*Signs*	*Forrer*	*Assyrian Forms*
kir, (*piš*)	—		88 (*gir*)	
—	GÌR *sword*		89	
—	GÌR *foot*		91	
—	GIR_4 *asphalt*		56 (DUL)	
—	GIŠ see under *iz*			
kiš			145	
—	KISLAḪ *granary*	(=KI.UD)	—	
—	GÍD see under *pu*			
kit_9 see under *kat*				
—	GIDIM *spirit of the dead*		81 (GEDIM)	
(*gu*)	GU		92	
—	GÚ 1) *neck*; 2) *leguminous plant*		93	
ku	1. DÚR *sit, sitting* 2. TUKUL (GIŠ) *weapon*		146	
—	KÚ *eat*		130	
—	KU(G) *bright*		23 (AZAG)	
—	GUL *strike, smite*		96	
(*kum*)	—		148	
—	KUN *tail*		149	
—	GUNNI *stove, hearth*	(=KI.IZI)	—	
—	GUB see under *du*			
—	GÚB see under *kap*			
—	KUBABBAR *silver*	(=KU(G).UD)	—	

Phonetic Values	Ideograms	Signs	Forrer	Assyrian Forms
(gur)	—		97	
(kur)	KUR *land, country; also as determ.*		150	
—	1. KÚR (LÚ) *enemy, (hostile* 2. PAB *protect*		216 (PAP)	
(ḫap)	KUR_4		86 (GIL)	
(su)	KUŠ *hide, leather; also as determ.*		240	
—	GUŠKIN *gold*		(=KU(G).GI) —	
—	GUD *ox*		94	
la	—		152	
—	LAL *bind*		154	
—	LÀL *honey*		156	
lam	—		157	
li	—		158	
(*lí*) see under *ni*				
(*lik*) see under *ur*				
(*lim*) see under *ši*				
(*liš*)	LIŠ *tray, bowl*		163	
lu	1. DIB *seize* 2. UDU *sheep*		164	
—	LÚ *man; determ. w. words denoting occupations*		166	
—	LUGAL *king*		168	

Phonetic Values	*Ideograms*	*Signs*	*Forrer*	*Assyrian Forms*
(*lum*)	—		170	
ma	—		171	
—	MÁ (GIŠ) *ship*		172	
(*maḫ*)	MAḪ *mighty, virile, strong*		173	
mar	—		178	
(*maš*) see under *pár*				
—	MÁŠ 1) *goat* 2) *relative*		179	
me	1. ME *place, set; take* 2. *ME* 100		180	
—	MÊ *battle*		9 (AG+ZAB)	
(*m*)*eš*	MEŠ *plural sign*		181	
mi	MI 1) *black* 2) *night*		182	
(*miš*) see under PISÀN				
(*mit*) see under *be*				
mu	1. MU *year* 2. MU (LÚ) *cook*		185	
(*mur*) see under *ḫar*				
—	MUŠEN see under *ḫu*			
na	—		193	
—	NAG *drink*		179 (Delaporte KA+A).	
nam	NAM *Sum. prefix forming abstract nouns*		199	
(*nap*)	—		195	

Phonetic Values	Ideograms	Signs	Forrer	Assyrian Forms
—	NA(D) (GIŠ) *bed*		196 (Forrer NAD, Delaporte NA_2)	
ne	1. IZI *fire* 2. BIL *burn*		201	
ni, (*lí*)	YÀ *oil, fat*		203	
—	NÍ see under *im*			
—	NÍG see under GAR			
—	NIN *sister*		206	
—	NINDA see under GAR			
nir	NIR		208	
—	NITA see under *uš*			
—	NITÁ see under ERUM			
nu	NU *Sum. negative prefix*		210	
—	NUMUN *seed; offspring, descendant*		147 (KUL)	
—	NUN *large, powerful*		211	
—	NUNUZ (ZÁ) *pearl*		212	
(*ba*)	BA		24	
pa, (*ḫat*)	1. PA *foreman* 2. PA (GIŠ) *staff*		213	
pal	BAL 1) *revolt;* 2) *pour a libation;* 3) *time, occasion*		27	
—	PAN (GIŠ) *bow*		215	
—	BANŠUR (GIŠ) *sacrificial table*	(=URU.URUDU)	—	
—	PAB see under KÚR			

Phonetic Values	Ideograms	Signs	Forrer	Assyrian Forms
—	BABBAR see under *ut*			
pár, (*maš*)	1. BAR 2. numeral ½		30	
pat, *bat*,	BAD see under *be*			
—	BÀD *fortification*		26	
be, *pat*, *pít*, (*mit*)	1. BAD 2. TIL *end, complete* 3. UG_6 *death; die*		25	
pí, (*bi*)	KAŠ *beer*		32	
—	BIL see under *ne*			
(*bíl*), (*píl*)	GIBIL *new*		33	
pir see under *ut*				
(*piš*) see under *kir*				
(*miš*)	PISÀN *a kind of vessel*		218	
pít see under *be*				
pu, (*bu*)	GÍD *long*		35	
(*bur*)	—		37	
ra	—		221	
ri, *tal*	—		223	
ru	ŠUB (GIŠ) *inventory*		225	
(*rum*) see under *aš*				
(*sa*)	—		226	
ša	—		244	
—	ŠAḪ *pig*		248	

For *ṣa*, *ṣi*, etc. (Akkadian only) see under *z*.

Phonetic Values	*Ideograms*	*Signs*	*Forrer*	*Assyrian Forms*
—	SAG *head, person*		228	
—	ŠA(G) *heart, interior; within*		246	
šal	SAL *woman; also determinative*		249	
—	ŠÁM *buy; price*		250	
—	SANGA (LÚ) *priest*		230	
(*šap*)	—		245	
šar	1. ŠAR *orchard, garden; vegetable; also post-determ. w. names of vegetables.* 2. SAR *write*		251	
še	ŠE 1) *grain;* 2) (*of domestic animals*) *fat*		252	
—	$ŠE_{12}$ 1) *winter, pass the winter;* 2) *rest, be quiet*		108 (HU+A) (Delaporte, $ŠE_{4}$)	
—	ŠEŠ *brother*		254	
—	SI *horn*		232	
ši, (*lim*)	IGI *eye, face; first; opposite*		255	
—	SIG *thin, weak*		235	
—	SÍG *wool; also as determ.*		236	

Phonetic Values	Ideograms	Signs	Forrer	Assyrian Forms
—	SÍG + SAL *mother-sheep*		95 (GUKKAL)	
—	SIG_5 *right, auspicious*		256 (ŠIG)	
—	SIG_7 *yellow*		229 (SAMAG)	
—	SILÁ *lamb*		237 (SÍL)	
—	^{D}*SIN* see under *eš*			
—	SIPAD (LÚ) *shepherd*		234 (SIB)	
—	SIR		239	
—	SÌR *sing*		231 (SER)	
šir	—		259	
—	SISKUR *sacrifice*		327 (ZÚR) (Delaporte SIGISSE)	
(*su*) see under KUŠ				
šu	ŠU *hand*		261	
(*šú*)	—		262	
—	ŠUKUR (GIŠ) *staff, scepter*	(= ŠI.GAG)	—	
—	SUM *set, place, give*		243	
(*šum*)	ŠUM *name*		267	
—	ŠUB see under *ru*			
(*šur*)	—		268	
—	ŠUDUN (GIŠ) *yoke*		264 (Delaporte ŠUDUL)	
da	—		38	
ta	—		269	
taḫ, tùḫ	—		40 (*daḫ*)	
ták	DAG (GIŠ or D) *sacred throne*		39 (*dag*)	
tal see under *ri*				

Phonetic Values	Ideograms	Signs	Forrer	Assyrian Forms
dam	DAM *wife*		41	
(tam) see under *ut*				
dan see under *kal*				
tap	TAB *cover*		270	
—	DAR *bright, varicolored*		42	
tar, (haš)	—		271	
(tàš)	ZÍZ *a kind of spelt*		272	(*dš*)
—	DÉ		43	
te	TE		273	
di	1. DI *judgement, lawsuit* 2. SILIM *health, safety*		44	
ti	TI *live; life*		275	
—	TIL see under *be*			
(tim)	—		276	
tin, (din)	TIN *beverage*		277	
—	DINGIR see under *an*			
—	DIB see under *lu*			
(dir)	SA$_5$ *red*		49	
(tir)	TIR (GIŠ) *forest*		278	
(diš)	numeral 1; also used as determ. w. names of men, read I		50	
du	GUB *stand, standing*		51	
—	DÙ see under GAG			
—	DU$_6$, *TÍL mound of a ruined city*		274 (TEL)	

Phonetic Values	Ideograms	Signs	Forrer	Assyrian Forms
—	1. DU_8 2. GAB *breast*		70	
tu	—		279	
tu_4 see under *tum*				
tuḫ see under *taḫ*				
—	DUG *pot, vessel; also as determ.*		54	
—	TÚG *cloth, clothing; also as determ.*		281	(Ass. same as ku)
—	TUKU *be angry*		280 (TUG)	
—	TUKUL see under *ku*			
(*túl*)	TÚL *well, spring*		282	
tum, *tu_4*	—		283	
—	1. DUMU *child, son* 2. TUR *small*		286	
(*tup*), (*dup*)	DUB *writing-tablet*		52	
—	DUBBIN (GIŠ) *wheel*		53	
(*dur*)	—		57	
—	DÚR see under *ku*			
—	TUR see under DUMU			
u	1. numeral 10 2. U (D) *god Dattaš or Tešup*		288	
ú	Ú, ŠAM *grass, plant; also as determ.*		289	

Phonetic Values	Ideograms	Signs	Forrer	Assyrian Forms
—	1. Ù *dream* 2. Ù *and*		290	
uḫ see under *aḫ*				
uk	—		293	
—	UG₆ see under *be*			
—	UGU *over, upper*		187 (MUḪ)	
—	UKÙ see under *un*			
ul	—		295	
um	—		296	
un	UKÙ *person, people*		297	
up	—		291	
ur, (*lik*)	UR *dog*		299	
úr	ÚR *lap; body-member*		300	
—	1. URU *city; also as determ.* 2. GÀL		303	
—	ÙRU		98 (GÚR)	
—	URUD(U) *copper*		304	
uš	NITA *male*		305	
ut, pir, (*tam*)	1. UD *day* 2. BABBAR *white* 3. UTU (D) *sun-god, sun;* DUTU-ŠI *title of Hittite monarch*		292	
—	UDU see under *lu*			

Phonetic Values	*Ideograms*	*Signs*	*Forrer*	*Assyrian Forms*
—	UTÚL see under KAM			
uz	—		308	
—	UZU *flesh, meat; also as determ.*		309	
wa	GEŠTU(G) *ear*		310	(*pi*)
wi	1. GEŠTIN *wine* 2. GEŠTIN (GIŠ) *vine*		311	
ya	—		112	
—	YÀ see under *ni*			
za, (*ṣa*)	—		317	
—	ZÁ *stone; also as determ.*		194 (NÁ) (Delaporte, NA₄)	
—	ZAG 1) *right, suitable* 2) *side* 3) *border, limit, territory*		320	
—	ZABAR *bronze*	(=UD.KA.BAR)	—	
zé, (*ṣe*)	—		322	
zi, (*ṣí*)	ZI *will, desire*		323	
zu, (*ṣú*)	*ZÚ half-shekel*		324	
	"Glossenkeil"		328, 329	
	Sign used by scribe to show gap in copy		330	

NUMERALS: 1 2 3 4 5 6 7 8 9
10 11 etc.; 20 30 40 50
60 (*ŠU-ŠI*) 70 80 90 100 (*ME*) (1 *ME*)
1000 (*LI-IM*) ½ (BAR)

THE APOLOGY OF HATTUSILIS

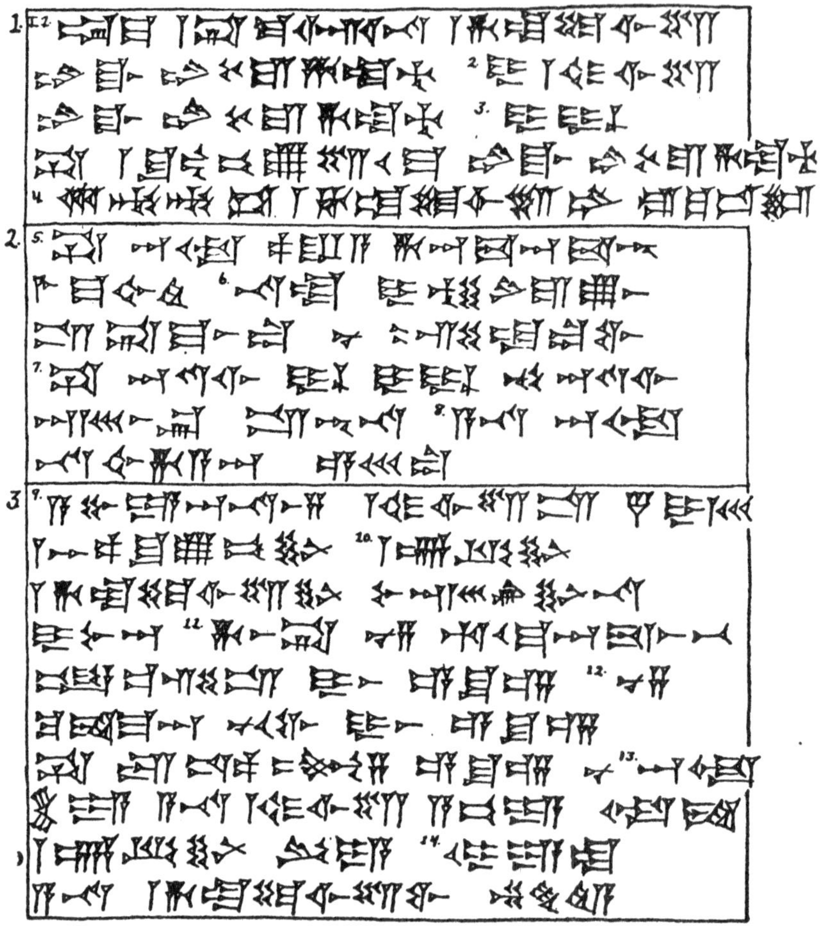

THE APOLOGY OF HATTUSILIS

1

(1.1) *UM-MA* ^{I}*TA-BA-AR-NA* ^{I}*ḪA-AT-TU-ŠI-LI* LUGAL.GAL LUGAL KUR ^{URU}*ḪA-AT-TI* (1.2) DUMU ^{I}*MUR-ŠI-LI* LUGAL.GAL LUGAL KUR ^{URU}*ḪA-AT-TI* (1.3) DUMU.DUMU-*ŠÚ ŠA* ^{I}*ŠU-UP-PÍ-LU-LI-U-MA* LUGAL.GAL LUGAL KUR ^{URU}*ḪA-AT-TI* (1.4) ŠA(G).BAL.BAL *ŠA* ^{I}*ḪA-AT-TU-ŠI-LI* LUGAL ^{URU}*KU-UŠ-ŠAR*

2

(1.5) *ŠA* ^{D}*IŠTAR pa-ra-a ḫa-an-da-an-da-tar me-ma-aḫ-ḫi* (1.6) *na-at* DUMU.NAM.LÚ.GÀL.LU-*aš iš-ta-ma-aš-du nu* ⸗*zi-la-du-wa* (1.7) *ŠA* ^{D}UTU-*ŠI* DUMU-*ŠÚ* DUMU.DUMU-*ŠÚ* NUMUN ^{D}UTU-*ŠI* DINGIR.MEŠ-*aš-kán iš-tar-na* (1.8) *A-NA* ^{D}*IŠTAR na-aḫ-ḫa-a-an e-eš-du*

3

(1.9) *A-BU-YA-an-na-aš-za* ^{I}*Mur-ši-li-iš* 4 DUMU.MEŠ ^{I}*Ḫal-pa-šu-lu-pí-in* (1.10) ^{I}NIR.GÁL-*in* ^{I}*Ḫa-at-tu-ši-li-in* ^{SAL}DINGIR.MEŠ.IR-*in-na* DUMU.SAL-*an* (1.11) *ḫa-aš-ta nu-za ḫu-u-ma-an-da-aš-be* EGIR-*iz-zi-iš* DUMU-*aš e-šu-un* (1.12) *nu-za ku-it-ma-an nu-u-wa* DUMU-*aš e-šu-un ŠA* KUŠ.KA.TAB.ANŠU-*za e-šu-un nu* (1.13) ^{D}*IŠTAR* GAŠAN-*YA A-NA* ^{I}*MUR-ŠI-LI A-BI-YA* Ù-*it* ^{I}NIR.GÁL-*in* ŠEŠ-*YA* (1.14) *u-i-ya-at A-NA* ^{I}*ḪA-AT-TU-ŠI-LI-wa* MU.KAM.ḪI.A *ma-ni-in-ku-*

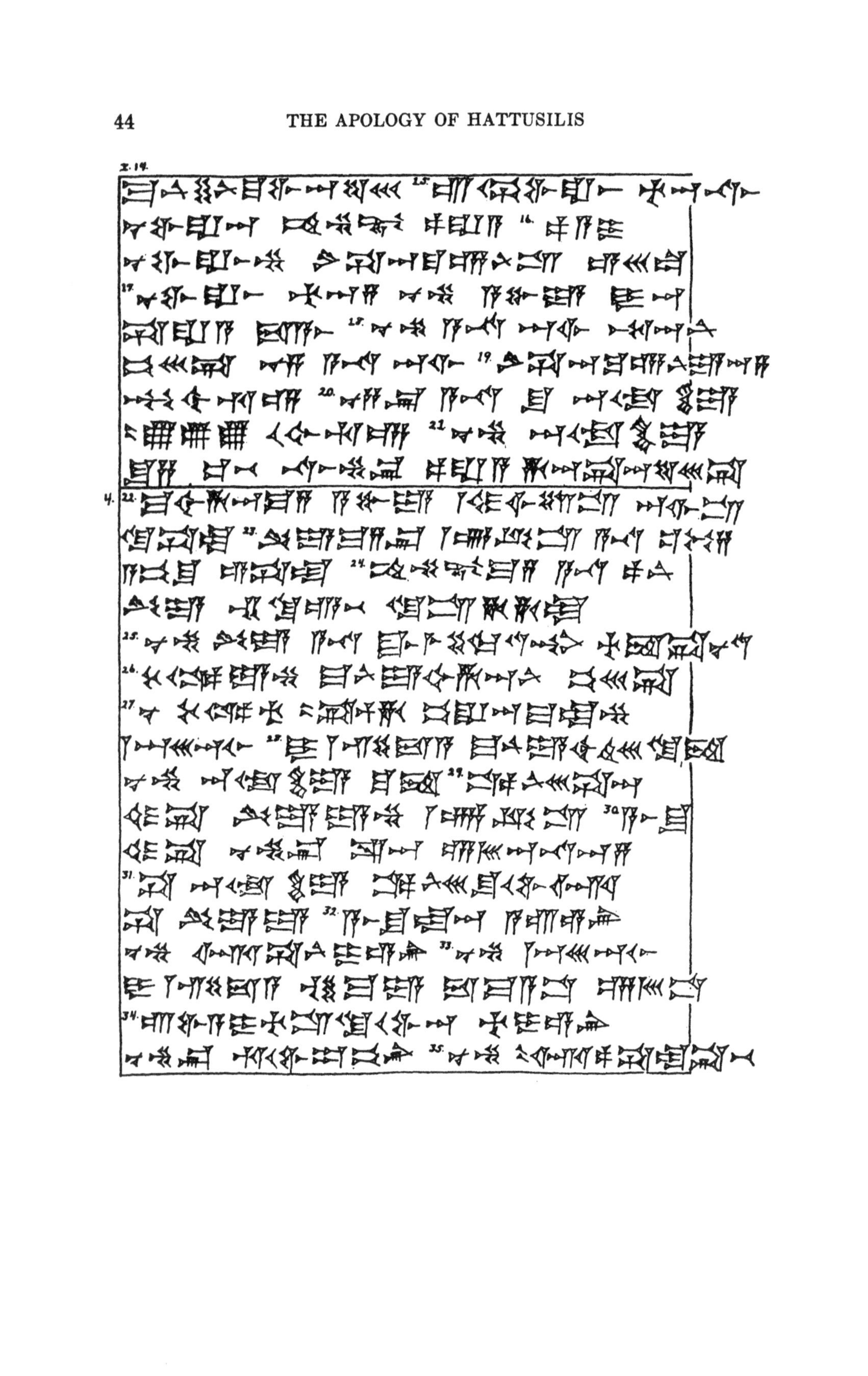

I. 14.

wa-an-te-eš (1.15) *Ú-UL-wa-ra-aš* TI-*an-na-aš nu-wa-ra-an am-mu-uk pa-ra-a* (1.16) *pa-a-i nu-wa-ra-aš-mu* ^{LÚ}*ša-an-ku-un-ni-iš e-eš-du* (1.17) *nu-wa-ra-aš* TI-*an-za nu-mu A-BU-YA* DUMU-*an ša-ra-a da-a-aš* (1.18) *nu-mu A-NA* DINGIR-*LIM* ERUM-*an-ni pí-eš-ta nu-za A-NA* DINGIR-*LIM* (1.19) ^{LÚ}*ša-an-ku-un-ni-ya-an-za* BAL-*aḫ-ḫu-un* (1.20) *nu-za-kán A-NA* ŠU ^{D}*IŠTAR* GAŠAN-*YA* ⸗*lu-ú-lu u-uḫ-ḫu-un* (1.21) *nu-mu* ^{D}*IŠTAR* GAŠAN-*YA* ŠU-*za IṢ-BAT na-aš-mu-kán pa-ra-a ḫa-an-ta-an-te-eš-ta*

4

(1.22) *ma-aḫ-ḫa-an-ma-za A-BU-YA* ^{I}*Mur-ši-li-iš* DINGIR-*LIM-iš ki-ša-at* (1.23) ŠEŠ-*YA-ma-za-kán* ^{I}NIR.GÁL-*iš A-NA* ^{GIŠ}GU.ZA *A-BI-ŠU e-ša-at* (1.24) *am-mu-uk-ma-za A-NA PA-NI* ŠEŠ-*YA* EN KARAŠ *ki-iš-ḫa-ḫa-at* (1.25) *nu-mu* ŠEŠ-*YA A-NA* GAL-*ME-ŠE-DI-UT-TIM ti-it-ta-nu-ut* (1.26) KUR.UGU-*ya-mu ma-ni-ya-aḫ-ḫa-an-ni pí-eš-ta* (1.27) *nu* KUR.UGU-*TI* ⸗*ta-pár-ḫa pí-ra-an-ma-at-mu* ^{I} ^{D}*SIN*.^{D}U-*aš* (1.28) DUMU ^{I}*ZI-DA-A ma-ni-ya-aḫ-ḫi-eš-ki-it nu-mu* ^{D}*IŠTAR* GAŠAN-*YA ku-it* (1.29) *ka-ni-eš-ša-an ḫar-ta* ŠEŠ-*YA-ya-mu* ^{I}NIR.GÁL-*iš* (1.30) *a-aš-šu ḫar-ta nu-mu-kán* GIM-*an* UKÙ.MEŠ-*an-na-an-za* (1.31) *ŠA* ^{D}*IŠTAR* GAŠAN-*YA ka-ni-eš-šu-u-wa-ar ŠA* ŠEŠ-*YA-ya* (1.32) *a-aš-šu-la-an a-ú-e-ir nu-mu ar-ša-ni-i-e-ir* (1.33) *nu-mu* ^{I} ^{D}*SIN*.^{D}U-*aš* DUMU ^{I}*ZI-DA-A nam-ma-ya da-ma-a-uš* UKÙ.MEŠ-*uš* (1.34) *ú-wa-a-i-ti-iš-ki-u-wa-an ti-i-e-ir nu-mu-kán ḫu-u-wa-ap-pí-ir* (1.35)

nu-mu 𒑱*ar-pa-ša-at-ta-be* [*nu-*]*mu* ŠEŠ-*YA* ^{I}NIR.GÁL-*iš* (1.36) *A-NA* ^{GIŠ}DUBBIN *lam-ni-ya-at* ^{D}*IŠTAR-ma-mu* GAŠAN-*YA* Ù-*at* (1.37) *nu-mu* Ù-*it ki-i me-mi-iš-ta* DINGIR-*LIM-ni-wa-at-ta* (1.38) *am-mu-uk tar-na-aḫ-ḫi nu-wa li-e na-aḫ-ti* (1.39) *nu* DINGIR-*LIM-za pár-ku-u-e-eš-šu-un nu-mu* DINGIR-*LUM ku-it* GAŠAN-*YA* ŠU-*za ḫar-ta* (1.40) *nu-mu* 𒑱*ḫu-u-wa-ap-pí* DINGIR-*LIM-ni* 𒑱*ḫu-u-wa-ap-pí ḫa-an-ne-eš-ni* (1.41) *pa-ra-a Ú-UL ku-wu-pí-ik-ki tar-na-aš Ú-UL-ma-mu* (1.42) ^{GIŠ}TUKUL ^{LÚ}KÚR *ku-wa-pí-ik-ki še-ir wa-aḫ-nu-ut* (1.43) ^{D}*IŠTAR-mu-za-kán* GAŠAN-*YA ḫu-u-ma-an-da-za-be da-aš-ki-it* (1.44) *ma-a-an-mu iš-tar-ak-zi ku-wa-pí nu-za-kán ir-ma-la-aš-be* (1.45) *ŠA* DINGIR-*LIM ḫa-an-da-an-da-tar še-ir uš-ki-nu-un* (1.46) DINGIR-*LUM-mu* GAŠAN-*YA ḫu-u-ma-an-da-za-be* ŠU-*za ḫar-ta am-mu-uk-ma-za* (1.47) *pa-ra-a ḫa-an-da-a-an-za ku-it* UKÙ-*aš e-šu-un* (1.48) *A-NA PA-NI* DINGIR.MEŠ *ku-it pa-ra-a ḫa-an-da-an-da-an-ni i-ya-aḫ-ḫa-at* (1.49) *ŠA* DUMU.NAM.LÚ.GÀL.LU-*UT-TI* ḪUL-*lu ut-tar Ú-UL ku-wa-pí-ik-ki* (1.50) *i-ya-nu-un* DINGIR-*LUM-mu-za-kán* GAŠAN-*YA ḫu-u-ma-an-da-za-be da-aš-ki-ši* (1.51) *Ú-UL e-eš-ta nu-mu* DINGIR-*LUM* GAŠAN-*YA* 𒑱*ku-wa-ya-mi me-e-ḫu-ni* (1.52) *Ú-UL ku-wa-pí-ik-ki še-ir ti-ya-at A-NA* ^{LÚ}KÚR-*mu* (1.53) *pí-ra-an kat-ta Ú-UL ku-wa-pí-ik-ki tar-na-aš* (1.54) *Ú-UL-ma-mu A-NA* EN *DI-NI-YA* $^{\text{LÚ.MEŠ}}$*ar-ša-na-at-tal-la-aš* (1.55) *ku-wa-pí-ik-ki pí-ra-an kat-ta tar-na-aš ma-a-na-aš* INIM ^{LÚ}KÚR (1.56)

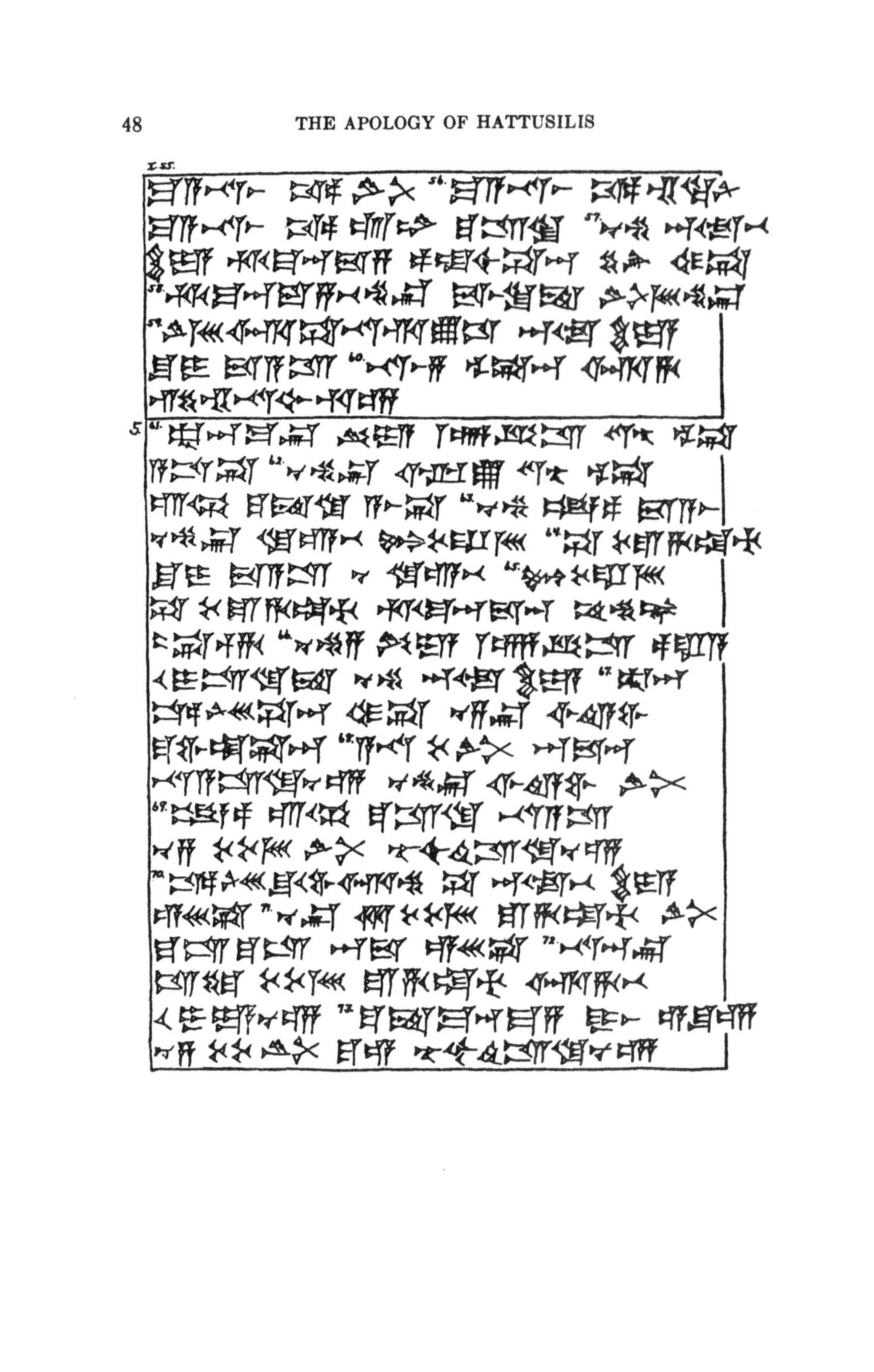

ma-a-na-aš INIM EN *DI-NI ma-a-na-aš* INIM É LUGAL *ku-iš-ki* (1.57) *nu-mu* ^{D}*IŠTAR-be* GAŠAN-*YA ḫu-u-ma-an-da-za pa-la-aḫ-ša-an še-ir ḫar-ta* (1.58) *ḫu-u-ma-an-da-za-be-mu-kán da-aš-ki-it* ^{LÚ}KÚR.MEŠ-*mu-kán* (1.59) $^{LÚ.MEŠ}$*ar-ša-na-tal-lu-uš* ^{D}*IŠTAR* GAŠAN-*YA* ŠU-*i da-a-iš* (1.60) *na-aš-za kat-ta-an ar-ḫa zi-en-na-aḫ-ḫu-un*

5

(1.61) GIM-*an-ma-kán* ŠEŠ-*YA* ^{I}NIR.GÁL-*iš ut-tar kat-ta a-uš-ta* (1.62) *nu-mu-kán* ḪUL-*lu ut-tar kat-ta Ú-UL ku-it-ki a-aš-ta* (1.63) *nu-mu* EGIR-*pa da-a-aš nu-mu-kán* KARAŠ ANŠU.KUR.RA.MEŠ (1.64) *ŠA* KUR ^{URU}*ḪA-AT-TI* ŠU-*i da-a-iš nu* KARAŠ (1.65) ANŠU.KUR.RA.MEŠ *ŠA* KUR ^{URU}*ḪA-AT-TI ḫu-u-ma-an-da-an am-mu-uk ta-pár-ḫa* (1.66) *nu-mu-za* ŠEŠ-*YA* ^{I}NIR.GÁL-*iš pa-ra-a u-i-iš-ki-it nu-mu* ^{D}*IŠTAR* GAŠAN-*YA* (1.67) GIM-*an ka-ni-eš-ša-an ḫar-ta nu-za-kán* IGI.ḪI.A-*wa ku-wa-at-ta-an* (1.68) *A-NA* KUR ^{LÚ}KÚR *an-da-an na-a-iš-ki-nu-un nu-mu-kán* IGI.ḪI.A-*wa* ^{LÚ}KÚR (1.69) EGIR-*pa Ú-UL ku-iš-ki na-a-iš nu-za* KUR.KUR.MEŠ ^{LÚ}KÚR *tar-aḫ-ḫi-iš-ki-nu-un* (1.70) *ka-ni-eš-šu-u-wa-ar-mu ŠA* ^{D}*IŠTAR-be* GAŠAN-*YA e-eš-ta* (1.71) *nu-kán* ŠA(G) KUR.KUR.MEŠ ^{URU}*ḪA-AT-TI* ^{LÚ}KÚR *ku-iš ku-iš an-da e-eš-ta* (1.72) *na-an-kán IŠ-TU* KUR.KUR.MEŠ ^{URU}*ḪA-AT-TI ar-ḫa-be u-i-ya-nu-un* (1.73) *ku-it-ma-an-ma-za* DUMU-*aš e-šu-un nu-za* KUR.KUR ^{LÚ}KÚR *ku-e tar-aḫ-ḫi-iš-ki-nu-un* (1.74) *na-at*

DUP-PU ḫa-an-ti-i DÙ-*mi na-at PA-NI* DINGIR-*LIM te-iḫ-ḫi*

6

(1.75) GIM-*an-ma* ŠEŠ-*YA* ^{I}NIR.GÁL-*iš IŠ-TU A-MA-AT* DINGIR-*LIM-ŠÚ* (1.76) *I-NA* KUR *ŠAP-LI-TI kat-ta pa-it* ^{URU}*Ḫa-at-tu-ša-an-ma ar-ḫa tar-na-aš* (2.1) *nu* ŠEŠ-*YA* DINGIR.MEŠ ^{URU}KUBABBAR-*TI* GIDIM.ḪI.A-*ya ša-ra-a da-a-aš* (2.2) *na-aš I-NA* KUR ^{URU}[*ŠAP-LI-TI kat-ta*] *pí-e-da-aš* EGIR-*az-ma* (2.3) KUR ^{URU}*GA-AŠ-GA*.ḪI.A *ḫu-u-ma-an-te-eš* KUR [*PÍ-*]*IŠ-ḪU-RU* KUR *IŠ-*[*ḪU-PÍ-I*]*T-TA* (2.4) KUR ^{URU}*DA-IŠ-TI-PA-AŠ-ŠA* BAL-*i-ya-at nu* KUR *L*[*A-AN-DA*] KUR ^{URU}*MA-RI-IŠ-TA* (2.5) URU.AŠ.AŠ.ḪI.A BÀD-*ya ar-ḫ*[*a da-*]*a-*[*ir*] *nu-kán* ^{LÚ}KÚR ^{ID}*Ma-ra-aš-ša-an-da-an* (2.6) *za-a-iš nu* KUR ^{URU} . . . [*wa-al*]*-aḫ-ḫi-eš-ki-u-wa-an da-a-iš* (2.7) *nu* KUR ^{URU}*KA-NI-EŠ wa-al-aḫ-ḫi-eš-ki-u-wa-an da-a-iš* (2.7b) . . . (2.8) ^{URU}*Ḫa-* . . . -[*ma*] ^{URU}*Ku-ru-uš-ta-ma-aš* ^{URU}*Gaz-zi-ú-ra-aš-ša* (2.9) *pí-di ku-ru-ri-ya-aḫ-ḫi-ir nu* URU.DU$_6$.ḪI.A ^{URU}*ḪA-AT-TI* (2.10) *wa-al-ḫi-iš-ki-u-wa-an ti-e-ir* ^{LÚ}KÚR KUR ^{URU}*DUR-MI-IT-TA-ma* (2.11) [KUR ^{URU}*TU-*]*ḪU-UP-PÍ-YA wa-al-ḫi-iš-ki-u-wa-an da-a-iš* (2.12) [*nu ku-it*] KUR *IP-PA-AŠ-ŠA-NA-MA dan-na-at-ta-an e-eš-ta* (2.13) [*nu-kán pa-*]*ra-a I-NA* KUR ^{URU}*ŠU-WA-TA-RA a-ar-aš-ki-it* (2.14) [^{URU}] . . . *-ša-aš-ma-kán* ^{URU}*Iš-ta-ḫa-ra-aš-ša* 2-*e-el iš-pár-zi-ir* (2.15) [*ku-e-ma* KUR.KUR.ḪI.A]-*TIM iš-tap-pa-an e-eš-ta nu-uš-ma-aš I-NA* MU 10 KAM (2.16) Š[E] NUMUN *Ú-UL an-ni-eš-ki-ir pa-ra-a-ma* MU.KAM.ḪI.A-*aš ku-it-ma-an*

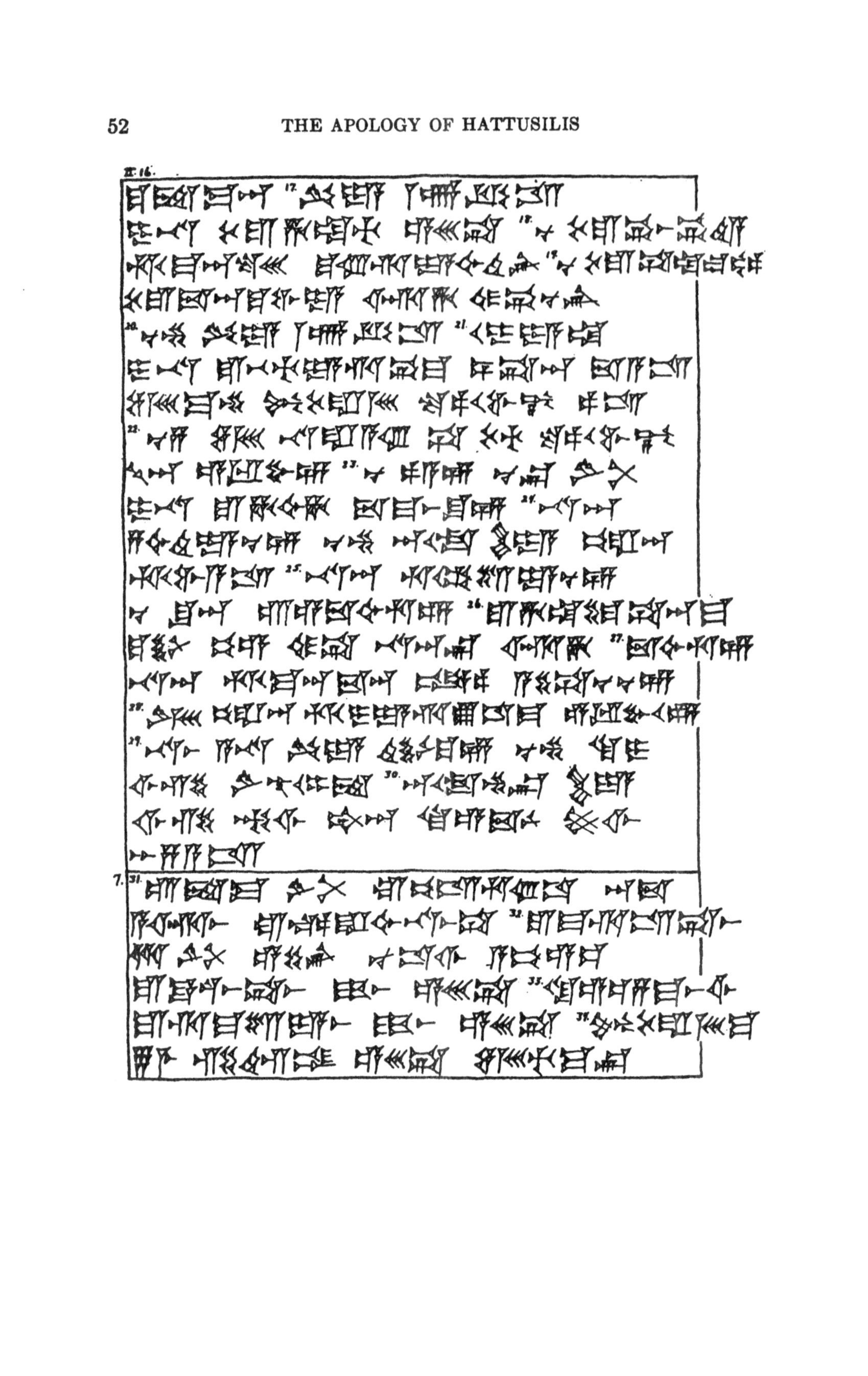

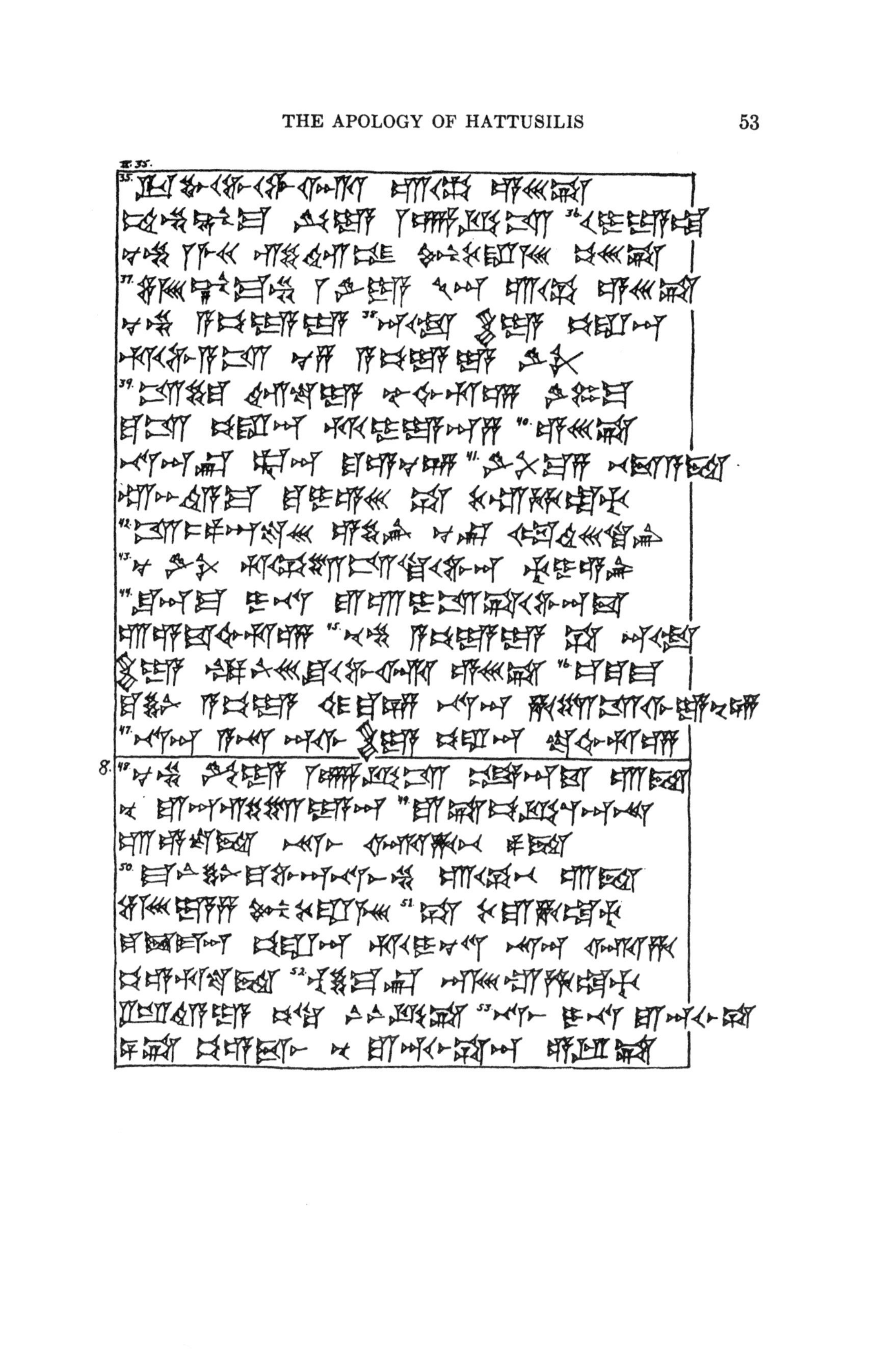

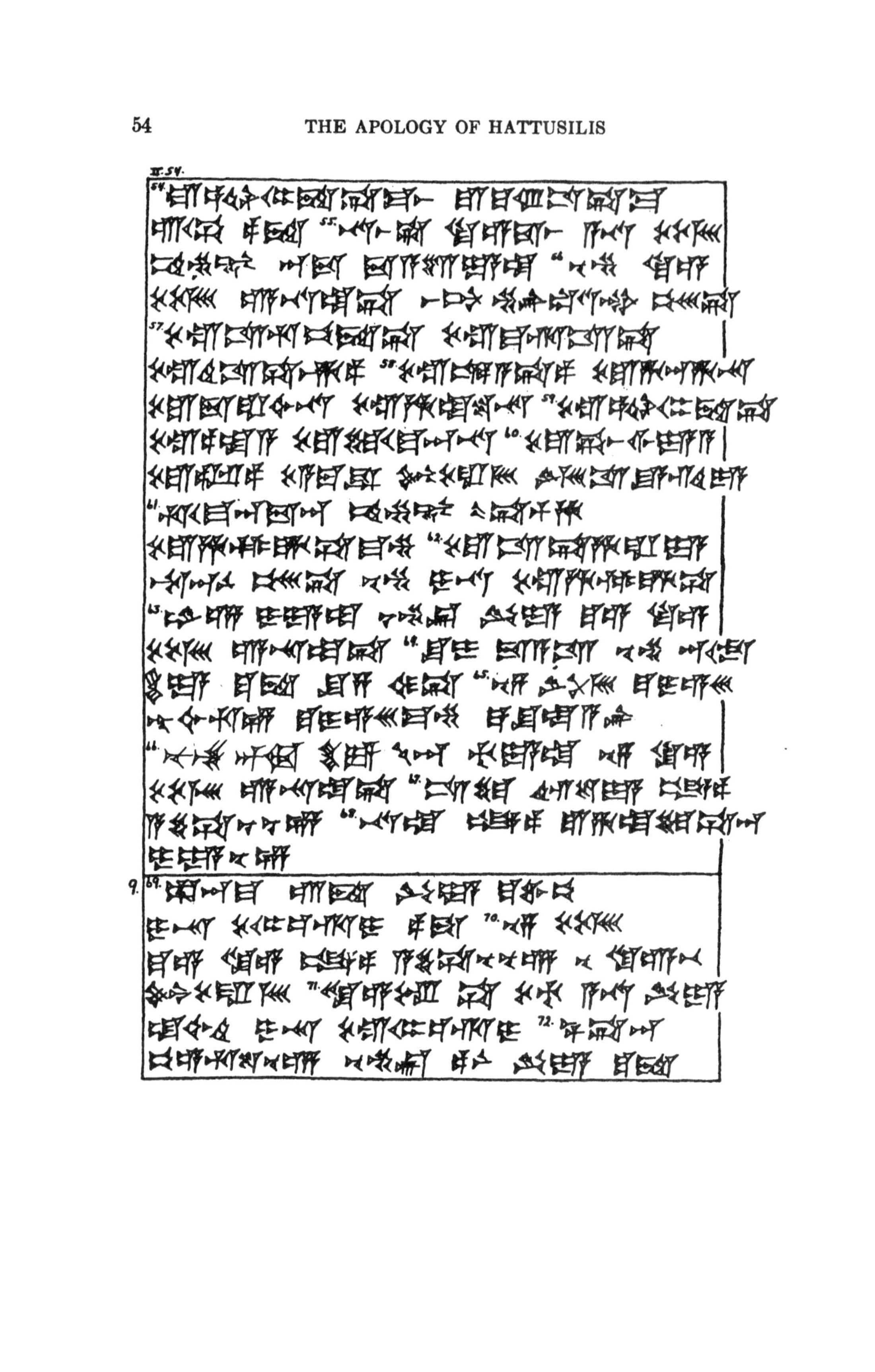

II. 54.

9.

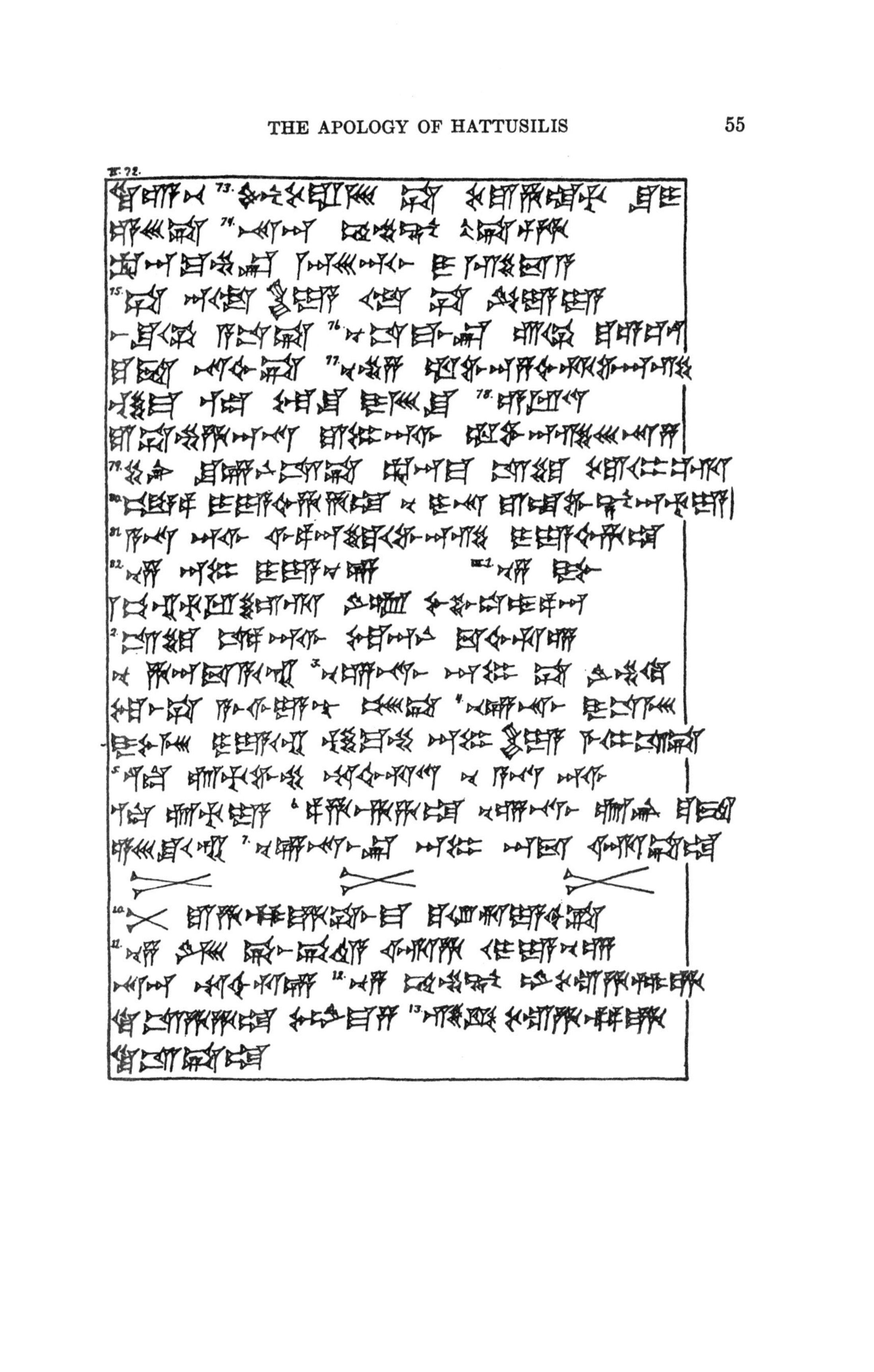

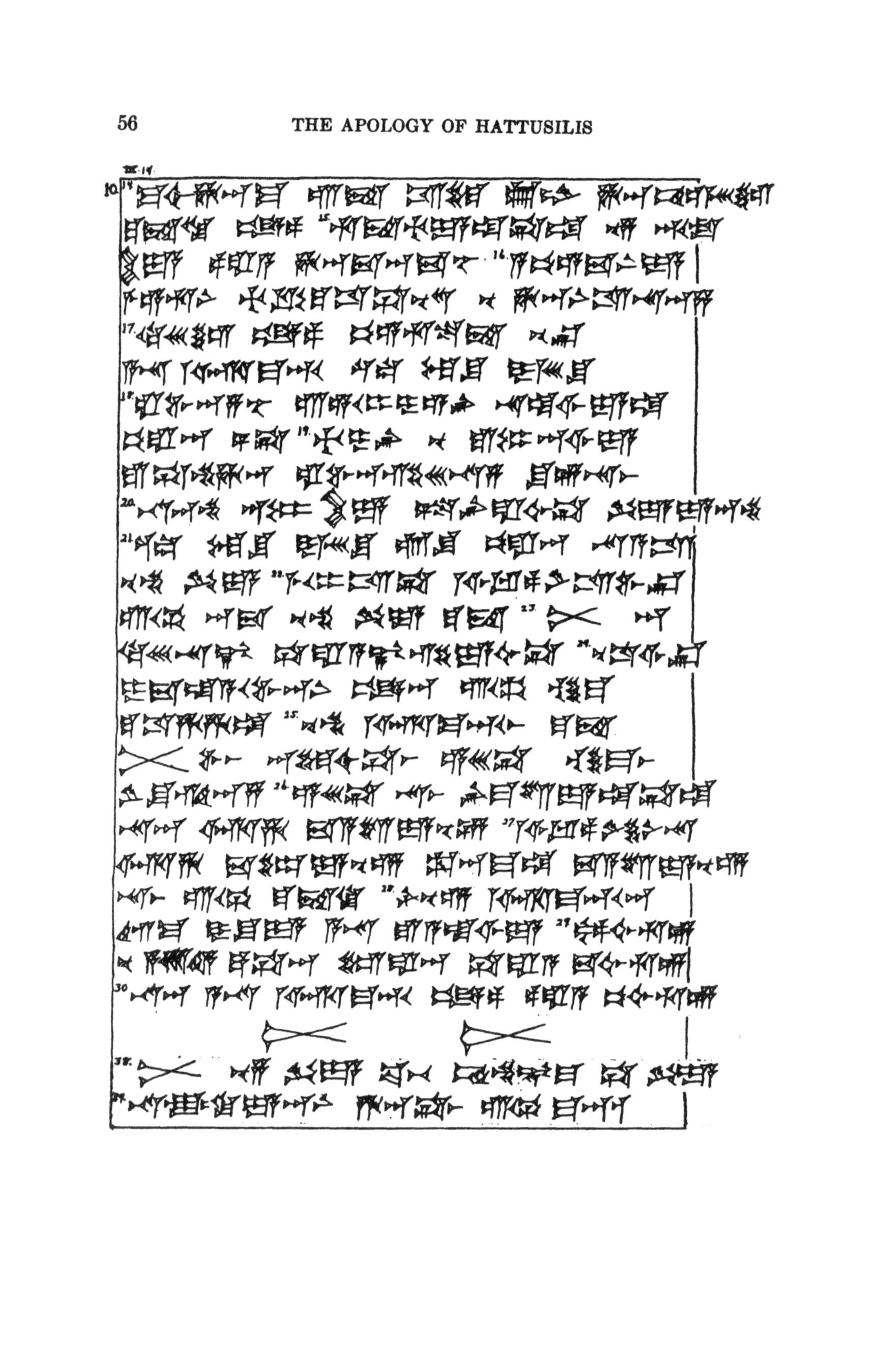

III. 14

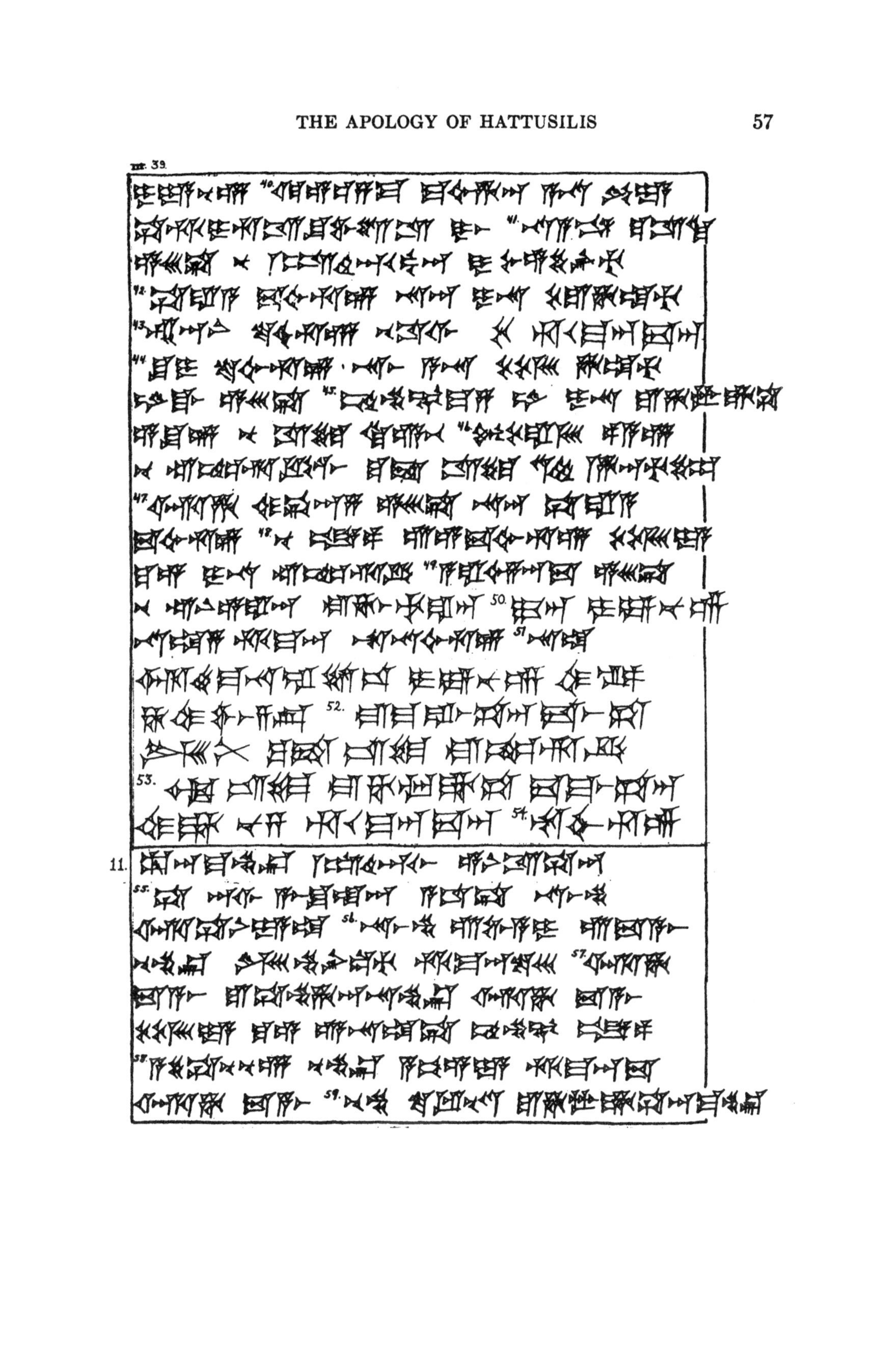

III. 39

11.

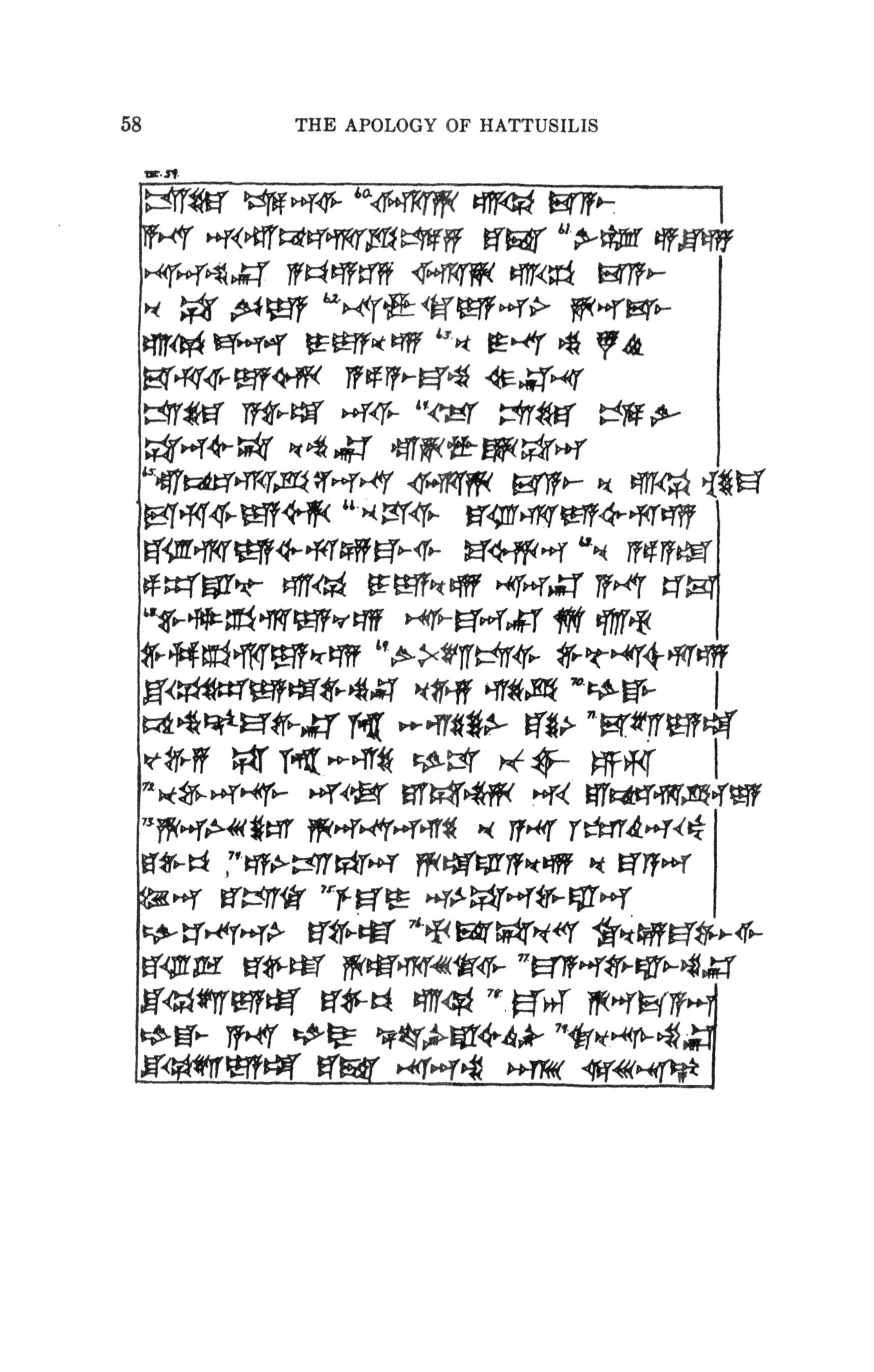

III. 59.

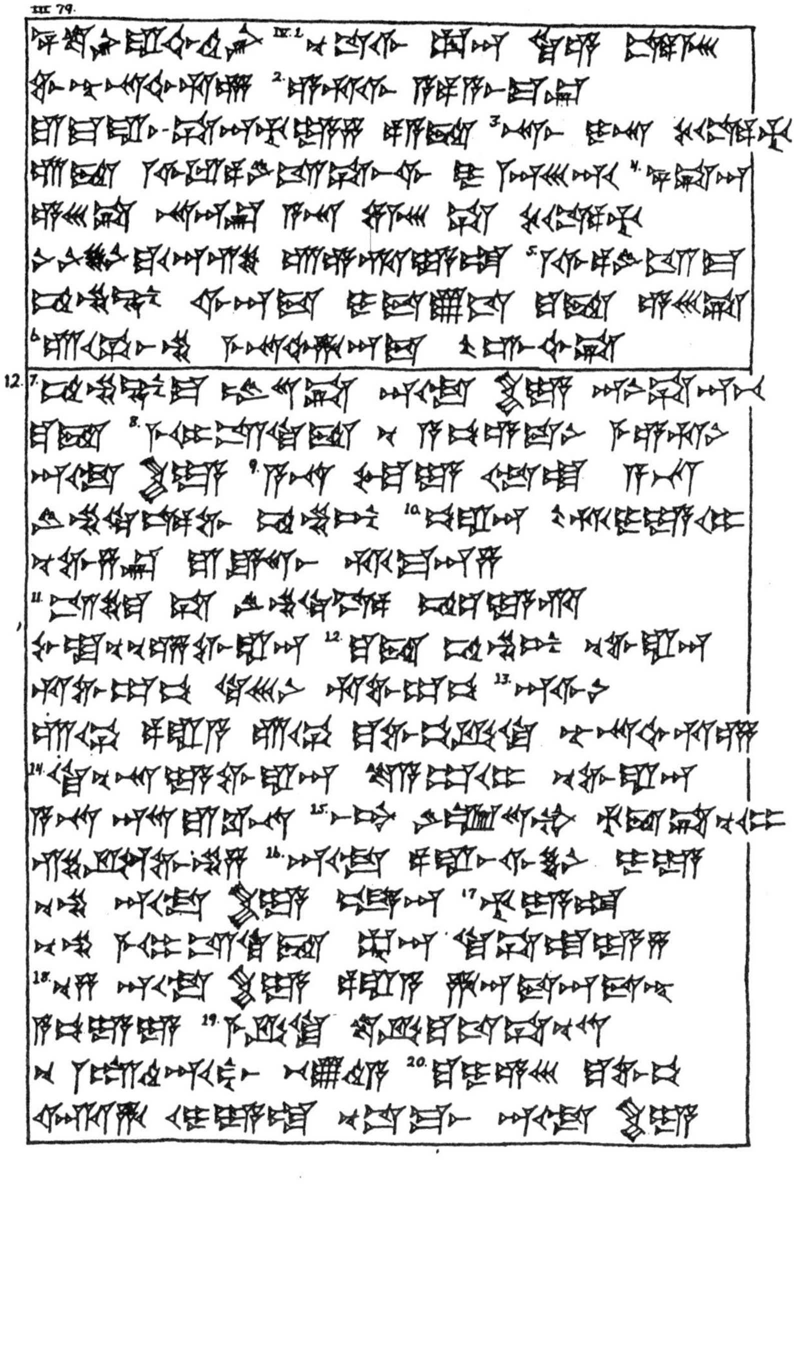

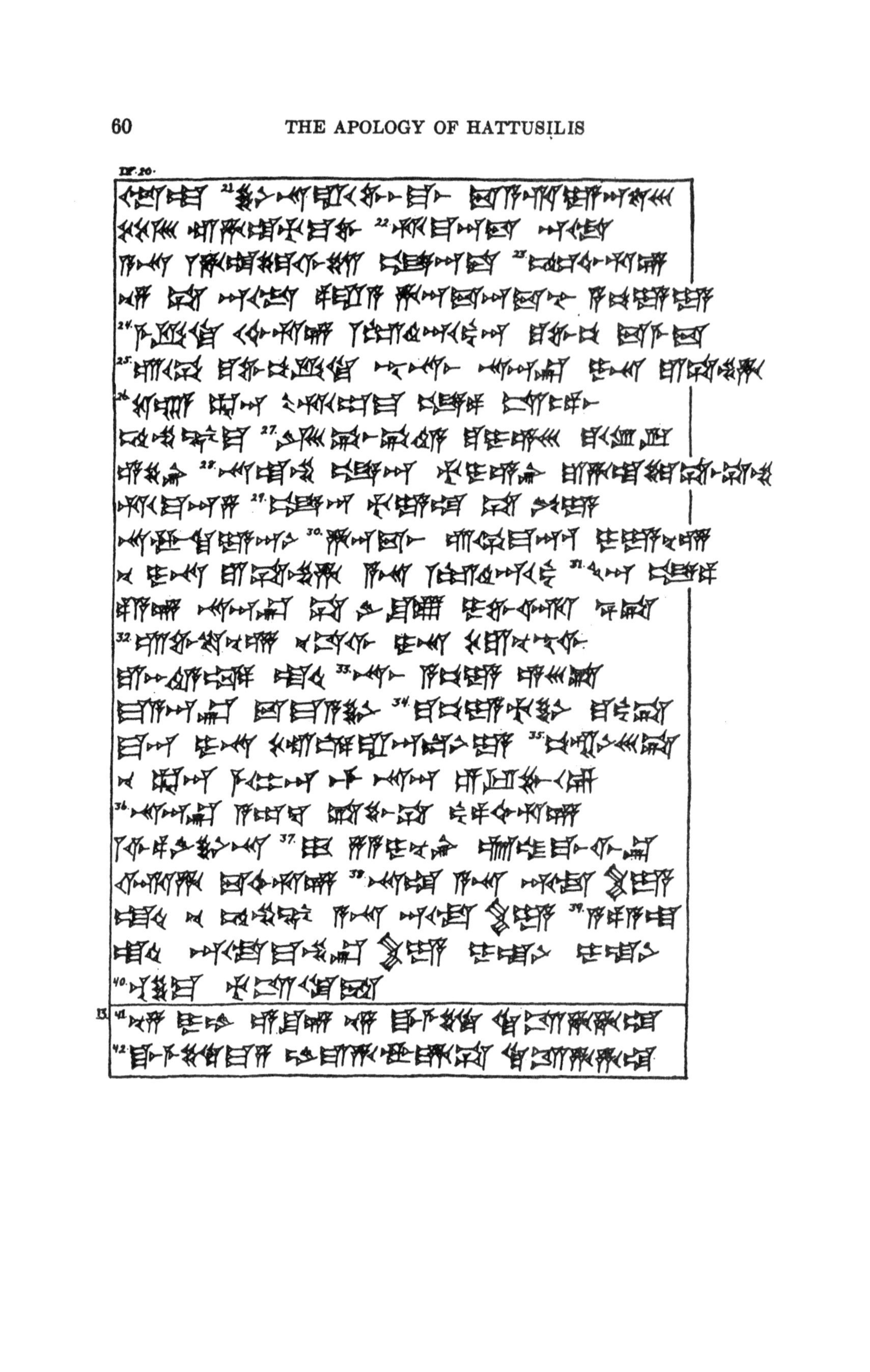

IV. 20.

IV 42.

43. 44. 45. 46. 47. 48. 49. 50. 51. 52. 53. 54. 55. 56. 57. 58. 59. 60. 61. 62.

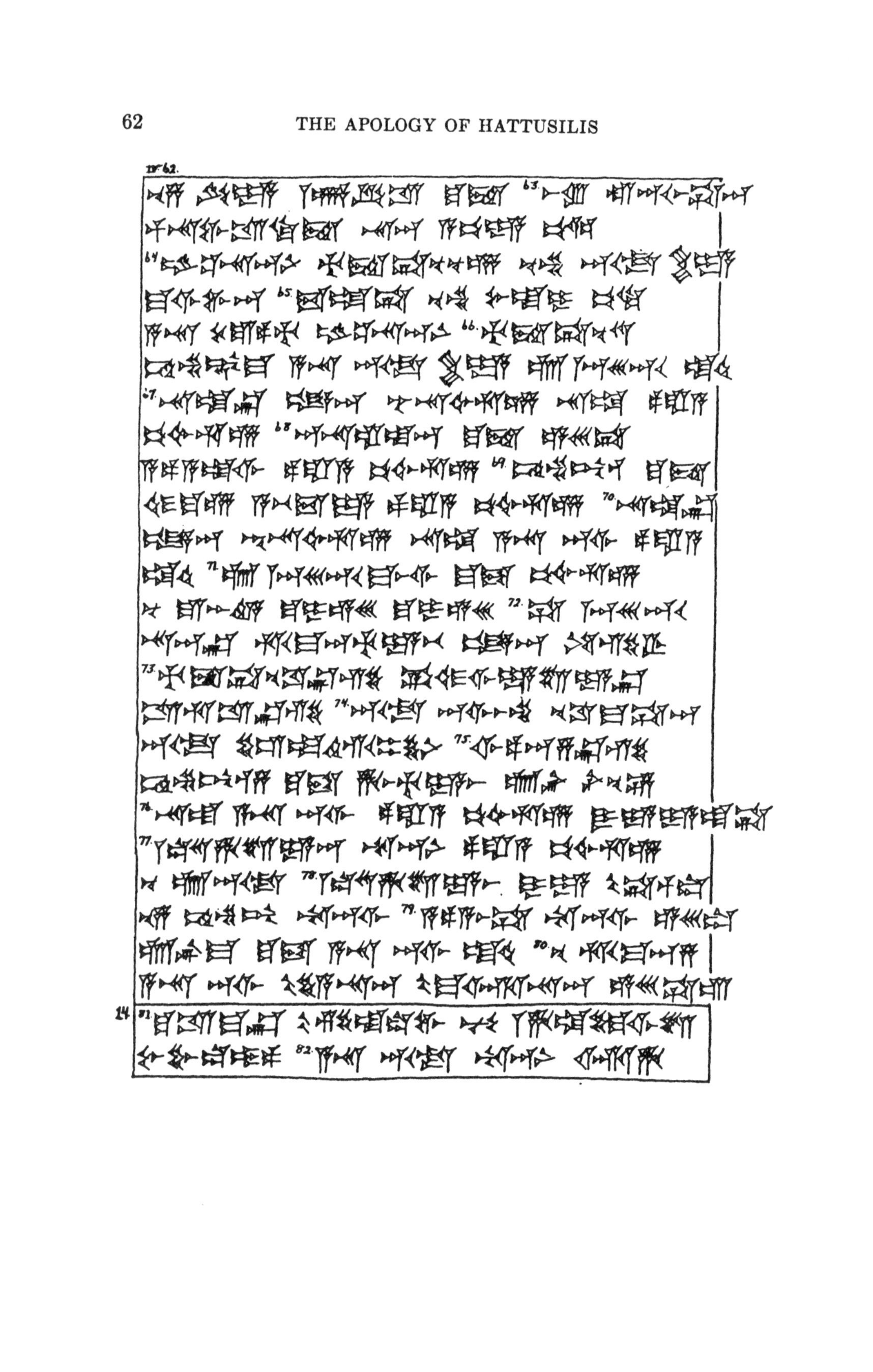

IV 62.

14

THE APOLOGY OF HATTUSILIS

1

(1.1) *UM-MA* ^{I}*TA-BA-AR-NA* ^{I}*ḪA-AT-TU-ŠI-LI* LUGAL.GAL LUGAL KUR ^{URU}*ḪA-AT-TI* (1.2) DUMU ^{I}*MUR-ŠI-LI* LUGAL.GAL LUGAL KUR ^{URU}*ḪA-AT-TI* (1.3) DUMU.DUMU-*ŠÚ ŠA* ^{I}*ŠU-UP-PÍ-LU-LI-U-MA* LUGAL.GAL LUGAL KUR ^{URU}*ḪA-AT-TI* (1.4) ŠA(G).BAL.BAL *ŠA* ^{I}*ḪA-AT-TU-ŠI-LI* LUGAL ^{URU}*KU-UŠ-ŠAR*

2

(1.5) *ŠA* ^{D}*IŠTAR pa-ra-a ḫa-an-da-an-da-tar me-ma-aḫ-ḫi* (1.6) *na-at* DUMU.NAM.LÚ.GÀL.LU-*aš iš-ta-ma-aš-du nu* ⸗*zi-la-du-wa* (1.7) *ŠA* ^{D}UTU-*ŠI* DUMU-*ŠÚ* DUMU.DUMU-*ŠÚ* NUMUN ^{D}UTU-*ŠI* DINGIR.MEŠ-*aš-kán iš-tar-na* (1.8) *A-NA* ^{D}*IŠTAR na-aḫ-ḫa-a-an e-eš-du*

3

(1.9) *A-BU-YA-an-na-aš-za* ^{I}*Mur-ši-li-iš* 4 DUMU.MEŠ ^{I}*Ḫal-pa-šu-lu-pí-in* (1.10) ^{I}NIR.GÁL-*in* ^{I}*Ḫa-at-tu-ši-li-in* ^{SAL}DINGIR.MEŠ.IR-*in-na* DUMU.SAL-*an* (1.11) *ḫa-aš-ta nu-za ḫu-u-ma-an-da-aš-be* EGIR-*iz-zi-iš* DUMU-*aš e-šu-un* (1.12) *nu-za ku-it-ma-an nu-u-wa* DUMU-*aš e-šu-un ŠA* KUŠ.KA.TAB.ANŠU-*za e-šu-un nu* (1.13) ^{D}*IŠTAR* GAŠAN-*YA A-NA* ^{I}*MUR-ŠI-LI A-BI-YA* Ù-*it* ^{I}NIR.GÁL-*in* ŠEŠ-*YA* (1.14) *u-i-ya-at A-NA* ^{I}*ḪA-AT-TU-ŠI-LI-wa* MU.KAM.ḪI.A *ma-ni-in-ku-wa-an-te-eš* (1.15) *Ú-UL-wa-ra-aš* TI-*an-na-aš nu-wa-ra-an am-mu-uk pa-ra-a* (1.16) *pa-a-i nu-wa-ra-aš-mu* ^{LÚ}*ša-an-ku-un-ni-iš e-eš-du* (1.17) *nu-wa-ra-aš* TI-*an-za nu-mu A-BU-YA* DUMU-*an ša-ra-a da-a-aš* (1.18) *nu-mu A-NA* DINGIR-*LIM* ERUM-*an-ni pí-eš-ta nu-za A-NA* DINGIR-*LIM* (1.19) ^{LÚ}*ša-an-ku-un-ni-ya-an-za* BAL-*aḫ-ḫu-un* (1.20) *nu-za-kán A-NA* ŠU ^{D}*IŠTAR* GAŠAN-*YA* ⸗*lu-ú-lu u-uḫ-ḫu-un* (1.21) *nu-mu* ^{D}*IŠTAR* GAŠAN-*YA* ŠU-*za IṢ-BAT na-aš-mu-kán pa-ra-a ḫa-an-ta-an-te-eš-ta*

4

(1.22) *ma-aḫ-ḫa-an-ma-za A-BU-YA* ^{I}*Mur-ši-li-iš* DINGIR-*LIM-iš ki-ša-at* (1.23) ŠEŠ-*YA-ma-za-kán* ^{I}NIR.GÁL-*iš A-NA* ^{GIŠ}GU.ZA *A-BI-ŠU e-ša-at* (1.24) *am-mu-uk-ma-za A-NA PA-NI* ŠEŠ-*YA* EN

THE APOLOGY OF HATTUSILIS

1

(1) Thus (speaks) King Hattusilis, the great king, king of the land of Hatti, son of Mursilis, the great king, king of the land of Hatti, grandson of Suppilulyumas, the great king, king of the land of Hatti, descendant of Hattusilis, king of the city of Kussaras.

2

(5) I tell Ishtar's divine power; let mankind hear it. (6) And in the future among the gods of My Majesty, of his son, of his grandson, of the descendants of My Majesty, let there be reverence to Ishtar.

3

(9) My father Mursilis begot us four children, Halpasulupis, Muwattallis, Hattusilis, and DINGIR.MEŠ.IR-is, a daughter. (11) Now of them all I was the last child. (12) And while I was still a child (and) was groom, (13) My Lady Ishtar by means of a dream sent to my father Mursilis my brother Muwattallis (with this message): 'For Hattusilis the years (are) short; he is not to live. (15) Now give him to me; and let him be my priest. (17) Then he (shall be) alive.' (17) And my father took me, (still) a child, and gave me to the goddess for service. (18) And, serving as priest to the goddess, I poured libations. (20) And so at the hand of My Lady Ishtar I saw prosperity. (21) And My Lady Ishtar took me by the hand; and she guided me.

4

(22) But when my father Mursilis became a god, and my brother Muwattallis sat upon the throne of his father, I became a general in the

KARAŠ *ki-iš-ḫa-ḫa-at* (1.25) *nu-mu* ŠEŠ-*YA A-NA* GAL-*ME-ŠE-DI-UT-TIM ti-it-ta-nu-ut* (1.26) KUR.UGU-*ya-mu ma-ni-ya-aḫ-ḫa-an-ni pí-eš-ta* (1.27) *nu* KUR.UGU-*TI* ⸗*ta-pár-ḫa pí-ra-an-ma-at-mu* ^{I} ^{D}*SIN*. ^{D}U-*aš* (1.28) DUMU ^{I}*ZI-DA-A ma-ni-ya-aḫ-ḫi-eš-ki-it nu-mu* ^{D}*IŠTAR* GAŠAN-*YA ku-it* (1.29) *ka-ni-eš-ša-an ḫar-ta* ŠEŠ-*YA-ya-mu* ^{I}NIR. GÁL-*iš* (1.30) *a-aš-šu ḫar-ta nu-mu-kán* GIM-*an* UKÙ.MEŠ-*an-na-an-za* (1.31) *ŠA* ^{D}*IŠTAR* GAŠAN-*YA ka-ni-eš-šu-u-wa-ar ŠA* ŠEŠ-*YA-ya* (1.32) *a-aš-šu-la-an a-ú-e-ir nu-mu ar-ša-ni-i-e-ir* (1.33) *nu-mu* ^{I} ^{D}*SIN*. ^{D}U-*aš* DUMU ^{I}*ZI-DA-A nam-ma-ya da-ma-a-uš* UKÙ.MEŠ-*uš* (1.34) *ú-wa-a-i-ti-iš-ki-u-wa-an ti-i-e-ir nu-mu-kán ḫu-u-wa-ap-pí-ir* (1.35) *nu-mu* ⸗*ar-pa-ša-at-ta-be* [*nu-*]*mu* ŠEŠ-*YA* ^{I}NIR.GÁL-*iš* (1.36) *A-NA* ^{GIŠ}DUBBIN *lam-ni-ya-at* ^{D}*IŠTAR-ma-mu* GAŠAN-*YA* Ù-*at* (1.37) *nu-mu* Ù-*it ki-i me-mi-iš-ta* DINGIR-*LIM-ni-wa-at-ta* (1.38) *am-mu-uk tar-na-aḫ-ḫi nu-wa li-e na-aḫ-ti* (1.39) *nu* DINGIR-*LIM-za pár-ku-u-e-eš-šu-un nu-mu* DINGIR-*LUM ku-it* GAŠAN-*YA* ŠU-*za ḫar-ta* (1.40) *nu-mu* ⸗*ḫu-u-wa-ap-pí* DINGIR-*LIM-ni* ⸗*ḫu-u-wa-ap-pí ḫa-an-ne-eš-ni* (1.41) *pa-ra-a Ú-UL ku-wa-pí-ik-ki tar-na-aš Ú-UL-ma-mu* (1.42) ^{GIŠ}TUKUL ^{LÚ}KÚR *ku-wa-pí-ik-ki še-ir wa-aḫ-nu-ut* (1.43) ^{D}*IŠTAR-mu-za-kán* GAŠAN-*YA ḫu-u-ma-an-da-za-be da-aš-ki-it* (1.44) *ma-a-an-mu iš-tar-ak-zi ku-wa-pí nu-za-kán ir-ma-la-aš-be* (1.45) *ŠA* DINGIR-*LIM ḫa-an-da-an-da-tar še-ir uš-ki-nu-un* (1.46) DINGIR-*LUM-mu* GAŠAN-*YA ḫu-u-ma-an-da-za-be* ŠU-*za ḫar-ta am-mu-uk-ma-za* (1.47) *pa-ra-a ḫa-an-da-a-an-za ku-it* UKÙ-*aš e-šu-un* (1.48) *A-NA PA-NI* DINGIR. MEŠ *ku-it pa-ra-a ḫa-an-da-an-da-an-ni i-ya-aḫ-ḫa-at* (1.49) *ŠA* DUMU. NAM.LÚ.GÀL.LU-*UT-TI* ḪUL-*lu ut-tar Ú-UL ku-wa-pí-ik-ki* (1.50) *i-ya-nu-un* DINGIR-*LUM-mu-za-kán* GAŠAN-*YA ḫu-u-ma-an-da-za-be da-aš-ki-ši* (1.51) *Ú-UL e-eš-ta nu-mu* DINGIR-*LUM* GAŠAN-*YA* ⸗*ku-wa-ya-mi me-e-ḫu-ni* (1.52) *Ú-UL ku-wa-pí-ik-ki še-ir ti-ya-at A-NA* ^{LÚ}KÚR-*mu* (1.53) *pí-ra-an kat-ta Ú-UL ku-wa-pí-ik-ki tar-na-aš* (1.54) *Ú-UL-ma-mu A-NA* EN *DI-NI-YA* $^{LÚ.MEŠ}$*ar-ša-na-at-tal-la-aš* (1.55) *ku-wa-pí-ik-ki pí-ra-an kat-ta tar-na-aš ma-a-na-aš* INIM ^{LÚ}KÚR (1.56) *ma-a-na-aš* INIM EN *DI-NI ma-a-na-aš* INIM É LUGAL *ku-iš-ki* (1.57) *nu-mu* ^{D}*IŠTAR-be* GAŠAN-*YA ḫu-u-ma-an-da-za pa-la-aḫ-ša-an še-ir ḫar-ta* (1.58) *ḫu-u-ma-an-da-za-be-mu-kán da-aš-ki-it* ^{LÚ}KÚR.MEŠ-*mu-kán* (1.59) $^{LÚ.MEŠ}$*ar-ša-na-tal-lu-uš* ^{D}*IŠTAR* GAŠAN-*YA* ŠU-*i da-a-iš* (1.60) *na-aš-za kat-ta-an ar-ḫa zi-en-na-aḫ-ḫu-un*

5

(1.61) GIM-*an-ma-kán* ŠEŠ-*YA* ^{I}NIR.GÁL-*iš ut-tar kat-ta a-uš-ta* (1.62) *nu-mu-kán* ḪUL-*lu ut-tar kat-ta Ú-UL ku-it-ki a-aš-ta* (1.63)

presence of my brother, and then my brother appointed me to the office of chief of the *Mešedi*, and gave me the Upper Country to rule. (27) Then I governed the Upper Country. (27) Before me, however, Armadattas, son of Zidas, had been ruling it. (28) Now because My Lady Ishtar had favored me and my brother Muwattallis was well disposed toward me, when people saw My Lady Ishtar's favor toward me and my brother's kindness, they envied me. (33) And Armadattas, son of Zidas, and other men too began to stir up ill will against me. (34) They brought malice against me, and I had bad luck; and my brother Muwattallis named me for the wheel (?). (36) My Lady Ishtar, however, appeared to me in a dream, and by means of the dream said this to me: 'Shall I abandon you to a (hostile) deity? (38) Fear not.' (39) And I was cleared from the (hostile) deity. (39) And since the goddess, My Lady, held me by the hand, she did not ever abandon me to the hostile deity, the hostile court; and the weapon of (my) enemy never overthrew me. (43) My Lady Ishtar always rescued me. (44) If ever ill-health befell me, even (while) ill I observed the goddess's divine power. (46) The goddess, My Lady, always held me by the hand. (46) Because I, for my part, was an obedient man, (and) because I walked before the gods in obedience, I never pursued the evil course of mankind. (50) Thou, goddess, My Lady, dost always rescue me. (51) Has it not been (so)? (51) In fact, the goddess, My Lady, did not ever in time of danger (?) pass me by; to an enemy she did not ever abandon me, and no more to my opponents in court, my enviers, did she abandon me. (55) If it was a plot of an enemy, if it was a plot of an opponent at law, if it was a plot of the palace, My Lady Ishtar always held over me protection. (58) She always rescued me. (58) Envious enemies My Lady Ishtar put into my hand; and I destroyed them utterly.

5

(61) When, however, my brother Muwattallis came to understand the matter, and there remained no ill repute against me, (63) he took

nu-mu EGIR-*pa da-a-aš nu-mu-kán* KARAŠ ANŠU.KUR.RA.MEŠ (1.64) *ŠA* KUR URU*ḪA-AT-TI* ŠU-*i da-a-iš nu* KARAŠ (1.65) ANŠU. KUR.RA.MEŠ *ŠA* KUR URU*ḪA-AT-TI ḫu-u-ma-an-da-an am-mu-uk ta-pár-ḫa* (1.66) *nu-mu-za* ŠEŠ-*YA* INIR.GÁL-*iš pa-ra-a u-i-iš-ki-it nu-mu* D*IŠTAR* GAŠAN-*YA* (1.67) GIM-*an ka-ni-eš-ša-an ḫar-ta nu-za-kán* IGI.ḪI.A-*wa ku-wa-at-ta-an* (1.68) *A-NA* KUR LÚKÚR *an-da-an na-a-iš-ki-nu-un nu-mu-kán* IGI.ḪI.A-*wa* LÚKÚR (1.69) EGIR-*pa Ú-UL ku-iš-ki na-a-iš nu-za* KUR.KUR.MEŠ LÚKÚR *tar-aḫ-ḫi-iš-ki-nu-un* (1.70) *ka-ni-eš-šu-u-wa-ar-mu ŠA* D*IŠTAR-be* GAŠAN-*YA e-eš-ta* (1.71) *nu-kán* ŠA(G) KUR.KUR.MEŠ URU*ḪA-AT-TI* LÚKÚR *ku-iš ku-iš an-da e-eš-ta* (1.72) *na-an-kán IŠ-TU* KUR.KUR.MEŠ URU*ḪA-AT-TI ar-ḫa-be u-i-ya-nu-un* (1.73) *ku-it-ma-an-ma-za* DUMU-*aš e-šu-un nu-za* KUR.KUR LÚKÚR *ku-e tar-aḫ-ḫi-iš-ki-nu-un* (1.74) *na-at DUP-PU ḫa-an-ti-i* DÙ-*mi na-at PA-NI* DINGIR-*LIM te-iḫ-ḫi*

6

(1.75) GIM-*an-ma* ŠEŠ-*YA* INIR.GÁL-*iš IŠ-TU A-MA-AT* DINGIR-*LIM-ŠÚ* (1.76) *I-NA* KUR *ŠAP-LI-TI kat-ta pa-it* URU*Ḫa-at-tu-ša-an-ma ar-ḫa tar-na-aš* (2.1) *nu* ŠEŠ-*YA* DINGIR.MEŠ URUKUBABBAR-*TI* GIDIM.ḪI.A-*ya ša-ra-a da-a-aš* (2.2) *na-aš I-NA* KUR URU[*ŠAP-LI-TI kat-ta*] *pí-e-da-aš* EGIR-*az-ma* (2.3) KUR URU*GA-AŠ-GA*.ḪI.A *ḫu-u-ma-an-te-eš* KUR [*PÍ*-]*IŠ-ḪU-RU* KUR *IŠ*-[*ḪU-PÍ-I*]*T-TA* (2.4) KUR URU*DA-IŠ-TI-PA-AŠ-ŠA* BAL-*i-ya-at nu* KUR *L*[*A-AN-DA*] KUR URU*MA-RI-IŠ-TA* (2.5) URU.AŠ.AŠ.ḪI.A BÀD-*ya ar-ḫ*[*a da-*]*a-*[*ir*] *nu-kán* LÚKÚR ÍD*Ma-ra-aš-ša-an-da-an* (2.6) *za-a-iš nu* KUR URU . . . [*wa-al*]*-aḫ-ḫi-eš-ki-u-wa-an da-a-iš* (2.7) *nu* KUR URU*KA-NI-EŠ wa-al-aḫ-ḫi-eš-ki-u-wa-an da-a-iš* (2.7b) . . . (2.8) URU*Ḫa-* . . . -[*ma*] URU*Ku-ru-uš-ta-ma-aš* URU*Gaz-zi-ú-ra-aš-ša* (2.9) *pí-di ku-ru-ri-ya-aḫ-ḫi-ir nu* URU.DU$_6$.ḪI.A URU*ḪA-AT-TI* (2.10) *wa-al-ḫi-iš-ki-u-wa-an ti-e-ir* LÚKÚR KUR URU*DUR-MI-IT-TA-ma* (2.11) [KUR URU*TU-*]*ḪU-UP-PÍ-YA wa-al-ḫi-iš-ki-u-wa-an da-a-iš* (2.12) [*nu ku-it*] KUR *IP-PA-AŠ-ŠA-NA-MA dan-na-at-ta-an e-eš-ta* (2.13) [*nu-kán pa-*]*ra-a I-NA* KUR URU*ŠU-WA-TA-RA a-ar-aš-ki-it* (2.14) [URU] . . . *-ša-aš-ma-kán* URU*Iš-ta-ḫa-ra-aš-ša* 2-*e-el iš-pár-zi-ir* (2.15) [*ku-e-ma* KUR.KUR.ḪI.A]-*TIM iš-tap-pa-an e-eš-ta nu-uš-ma-aš I-NA* MU 10 KAM (2.16) Š[E] NUMUN *Ú-UL an-ni-eš-ki-ir pa-ra-a-ma* MU.KAM.ḪI.A-*aš ku-it-ma-an* (2.17) ŠEŠ-*YA* INIR.GÁL-*iš I-NA* KUR URU*ḪA-AT-TI e-eš-ta* (2.18) *nu* KUR URU*GA-AŠ-GA*.ḪI.A *ḫu-u-ma-an-te-eš ku-ru-ri-ya-aḫ-ḫi-ir* (2.19) *nu* KUR URU*ŠA-AD-DU-UP-PA* KUR URU*DA-AN-KU-WA-ya ar-ḫa ḫar-ga-nu-ir* (2.20) *nu-mu* ŠEŠ-*YA* INIR.GÁL-*iš* (2.21) *u-i-ya-at*

me back; and he put the infantry (and) charioteers of the land of Hatti into my hand, and I commanded all the infantry (and) charioteers of the land of Hatti. (66) And my brother Muwattallis used to send me on expeditions. (66) And as My Lady Ishtar had granted me her favor, wherever among the countries of the enemy I turned my eyes, not an enemy turned back his eyes upon me. (69) And I kept conquering the countries of the enemy. (70) The favor of My Lady Ishtar, as ever, was mine. (71) And whatever enemy there was within the lands of Hatti, I drove clear out of the lands of Hatti. (73) However, what countries of the enemy I conquered while I was a minor, that I shall make (into) a tablet separately; and I shall set it up before the goddess.

6

(75) When, however, my brother Muwattallis at the command of his (patron) deity went down to the Lower Country and left Hattusas, my brother took the gods of Hatti and the Manes and carried them down into the Lower Country. (2) During (his) absence all the land of Gasgā, the land of Pishurus, the land of Ishupitta, (and) the land of Daistipassa revolted. (4) And they took away the land of Landas (?) and the land of Maristas and the fortified cities. (5) And the enemy crossed the Halys and he began to attack the land of . . . and he began to attack the land of Kanes. . . . (8) However H . . . , Kurustamas, and Gaziuras immediately made war, and they began to attack the ruined cities of Hatti. (10) The enemy from the land of Durmittas, however, began to attack the land of Tuhuppiya. (12) And since the land of Ippassanama was deserted, he kept making incursions into the country of Suwatara. (14) And only the cities of . . . and Istaharas escaped. (15) But in the districts that had been cut off they did not plant seed for ten years. (16) Thenceforth, moreover, during the years while my brother Muwattallis was in the land of Hatti, all the Gasgā countries made war; and they devastated the land of Sadduppa and the land of Dankuwa. (20) Now my brother Muwattallis sent me (into the field),

I-NA ^{URU}*PÁT-TI-YA-RI-GA-ma kat-ta-an da-a-iš* ERÍN.MEŠ-*ma-mu* ANŠU.KUR.RA.MEŠ *te-pa-u-wa-az pa-iš* (2.22) *nu-za* ERÍN.MEŠ *NA-RA-A-RU ŠA* KUR-*TI te-pa-u-wa-az* GAM-*an e-ip-pu-un* (2.23) *nu pa-a-un nu-kán* ^{LÚ}KÚR *I-NA* ^{URU}*ḪA-AḪ-ḪA da-ma-aš-šu-un* (2.24) *na-an za-aḫ-ḫi-ya-nu-un nu-mu* ^{D}*IŠTAR* GAŠAN-*YA pí-ra-an ḫu-u-wa-a-iš* (2.25) *na-an ḫu-ul-li-ya-nu-un nu* ŠU-*an ú-e-da-aḫ-ḫu-un* (2.26) ^{URU}*Ḫa-at-tu-ša-an-ma ku-in pí-e ḫar-ta na-an-kán ar-ḫa* (2.27) *da-aḫ-ḫu-un na-an ḫu-u-ma-an-da-an* EGIR-*pa a-še-ša-nu-nu-un* (2.28) $^{\text{LÚ.MEŠ}}$*pí-ra-an ḫu-u-i-ya-tal-lu-uš-ma e-ip-pu-u-un* (2.29) *na-aš A-NA* ŠEŠ-*YA ḫi-in-ku-un nu-mu ki-i* IGI-*zi* LÚ-*tar-mi-it* (2.30) ^{D}*IŠTAR-mu-kán* GAŠAN-*YA* IGI-*zi* BAL-*ši ŠUM-an ki-e-da-ni* KASKAL-*ši ḫal-za-a-iš*

7

(2.31) *ú-it-ma* ^{LÚ}KÚR ^{URU}*Pí-iš-ḫu-ru-uš an-da a-ar-aš* ^{URU}*Ka-ra-aḫ-na-aš-ša* (2.32) ^{URU}*Ma-ri-iš-ta-aš* ŠA(G) ^{LÚ}KÚR [*e-še-ir*] *nu-uš-ši a-pí-e-iz* ^{URU}*Táq-qa-aš-ta-aš* ZAG-*aš e-eš-ta* (2.33) *ki-e-iz-za-ma-aš-ši* ^{URU}*Tal-ma-li-ya-aš* ZAG-*aš e-eš-ta* (2.34) ANŠU.KUR.RA.MEŠ-*ma* 8 *ME ṢI-IM-TUM e-eš-ta* ERÍN.MEŠ-*TI-ma-kán* (2.35) *kap-pu-u-wa-u-wa-ar Ú-UL e-eš-ta am-mu-uk-ma* ŠEŠ-*YA* ^{I}NIR.GÁL-*iš* (2.36) *u-i-ya-at nu-mu* 1 *ME* 20 *ṢI-IM-TUM* ANŠU.KUR.RA.MEŠ *pí-eš-ta* (2.37) ERÍN.MEŠ-*az-ma-mu* 1 LÚ-*ya* GAM-*an Ú-UL e-eš-ta nu-mu a-pí-ya-ya* (2.38) ^{D}*IŠTAR* GAŠAN-*YA pí-ra-an ḫu-u-wa-a-iš nu-za a-pí-ya-ya* ^{LÚ}KÚR (2.39) *IŠ-TU* NÍ.TE-*YA tar-aḫ-ḫu-un* LÚ-*LUM-ma ku-iš pí-ra-an ḫu-u-i-ya-an-za* (2.40) *e-eš-ta na-an-kán* GIM-*an ku-e-nu-un* (2.41) ^{LÚ}KÚR-*ma-za píd-da-a-it* URU.AŠ.AŠ.ḪI.A-*ma ku-i-e-eš ŠA* KUR ^{URU}*ḪA-AT-TI* (2.42) *iš-tap-pa-an-te-eš e-še-ir nu-kán* GUL-*ḫi-eš-ki-ir* (2.43) *nu* ^{LÚ}KÚR *ḫu-ul-li-iš-ki-u-wa-an ti-i-e-ir* (2.44) ŠU-*an-ma I-NA* ^{URU}*Ú-I-IŠ-TA-U-WA-AN-DA ú-e-da-aḫ-ḫu-un* (2.45) *nu-mu a-pí-ya-ya ŠA* ^{D}*IŠTAR* GAŠAN-*YA ka-ni-eš-šu-u-wa-ar e-eš-ta* (2.46) ^{GIŠ}TUKUL-*ma ku-in a-pí-ya ḫar-ku-un na-an ḫa-li-iš-ši-ya-nu-un* (2.47) *na-an A-NA* DINGIR-*LIM* GAŠAN-*YA pí-ra-an te-iḫ-ḫu-un*

8

(2.48) *nu-mu* ŠEŠ-*YA* ^{I}NIR.GÁL-*iš* EGIR-*an-da ú-it nu* ^{URU}*An-zi-li-ya-an* (2.49) ^{URU}*Ta-pí-iq-qa-an-na ú-e-te-it na-aš ar-ḫa-be pa-it* (2.50) *ma-ni-in-ku-wa-an-na-aš-mu Ú-UL-be ú-it* ERÍN.MEŠ-*ya-za* ANŠU. KUR.RA.MEŠ (2.51) *ŠA* KUR ^{URU}*ḪA-AT-TI* [*ku-it*]-*ma-an pí-ra-an ḫu-u-i-nu-ut na-an ar-ḫa pí-e-ḫu-te-it* (2.52) *nam-ma-kán* DINGIR.MEŠ ^{URU}*ḪA-AT-TI* GIDIM.ḪI.A-*ya pí-di ni-ni-ik-ta* (2.53) *na-aš I-NA* ^{URU} ^{D}U-*AŠ-ŠA kat-ta pí-e-da-aš nu* ^{URU} ^{D}U-*aš-ša-an e-ip-ta* (2.54)

and established (my headquarters) in Pattiyarigas. (21) However, he gave me troops (and) charioteers in small numbers. (22) Now I took with me auxiliary troops of the country in small numbers; and I marched and cut the enemy off in Hahhas, and I gave him battle. (24) Then My Lady Ishtar marched before me, and I defeated him. (25) And I set up a trophy (?). (26) And every Hittite he had brought with him I took away and established again (in his former dwelling place). (28) Moreover, I took (his) allies and delivered them to my brother. (29) And this was my first manly deed; My Lady Ishtar in this campaign for the first time proclaimed my name.

7

(31) The Pishuruwian enemy, however, came (and) made an incursion, and Karahnas (and) Maristas were in the midst of the enemy; and on that side Takkastas was his boundary, and on this side Talmaliyas was his boundary. (34) (His) horses were 800 teams, while it was impossible to count the infantry. (35) My brother Muwattallis, however, sent me (to meet him), and he gave me 120 teams of horses, but as to infantry not even a single man was with me. (37) And then also My Lady Ishtar marched before me; and then also with my own resources I conquered the enemy. (39) But when I slew every man who was an ally, the enemy fled. (41) The cities of the land of Hatti, however, which had been cut off were now taking up arms, and they began to attack the enemy. (44) But I set up a trophy (?) in Wistawanda. (45) And then also the favor of My Lady Ishtar was mine. (46) The weapon, moreover, which I carried on that occasion I enclosed (in a case?), and I set it up before the goddess, My Lady.

8

(48) And after me my brother Muwattallis came and fortified (?) Anziliyas and Tapikkas; and he went right back; he did not come near me at all. (50) And he caused the troops (and) charioteers of the land of Hatti to march before him for a while, and he took them back. (52) Then he gathered in (one) spot the gods of Hatti and the Manes, and carried them down to Dattassas; and he took Dattassas (for his resi-

URU*Dur-mi-it-ta-ma-aš* URU*Ku-ru-uš-ta-ma Ú-UL pa-it* (2.55) *na-aš-ta ki-e-da-aš A-NA* KUR.KUR.MEŠ *am-mu-uk an-da da-a-li-ya-at* (2.56) *nu-mu ki-e* KUR.KUR.MEŠ *dan-na-at-ta AŠ-ŠUM MU-IR-DU-UT-TIM pí-eš-ta* (2.57) KUR URU*IŠ-ḪU-PÍ-IT-TA* KUR URU*MA-RI-IŠ-TA* KUR URU*ḪI-IŠ-ŠA-AŠ-ḪA-PA* (2.58) KUR URU*KA-A-TA-PA* KUR URU*ḪA-AN-ḪA-NA* KUR URU*DA-RA-AḪ-NA* KUR URU*ḪA-AT-TE-NA* (2.59) KUR URU*DUR-MI-IT-TA* KUR URU*PA-LA-A* KUR URU*TU-U-MA-AN-NA* (2.60) KUR URU*GA-AŠ-ŠI-YA-A* KUR URU*ŠAP-PA* KUR ÍD SIG₇ ANŠU.KUR.RA.MEŠ LÚ.MEŠIŠ.GUŠKIN-*ya* (2.61) *ḫu-u-ma-an-da-an am-mu-uk* *ta-pár-ḫa* KUR URU*ḪA-AK-PIŠ-ŠA-ma-mu* (2.62) KUR URU*IŠ-TA-ḪA-RA-ya* ERUM-*an-ni pí-eš-ta nu-mu I-NA* KUR URU*ḪA-AK-PIŠ-ŠA* (2.63) LUGAL-*un i-ya-at nu-mu-kán* ŠEŠ-*YA ku-e ki-e* KUR.KUR.MEŠ *dan-na-at-ta* (2.64) ŠU-*i da-a-iš nu-mu* D*IŠTAR* GAŠAN-*YA ku-it* ŠU-*za ḫar-ta* (2.65) *nu-za* LÚKÚR.MEŠ *ku-i-e-eš tar-aḫ-ḫu-un ku-i-e-eš-ma-mu ták-šu-la-a-ir* (2.66) *nu-mu* D*IŠTAR* GAŠAN-*YA* GAM-*an ti-ya-at nu-za ki-e* KUR.KUR. MEŠ *dan-na-at-ta* (2.67) *IŠ-TU* NÍ.TE-*YA* EGIR-*pa a-še-ša-nu-nu-un* (2.68) *na-at* EGIR-*pa* URU*Ḫa-at-tu-ša-an i-ya-nu-un*

9

(2.69) GIM-*an-ma ú-it* ŠEŠ-*YA ku-wa-pí I-NA* KUR *MI-IṢ-RI-I pa-it* (2.70) *nu-za* KUR.KUR.MEŠ *ku-e ki-e* EGIR-*pa a-še-ša-nu-nu-un nu* KARAŠ ANŠU.KUR.RA.MEŠ (2.71) *ki-e-el ŠA* KUR-*TI A-NA* ŠEŠ-*YA la-aḫ-ḫi I-NA* KUR URU*MI-IṢ-RI-I* (2.72) *kat-ta-an pí-e-ḫu-te-nu-un nu-mu-kán PA-NI* ŠEŠ-*YA ku-it* KARAŠ (2.73)ANŠU.KUR. RA.MEŠ *ŠA* KUR URU*ḪA-AT-TI* ŠU-*i e-eš-ta* (2.74) *na-an am-mu-uk* *ta-pár-ḫa* GIM-*an-ma-mu-kán* ID*SIN*.DU-*aš* DUMU I*ZI-DA-A* (2.75) *ŠA* D*IŠTAR* GAŠAN-*YA Ú ŠA* ŠEŠ-*YA-ya aš-šu-ul a-uš-ta* (2.76) *nu-uš-ma-aš-kán Ú-UL ku-e-iz-qa ku-it* [*na-aḫ-ta*] (2.77) *nu-mu-za al-wa-an-za-aḫ-ḫu-u-wa-an-zi nam-ma QA-DU* [DAM-*ŠU* DUMU.MEŠ-*ŠU*] (2.78) *e-ip-pir* URU*Ša-mu-ḫa-an-na* URU-*LUM* DINGIR-*LIM al-wa-an-zi-*[*eš-na-za*] (2.79) *še-ir šu-un-ni-iš-ta* GIM-*an-ma IŠ-TU* KUR URU*MI-IṢ-RI* (2.80) EGIR-*pa i-ya-aḫ-ḫa-ḫa-at n*[*u I-NA* URU*LA-WA-A*]*Z-AN-TI-YA* (2.81) *A-NA* DINGIR-*LIM ši-pa-an-tu-u-wa-an-zi i-ya-aḫ-ḫa-at* (2.82) *nu-za* DINGIR-*LUM i-ya-nu-u*[*n*] (3.1) *nu-za* DUMU.SAL I*PÍ-EN-TI-IP-ŠAR-RI* LÚSANGA SAL*Pu-du-ḫé-pa-an* (3.2) *IŠ-TU* INIM DINGIR-*LIM* DAM-*an-ni da-aḫ-ḫu-un nu ḫa-an-da-a-u-en* (3.3) [*nu-un-n*]*a-aš* DINGIR-*LUM ŠA* LÚ*MU-DI* DA[M-*aš-ša*] *a-aš-ši-ya-tar pí-eš-ta* (3.4) *nu-un-na-aš* DUMU.NITA.MEŠ DUMU.SAL.MEŠ *i-ya-u-en nam-ma-mu* DINGIR-*LUM* GAŠAN-*YA*

dence). (54) But he did not go to Durmittas (and) Kurustamas. (55) At that time he left me in these countries. (56) And he gave me these depopulated countries to govern. (57) I ruled over the country of Ishupitta, the country of Maristas, the country of Hissashapa, the country of Katapas, the country of Hanhana, the country of Darahna, the country of Hattena, the country of Durmittas, the country of Palā, the country of Tumanna, the country of Gassiyā, the country of Sappa, the country of the Yellow River, the charioteers and all the golden grooms. (61) The land of Hakpissas, moreover, and the land of Istaharas he gave me to be my subjects; and he made me king in the land of Hakpissas. (63) Now (in) the above mentioned depopulated countries which my brother had put into my hands, since My Lady Ishtar held me by the hand, I conquered some enemies and others made peace with me. (66) And My Lady Ishtar stood with me. (66) And these depopulated countries I myself caused to be inhabited again. (68) And I made them Hittite again.

9

(69) When once my brother came (and) marched against the land of Egypt, these countries which I had caused to be inhabited again—the army (and) charioteers of this country I led for my brother's campaign against the land of Egypt. (72) Now because, in the presence of my brother, infantry and charioteers of the land of Hatti were in my hands, I commanded them. (74) Now when Armadattas, son of Zidas, saw the kindness to me of My Lady Ishtar and of my brother, he (nevertheless) did not in any respect show them any reverence; and thereupon he with his wife and his sons tried to bewitch me. (78) And he filled Samuhas, the city of the goddess, with witchcraft. (79) When, however, I was on my way back from the land of Egypt, I journeyed to Lawazantiyas to pour libations to the goddess; and I worshipped the goddess. (1) And at the command of the goddess I took in marriage Puduhepas, the daughter of Pentipsarris, the priest. (2) And we founded a family, and the goddess gave us the love of husband and wife. (4) And we got us sons (and) daughters. (4) Furthermore the god-

[*me-mi-iš-ta*] (3.5) *QA-DU* É-*TI-wa-mu* ERUM-*aḫ-ḫu-ut nu A-NA* [DING]IR-*LIM QA-DU* É-*TI-YA* (3.6) [*pa-ḫ*]*a-aš-ḫa-ḫa-at nu-un-na-aš* É-*ir ku-it e-eš-šu-u-en* (3.7) *nu-un-na-aš-kán* DINGIR-*LUM an-da ar-ta-at* . . .

* * * * *

(3.10) . . . ^{URU}*Ḫa-ak-piš-ša-aš-ma ku-ru-*[*ri-ya-aḫ-ta*] (3.11) [*nu-za*] LÚ.MEŠ *GA-AŠ-GA*.ḪI.A *ar-ḫa u-i-ya-nu-un na-an* ERUM-*aḫ-ḫu-un* (3.12) [*nu-za*] *am-mu-uk* LUGAL KUR ^{URU}*ḪA-AK-PIŠ ki-iš-ḫa-ḫa-at* SAL.LUGAL-*ma-za* (3.13) [*zi-ik* KUR ^{UR}]^{U}*ḪA-AK-PIŠ ki-iš-ta-at*

10

(3.14) *ma-aḫ-ḫa-an-ma ú-it IŠ-TU* É LUGAL *ḫa-an-ne-*(*m*)*eš-šar ku-it-ki* EGIR-*pa* (3.15) *ḫu-it-ti-ya-at-ta-at nu-za* ^{D}*IŠTAR* GAŠAN-*YA pa-ra-a ḫa-an-da-an-da-tar* (3.16) *a-pí-e-da-ni-ya me-e-ḫu-ni ti-ik-ku-uš-ša-nu-ut nu ḫa-an-ni-iš-na-an-za* (3.17) DI-*eš-šar* EGIR-*pa pí-e-ḫu-te-it nu-kán A-NA* ^{I}*AR-MA*-^{D}U *QA-DU* DAM-*ŠU* DUMU.MEŠ-*ŠU* (3.18) *al-wa-an-za-tar ú-e-mi-i-e-ir na-at-ši-ya-at pí-ra-an kat-ta* (3.19) *ti-i-ir nu* URU-*LUM* DINGIR-*LIM-ya* ^{URU}*Ša-mu-ḫa-an al-wa-an-zi-eš-na-za šu-un-na-aš* (3.20) *na-an-mu* DINGIR-*LUM* GAŠAN-*YA kat-te-ir-ra-aḫ-ta* ŠEŠ-*YA-ya-an-mu* (3.21) *QA-DU* DAM-*ŠU* DUMU.MEŠ-*ŠU* É-*ŠU pí-ra-an na-a-iš nu-mu* ŠEŠ-*YA* (3.22) *me-mi-iš-ta* ^{I}*Ši-ip-pa*-LÚ-*iš-wa-kán Ú-UL an-da nu-mu* ŠEŠ-*YA ku-it* (3.23) . . . . . *-an* DI-*eš-na-az ša-ra-a-az-zi-ya-aḫ-ta* (3.24) *nu-uš-ši-kán i-*[*d*]*a-la-a-u-wa-an-ni* EGIR-*an Ú-UL nam-ma ku-uš-ḫa-ḫa-at* (3.25) *nu-mu* ^{I}*Ar-ma*-^{D}U-*aš* [*ku-it* . . . *-w*]*a-aš an-tu-uḫ-ša-aš e-eš-ta nam-ma-aš* ^{LÚ}ŠU.GI-*an-za* (3.26) *e-eš-ta* [*na-aš ir-ma-li-y*]*a-at-ta-at* [*na-a*]*n ar-ḫa da-a-li-ya-nu-un* (3.27) ^{I}*Ši-ip-pa*-LÚ-*in-n*[*a ar-ḫa d*]*a-li-ya-nu-un* [GIM-*an-ma-a*]*t da-a-li-ya-nu-un na-aš Ú-UL ku-it-ki* (3.28) DÙ-*nu-un* [^{I}*Ar-ma*-^{D}U-*an*] *im-ma* DUMU-*ŠU-ya* [*A-N*]*A* ^{URU}*A-LA-ŠI-YA* (3.29) *up-pa-aḫ-ḫu-un* [*nu* A.ŠA(G).ḪI.A *ták-ša-a*]*n šar-ra-an ša-ra-a da-aḫ-ḫu-un* (3.30) *na-an A-NA* ^{I}*AR-MA*-^{D}U EGIR-*pa pa-ra-a pí-iḫ-ḫu-un*

* * * * *

(3.38) . . . [*nu-za* ŠEŠ-*YA* BA.UG$_6$] *am-mu-uk-ma ŠA* ŠEŠ-*YA* (3.39) [*na-ak-ki-ya-an-ni*] *ḫa-an-ta-aš Ú-UL ma-*[*an-qa i-ya-nu-u*]*n* (3.40) *ki-e-iz-za-ma ma-aḫ-ḫ*[*a-an*] *A-NA* ŠEŠ-*YA* [*ša-*]*ḫu-u-i-ḫu-iš-šu-wa-l*[*i-iš*] DUMU-*aš* (3.41) [*na-a-wi ku-iš-ki e-eš*]*-ta* [*nu* ^{I}*Ú*]*r-ḫi*-^{D}U-*up-an* DUMU ^{SAL}*E-ŠE-IR-TI* (3.42) *ša-ra-a da-aḫ-ḫu-un* [*na-an I-NA* KUR ^{URU}*ḪA-A*]*T-TI* (3.43) EN-*an-ni t*[*e-iḫ-ḫu-un nu-uš-ši* KUR] *ḫu-u-ma-an-da-an* (3.44) ŠU-*i te-iḫ-ḫu-un na-aš A-NA* KUR.KUR.MEŠ *Ḫ*[*A-AT-TI* LU-

dess, My Lady, said to me: 'Do you with (your) house be subject to me.' (5) And with my house I was true to the goddess. (6) And for us the goddess dwelt within the house that we were making us. . . . (10) Hakpissas, however, revolted; and I drove out the men of the Gasgā countries, and I subjected it. (12) And I became king of the land of Hakpissas and you became queen of the land of Hakpissas.

10

(14) When, however, an indictment was brought again from the palace, My Lady Ishtar at that time also showed her divine power. (16) And she brought a new indictment out of the indictment. (17) Now they found witchcraft in Armadattas along with his wife and his sons, and they established it against him; and he had filled even Samuhas, the city of the goddess, with witchcraft. (20) Now the goddess, My Lady, made him lose the case to me; and my brother delivered him to me with his wife, his sons, (and) his house. (21) Then my brother said to me 'Sippa-LÛ-is (is) not in (it).' (22) And because my brother made me, the innocent (? party), victorious in the trial, I did not thereafter repay him in malice. (25) Now because Armadattas was a man related (?) to me, (and) besides he was an aged man, and he was ill, I let him off. (27) And I let Sippa-LÛ-is off. (27) When, however, I had let them off and had done nothing to them, I actually sent Armadattas and his son to Alasiya, and I took half of his estate and gave it back to Armadattas.

* * * * *

(38) And my brother died. (38) I, however, firm in (my) respect for my brother, did not do anything; but, as at this time my brother did not yet have a legitimate son, I took Urhitesupas, the son of a secondary wife, and set him in authority in the land of Hatti. (43) And I put all the country in his hands. (44) And in the lands of Hatti he was the

GAL.GAL] *e-eš-ta* (3.45) *am-mu-uk-ma-za* LUGAL *I-*[*NA* ^{U}]^{RU}*ḪA-AK-PIŠ-ŠA e-šu-*[*un*] *nu IŠ-TU* KARAŠ (3.46) ANŠU.KUR.RA.[MEŠ *pa-a-un*] *nu* ^{URU}*Ne-ri-iq-qa-aš ku-it IŠ-TU* [UD.KAM ^{I}*ḪA-AN*]*-TI-LI* (3.47) *ar-ḫa ḫar-ga-an-za e-eš-ta na-an* [*ša-ra-a da-aḫ-ḫu-un*] (3.48) [*nu* EGIR*-pa ú-e-da-aḫ-*]*ḫu-un* KUR.KUR.MEŠ*-ya ku-e I-NA* ^{URU}*NE-RI-IK* (3.49) *a-ra-aḫ-za-an-da e-eš-ta* [*nu* ^{URU}]*Ni-e-ra-a*[*n*] ^{URU}*Ḫa-aš-ti-ra-an* (3.50) ZAG[*-an i*]*-ya-nu-un na-at-za ḫu-u-ma-an* [ERÍM*-n*]*a-aḫ-ḫu-un* (3.51) *n*[*a-a*]*t ar-kam-ma-na-al-li-uš* [*i-ya-nu-un* ḪUR.SAG] *Ḫa-ḫar-wa-aš-za-kán* (3.52) [^{UR}]^{U}*Ma-ra-aš-ša-an-da-aš-ša* ^{L}[$^{Ú.MEŠ}$KÚR *k*]*u-it IŠ-TU* ^{URU}*NE-RI-IK* (3.53) *Ù IŠ-TU* ^{URU}*ḪA-AK-PIŠ-ŠA da-ma-aš-ša-an ḫar-kir nu-za ḫu-u-ma-an-da-an* (3.54) ERÍM*-aḫ-ḫu-un*

11

GIM*-an-ma-mu-kán* ^{I}*Úr-ḫi-*^{D}[U*-aš e*]*-ni-iš-ša-an* (3.55) *ŠA* DINGIR*-LIM a-aš-šu-la-an a-uš-ta na-aš-mu ar-ša-ni-ya-at* (3.56) *n*[*a-aš-mu ú*]*-wa-a-i* [*ú-da*]*-a-aš nu-mu-kán* LÚ.MEŠ *MU-IR-DU-TI ḫu-u-ma-an-te-eš* (3.57) *ar-ḫa da-a-aš* ^{URU}*Š*[*a-mu-ḫa-a*]*n-na-mu-kán ar-ḫa da-a-aš* KUR.KUR.MEŠ*-ya ku-e dan-na-at-ta am-mu-uk* EGIR*-pa* (3.58) *a-še-ša-nu-nu-un nu-mu-kán a-pí-e-ya ḫu-u-ma-an-da ar-ḫa da-a-aš* (3.59) *nu-mu te-ip-nu-ut* ^{URU}*Ḫa-ak-piš-ša-an-ma-mu-kán IŠ-TU* INIM DINGIR*-LIM* (3.60) *ar-ḫa Ú-UL da-a-aš A-NA* ^{D}U ^{URU}*NE-RI-IK-KA-za k*[*u-it*] (3.61) ^{LÚ}SANGA *e-šu-un na-an-mu-kán a-pí-e-iz-za ar-ḫa Ú-UL da-a-aš nu ŠA* ŠEŠ*-YA* (3.62) *na-ak-ki-ya-an-ni ḫa-an-da-aš Ú-UL ma-an-qa i-ya-nu-un* (3.63) *nu I-NA* MU 7.KAM *da-ḫu-ši-ya-aḫ-ḫa a-pa-a-aš-ma-mu ḫar-kán-na IŠ-TU A-WA-AT* DINGIR*-LIM* (3.64) *Ù IŠ-TU* INIM LÚ *ša-an-aḫ-ta nu-mu-kán* ^{URU}*Ḫa-ak-piš-ša-an* (3.65) ^{URU}*Ne-ri-iq-qa-an-na ar-ḫa da-a-aš nu Ú-UL nam-ma da-ḫu-ši-ya-aḫ-ḫa* (3.66) *nu-uš-ši ku-ru-ri-ya-aḫ-ḫu-un ku-ru-ri-ya-aḫ-ḫu-un-ma-aš-ši ma-aḫ-ḫa-an* (3.67) *nu a-pa-a-at pa-ap-ra-tar Ú-UL i-ya-nu-un na-an-kán A-NA* ^{GIŠ}GIGIR (3.68) *wa-ag-ga-ri-ya-nu-un na-aš-ma-an-kán* ŠA(G) *É-TI wa-ag-ga-ri-ya-nu-un* (3.69) ^{LÚ}KÚR*-li-iš-ši wa-tar-na-aḫ-ḫu-un šu-ul-li-ya-at-wa-mu-kán nu-wa-za zi-ik* (3.70) LUGAL.GAL *am-mu-uk-ma-wa-kán* 1*-EN ḫal-zi-in ku-in* (3.71) *da-li-ya-at nu-wa-za ŠA* 1*-EN ḪAL-ṢÍ* LUGAL*-uš* [*nu-w*]*a e-ḫu* (3.72) *nu-wa-an-na-aš* ^{D}*IŠTAR* ^{URU}*ŠA-MU-ḪA* ^{D}U ^{URU}*NE-RI-IQ-QA-ya* (3.73) *ḫ*[*a*]*-an-ni-eš-šar ḫa-an-na-an-zi nu A-NA* ^{I}*ÚR-ḪI-*^{D}U*-UP ku-wa-pí* (3.74) *e-ni-iš-ša-an* [*ḫa*]*-at-ra-a-nu-un nu ma-a-an kiš-an ku-iš-ki* (3.75) *me-ma-i an-ni-ša-an-wa-ra-an* LUGAL*-iz-na-an-ni ku-wa-at* (3.76) *ti-it-ta-nu-ut ki-nu-un-ma-wa-aš-ši ku-u-ru-ur ku-wa-at ḫa-at-ri-eš-ki-ši* (3.77) *ma-a-an-wa-ra-aš-mu-kán šu-ul-li-ya-at ku-wa-pí Ú-UL* (3.78) *ma-an ḫa-an-da-a-an* LUGAL.GAL *A-NA* LUGAL.TUR *kat-te-ir-ra-aḫ-ḫi-ir* (3.79) *ki-nu-na-aš-mu-kán šu-ul-li-ya-at ku-it na-an-mu* DINGIR.

great king. (45) I, however, was king in Hakpissas. (45) And with army and charioteers I took the field. (46) And, since Nerikkas had been in ruins from the day of Hantilis, I took it and rebuilt it. (48) And the countries which were around Nerik—I made Neras (and) Hastiras (their) boundary—(51) all these I subjected and made tributaries. The mountain (country) of Haharwas and (52) the town of Marassandas, which the [enemy] (operating) out of Nerik and (53) Hakpis had oppressed, all of it (54) I subjected.

11

Now when Urhitesupas thus observed the kindness of the goddess to me, he envied me, and he brought ill will upon me. (56) He took away from me all (my) subjects; Samuhas also he took away from me; the depopulated lands also that I had settled again, all those too he took away from me, and he made me weak. (59) Hakpissas, however, according to the command of a god he did not take away from me. (60) Because I was priest of the storm god of Nerikkas, for that reason he did not take it away from me. (61) And, firm in (my) respect for my brother, I did not do anything. (62) And for seven years I submitted. (63) But he (Urhitesupas) at the command of a god and the suggestion of man tried to destroy me. (64) And he took Hakpissas and Nerikkas away from me. (65) And I did not submit any longer. (66) And I made war upon him. (66) But when I made war upon him, I did not do it (as) a crime. (67) Did I rebel against him in the chariot or rebel against him within the palace? (69) I sent him a declaration (of war) as an (open) enemy: 'You started hostilities with me. (69) Now you (are) a great king; but as for me, the one fortress that you have left me—of (that) one (I) am king. (71) Come! Ishtar of Samuhas and the storm god of Nerikkas shall decide the case for us.' (73) Now whereas I wrote Urhitesupas thus, if any one speaks as follows: 'Why did you formerly establish him on the throne? (76) And why are you now declaring war upon him?' (77) (I answer, 'Very well), if he had never started hostilities with me.' (78) Would (the gods) have subjected a great king (who was) upright to a small king? (79) Now because he

MEŠ DI-*eš-na-az kat-te-ir-ra-aḫ-ḫi-ir* (4.1) *nu-uš-ši* GIM-*an ki-e* INIM.MEŠ *wa-tar-na-aḫ-ḫu-un* (4.2) *e-ḫu-ši a-pa-a-aš-ma-kán* ^{URU}*Ma-ra-aš-ša-an-ti-ya-za* [*p*]*a-a-*[*it*] (4.3) *na-aš I-NA* KUR UGU-*TI ú-it* ^{I}*Ši-ip-pa-*LÚ-*iš-ša-aš-ši* DUMU ^{ID}*SIN*.^{D}U (4.4) *kat-ta-an e-eš-ta na-an-kán A-NA* ERÍN.MEŠ *ŠA* KUR UGU-*TI* [*ni*]-*ni-in-ku-u-an-zi ú-e-ri-ya-at* (4.5) ^{I}*Ši-pa-*LÚ-*iš-ma am-mu-uk* IGI-*an-da i-da-lu-uš ku-it e-eš-ta* (4.6) *Ú-UL-aš-mu me-na-aḫ-ḫa-an-da* ⸌*mar-aḫ-ta*

12

(4.7) *am-mu-uk-ma* LUGAL-*UT-TA* ^{D}*IŠTAR* GAŠAN-*YA an-ni-ša-an-be ku-it* (4.8) *me-mi-iš-ki-it nu a-pí-e-da-ni me-e-ḫu-ni* ^{D}*IŠTAR* GAŠAN-*YA* (4.9) *A-NA* DAM-*YA* Ù-*at A-NA* ^{LÚ}*MU-DI-KA-wa am-mu-uk* (4.10) *pí-ra-an* ⸌*ḫu-u-i-ya-mi nu-wa-za-kán* ^{URU}KUBAB-BAR-*aš ḫu-u-ma-an-za* (4.11) *IŠ-TU ŠA* ^{LÚ}*MU-DI-KA ne-ya-ri šal-la-nu-nu-un-wa-ra-an* (4.12) *ku-it am-mu-uk nu-wa-ra-an ḫu-wa-ap-pí* DI-*eš-ni ḫu-wa-ap-pí* (4.13) DINGIR-*LIM-ni Ú-UL pa-ra-a Ú-UL ku-wa-pí-ik-ki tar-na-aḫ-ḫu-un* (4.14) *ki-nu-na-ya-wa-ra-an kar-ap-mi nu-wa-ra-an A-NA* ^{D}UTU ^{URU}TÚL-*NA* (4.15) *AŠ-ŠUM* ^{LÚ}SANGA-*UT-TIM ti-it-ta-nu-mi zi-iq-qa-wa-mu-za* (4.16) ^{D}*IŠTAR pa-ra-aš-ši-in i-ya nu-mu* ^{D}*IŠTAR* GAŠAN-*YA* EGIR-*an* (4.17) *ti-ya-at nu-mu me-mi-iš-ki-it* GIM-*an ki-ša-at-ya-za* (4.18) *nu-za* ^{D}*IŠTAR* GAŠAN-*YA pa-ra-a ḫa-an-da-an-da-tar a-pí-ya-ya* (4.19) *me-ik-ki te-ik-ku-uš-ša-nu-ut nu* ^{I}*Úr-ḫi-*^{D}U-*up-aš BE-LU-*ḪI.A (4.20) *ku-i-e-eš ku-wa-pí ar-ḫa u-i-ya-at nu-uš-ma-aš* ^{D}*IŠTAR* GAŠAN-*YA* Ù-*at* (4.21) *in-na-ra-u-wa-aš-ma-aš da-a-ri-ya-an-te-eš* KUR.KUR.MEŠ ^{URU}*ḪA-AT-TI-ma-wa* (4.22) *ḫu-u-ma-an-da* ^{D}*IŠTAR A-NA* ^{I}*ḪA-AT-TU-ŠI-LI* EGIR-*an-da* (4.23) *ne-iḫ-ḫu-un nu-za ŠA* ^{D}*IŠTAR pa-ra-a ḫa-an-da-an-da-tar a-pí-ya-ya* (4.24) *me-ik-ki u-uḫ-ḫu-un* ^{I}*Úr-ḫi-*^{D}U-*up-an ku-wa-pí da-me-da* (4.25) *Ú-UL ku-wa-pí-ik-ki tar-na-aš na-an-kán I-NA* ^{URU}*ŠA-MU-ḪA* (4.26) ŠAḪ GIM-*an* ⸌*ḫu-u-um-ma* EGIR-*pa iš-tap-pa-aš am-mu-uk-ma* (4.27) LÚ.MEŠ *GA-AŠ-GA-*ḪI.A *ku-i-e-eš ku-u-ru-ur e-še-ir* (4.28) *na-at-mu* EGIR-*an ti-i-e-ir* ^{URU}*Ḫa-at-tu-ša-aš-ša-mu ḫu-u-ma-an-za* (4.29) EGIR-*an ti-ya-at ŠA* ŠEŠ-*YA na-ak-ki-ya-an-ni* (4.30) *ḫa-an-da-aš Ú-UL ma-an-qa i-ya-nu-un nu I-NA* ^{URU}*ŠA-MU-ḪA A-NA* ^{I}*ÚR-ḪI-*^{D}U-*UP* (4.31) GAM-*an* EGIR-*pa pa-a-un na-an-kán ŠA* ^{LÚ}ŠU.DIB *i-wa-ar kat-ta* (4.32) *ú-wa-te-nu-un nu-uš-ši I-NA* KUR ^{URU}*NU-ḪAŠ-ŠI* URU.AŠ.AŠ.ḪI.A BÀD *AD-DIN* (4.33) *na-aš a-pí-ya e-eš-ta ma-a-an-kán da-ma-a-in* (4.34) *ku-pí-ya-ti-in ku-up-ta ma-an I-NA* KUR ^{URU}*KA-RA-*^{D}*DU-NI-YA* (4.35) *pí-en-ni-eš-ta nu* GIM-*an me-mi-an AŠ-ME na-an e-ip-pu-u-un* (4.36) *na-an-kán* A.AB.BA *ta-*

started hostilities with me, they subjected him to me in the trial. (1) Now when I communicated these words to him (saying) 'Come on' to him, he marched out from Marassantiyas, and came to the Upper Country. (3) And Sippa-LÚ-is, the son of Armadattas, was with him. (4) And he appointed him to gather the troops of the Upper Country. (5) But because Sippa-LÚ-is was hostile to me, he did not succeed against me.

12

(7) Now, while My Lady Ishtar had even before this been promising me the kingship, at that time My Lady Ishtar appeared to my wife in a dream: 'I shall march before your husband. (10) And all Hattusas shall be led with your husband. (11) Since I thought highly of him, I did not—no, not ever—abandon him to the hostile trial, the hostile deity. (14) Now also I will exalt him, and make him priest of the sun goddess of Arinnas. (15) Do you also make me, Ishtar, (your) patron deity.' (16) And My Lady Ishtar stood behind (i.e. supported) me; and whatever she promised me occurred. (18) And My Lady Ishtar then also showed me her divine power abundantly. (19) To whatever nobles Urhitesupas had ever banished My Lady Ishtar appeared in a dream: 'You (are) summoned to your strength; but I, Ishtar, have turned all the lands of Hatti to the side of Hattusilis.' (23) And then also I saw the divine power of Ishtar abundantly. (24) Whereas she did not ever at another time abandon Urhitesupas, she shut him up in Samuhas like a pig in a sty. (26) As for me, however, the Gasgā men who had been hostile supported me; and all Hattusas supported me. (29) But, firm in (my) respect for my brother, I did not do anything. (30) And I marched back to Samuhas (to be) with Urhitesupas and I brought him down like a captive. (32) And I gave him fortified towns in the land of Nuhasse, and he dwelt there. (33) He would have planned another plan, (and) would have proceeded into the land of Karaduniya; but when I heard of the matter, I arrested him and ban-

pu-ša up-pa-aḫ-ḫu-un ^{I}*Ši-pa*-LÚ-*in-na* (4.37) ZAG *za-a-i-nu-ir* É-*TUM-ma-aš-ši-kán ar-ḫa da-aḫ-ḫu-un* (4.38) *na-at A-NA* ^{D}*IŠTAR* GAŠAN-*YA AD-DIN nu am-mu-uk A-NA* ^{D}*IŠTAR* GAŠAN-*YA* (4.39) *a-pa-a-at AD-DIN* ^{D}*IŠTAR-ma-mu-kán* GAŠAN-*YA i-la-ni i-la-ni* (4.40) *nam-ma ti-iš-ki-it*

13

(4.41) *nu-za* DUMU.LUGAL *e-šu-un nu-za* GAL *ME-ŠE-DI ki-iš-ḫa-ḫa-at* (4.42) GAL *ME-ŠE-DI-ma-za* LUGAL ^{URU}*ḪA-AK-PIŠ-ŠA ki-iš-ḫa-ḫa-at* LUGAL ^{URU}*ḪA-AK-PIŠ-ma-za* (4.43) LUGAL.GAL *nam-ma ki-iš-ḫa-ḫa-at nam-ma-mu-kán* ^{D}*IŠTAR* GAŠAN-*YA* (4.44) $^{LÚ.MEŠ}$*ar-ša-na-at-ta-lu-uš* $^{LÚ.MEŠ}$*ḫar-pa-na-al-li-uš* (4.45) *BE-LU*-ḪI.A *DI-NI-ya* ŠU-*i da-a-iš nu ku-i-e-eš IŠ-TU* ^{GIŠ}TUKUL *e-kir* (4.46) *ku-i-e-eš-ma* UD.KAM-*za e-kir na-aš-za ḫu-u-ma-an-te-eš-ḫe* GAM-*an ar-ḫa* (4.47) *zi-en-na-aḫ-ḫu-un nu-mu* ^{D}*IŠTAR* GAŠAN-*YA* LUGAL-*UT-TA ŠA* KUR ^{URU}*ḪA-AT-TI-ya* (4.48) *pí-eš-ta nu-za* LUGAL.GAL *ki-iš-ḫa-ḫa-at nu-mu* DUMU.LUGAL *da-a-aš* (4.49) *nu-mu-kán* ^{D}*IŠTAR* GAŠAN-*YA* LUGAL-*iz-na-an-ni an-da tar-ni-iš-ta* (4.50) *nu-mu* LUGAL.MEŠ *MAḪ-RU-YA a-aš-ša-u-wa-aš me-mi-ya-na-aš ku-i-e-eš e-šir* (4.51) *na-at-mu a-aš-ša-u-wa-aš-ḫe me-mi-ya-na-aš ki-ša-an-ta-at* (4.52) LÚ.MEŠ *TE-ME-ya-mu u-i-iš-ki-u-wa-an ti-i-e-ir up-pí-eš-šar*-ḪI.A-*ma-mu* (4.53) *up-pí-eš-ki-u-wa-an ti-i-e-ir up-pí-eš-šar*-ḪI.A-*ma-mu ku-i-e* (4.54) *up-pí-eš-ki-ir na-at A-NA* AB.BA.ḪI.A *Ú A-NA* AB.BA.AB.BA.ḪI.A-*YA* (4.55) *Ú-UL ku-e-da-ni-ik-ki up-pí-ir na-aḫ-ḫu-u-wa-aš-ma-mu ku-iš* LUGAL-*uš* (4.56) *e-eš-ta na-aš-mu-kán na-aḫ-ta ku-ru-ri*-ḪI.A-*ma-mu ku-e e-eš-ta* (4.57) *na-at-za tar-aḫ-ḫu-un A-NA* KUR.KUR.ḪI.A ^{URU}*ḪAT-TI-ma-za-kán* ZAG.ḪI.A *A-NA* ZAG.ḪI.A (4.58) *an-da da-aḫ-ḫu-un A-NA PA-NI* AB.BA.ḪI.A-*ya* AB.BA.AB.BA.ḪI.A-*ya* (4.59) *ku-i-e-eš ku-u-ru-ur e-šir am-mu-uk-ma ták-šu-la-a-ir* (4.60) *nu-mu* DINGIR-*LUM ku-it* GAŠAN-*YA kiš-an ka-ni-iš-ša-an ḫar-ta* (4.61) *nu ŠA* ŠEŠ-*YA na-ak-ki-ya-an-ni ḫa-an-da-aš Ú-UL ma-an-qa* DÙ-*nu-un* (4.62) [*nu* DUMU ŠE]Š-[*Y*]*A* ^{I} ^{D}KAL-*an ša-ra-a da-aḫ-ḫu-un nu-za* ŠEŠ-*YA* ^{I}NIR.GÁL-*iš ku*-[*it*] (4.63) *AŠ-RU* ^{URU} ^{D}U-*aš-ša-an pár-na-wa-iš-ki-it na-an a-pí-ya pí-di* (4.64) LUGAL-*iz-na-an-ni ti-it-ta-nu-nu-un nu-mu* ^{D}*IŠTAR* GAŠAN-*YA ma-ši-wa-an* (4.65) *da-a*[*t*]*-ta nu-mu šal-la-i pí-di A-NA* KUR ^{URU}*ḪAT-TI* LUGAL-*iz-na-an-ni* (4.66) *ti-it-ta-nu-ut am-mu-uk-ma A-NA* ^{D}*IŠTAR* GAŠAN-*YA* É ^{I} ^{D}*SIN*.^{D}U *AD-DIN* (4.67) *na-at-kán* EGIR-*an tar-na-aḫ-ḫu-un na-at pa-ra-a pí-iḫ-ḫu-un* (4.68) [*an*]*-na-al-la-an ku-it e-eš-ta a-pa-a-at-ši pa-ra-a pí-iḫ-ḫu-un* (4.69) *am-mu-uq-qa ku-it ḫar-ku-un a-pád-da-ya*

ished him across the sea. (36) And they sent Sippa-LÚ-is across the border; but I took (his) house from him, and gave it to My Lady Ishtar. (38) Now I gave that to My Lady Ishtar, and My Lady Ishtar thereafter granted me desire after desire.

13

(41) Now I was a prince, and became chief of the *Mešedi*. Again I, chief of the *Mešedi*, became king of Hakpissas. (42) Again I, king of Hakpissas, later became great king. (43) Thereupon My Lady Ishtar put into my hands (my) enviers, enemies, and opponents at law. (45) And some (of them) died by the weapon, but others died on the (appointed) day; and I completely got rid of them all. (47) And My Lady Ishtar gave me the kingship of the land of Hatti also, and I became a great king. (48) My Lady Ishtar took me (as a) prince and placed me on the throne. (50) And (those) who had been well disposed toward the kings, my predecessors, became well disposed toward me. (52) And they began to send me messengers, and they began to send me gifts as well. (53) But such gifts as they kept sending me, they had not sent to any of my fathers and forefathers. (55) On the other hand, whatever king owed me homage paid me homage. (56) But (the lands) that were hostile to me I conquered; I annexed district after district to the lands of Hatti. (58) And (those) who had been hostile in the time of my fathers and of my forefathers made peace with me. (60) And since the goddess, My Lady, had thus favored me, (being) firm in (my) loyalty to my brother, I did not act selfishly. (62) And I took my brother's son KAL-as, and set him upon a throne in the very spot, (namely) Dattasas, which my brother Muwattallis used for (his) palace. (64) Insignificant as I was when thou, My Lady Ishtar, didst take me, thou didst set me in the high place in the land of Hatti, upon the throne. (66) For my part I gave My Lady Ishtar the house of Armadattas. (67) I consecrated (?) it and gave it (to her). (68) What was (there) previously, I gave her; and what I had, that also I gave. (70) I conse-

pa-ra-a pi-iḫ-ḫu-un (4.70) *na-at-kán* EGIR-*an tar-na-aḫ-ḫu-un na-at A-NA* DINGIR-*LIM pa-ra-a AD-DIN* (4.71) É ^{I} ^{D}*SIN*.^{D}U-*ma-aš-ši ku-it pí-iḫ-ḫu-un nu* URU.AŠ.AŠ.ḪI.A *ku-i-e-eš ku-i-e-eš* (4.72) [*Š*]*A* ^{I} ^{D}*SIN*.^{D}U *na-an-kán ḫu-u-ma-an-ti-ya-be* EGIR-*an* ^{ZA}ZI.KIN (4.73) [*t*]*i-it-ta-nu-uš-kán-zi* DUG *ḫar-ši-ya-li-ya-kán iš-ḫu-iš-kán-zi* (4.74) ^{D}*IŠTAR* DINGIR-*LIM-aš-mu nu-uš-ma-ša-an* ^{D}*IŠTAR šar-la-im-mi-in* (4.75) [*ši*]*-pa-an-za-kán-zi am-mu-uq-qa-za ku-it ḫa-aš-ti-ya-aš* É-*ir* DÙ-*nu-un* (4.76) *na-at A-NA* DINGIR-*LIM pa-ra-a pí-iḫ-ḫu-un* DUMU-*YA-ya-at-ta* (4.77) ^{I}*Du-ut-ḫa-li-ya-an* ERUM-*an-ni pa-ra-a pí-iḫ-ḫu-un nu* É ^{D}*IŠTAR* (4.78) [^{I}*Du*]*-ut-ḫa-li-ya-aš* DUMU-*YA* 𒑱*ta-pár-du nu-za am-mu-uk* ERUM DINGIR-*LIM* (4.79) *a-pa-a-aš-ša* ERUM DINGIR-*LIM e-eš-du* É-*ir-ma ku-it A-NA* DINGIR-*LIM AD-DIN* (4.80) *nu ḫu-u-ma-an-za A-NA* DINGIR-*LIM* 𒑱*še-a-na-an* 𒑱*ma-ar-na-an e-eš-ša-ú*

14

(4.81) *ku-iš-ma-kán* 𒑱*zi-la-du-wa* NUMUN ^{I}*ḪA-AT-TU-ŠI-LI* ^{SAL}*PU-DU-ḪÉ-PA* (4.82) *A-NA* ^{D}*IŠTAR* ERUM-*an-ni ar-ḫa da-a-i ŠA* É *ga-ru-pa-ḫi-ya-aš-za* (4.83) *e-iz-za-an* ^{GIŠ}ŠUB KISLAḪ *ŠA* ^{D}*IŠTAR* ^{URU}*ŠA-MU-ḪA i-la-li-ya-zi* (4.84) *na-aš A-NA* ^{D}*IŠTAR* ^{URU}*ŠA-MU-ḪA* EN *DI-NI-ŠU e-eš-du* (4.85) *ša-aḫ-ḫa-ni-ya-aš lu-uz-zi li-e ku-iš-ki e-ip-zi*

15

(4.86) *ku-iš-ša-kán* 𒑱*zi-la-du-wa* DUMU-*ŠÚ* DUMU.DUMU-*ŠÚ* ŠA(G).BAL.BAL (4.87) 𒑱*zi-la-du-wa ŠA* ^{I}*ḪA-AT-TU-ŠI-LI* ^{SAL}*PU-DU-ḪÉ-PA ša-ra-a* (4.88) *iš-pár-za-zi na-aš-kán ŠA*(G) DINGIR.MEŠ *A-NA* ^{D}*IŠTAR* ^{URU}*ŠA-MU-ḪA* (4.89) *na-aḫ-ḫa-an-za e-eš-du*

crated it and gave it to the goddess. (71) Furthermore, as to the house of Armadattas that I gave her, and the cities that belonged to Armadattas, behind every one they are again setting up her statue (?), and distributing libation cups (?). (74) Ishtar is my goddess, and for themselves (men) pour libations to Ishtar, the Highest (?). (75) Whatever mausoleum I have built, that I have given to the goddess. (76) And my son Duthaliyas I gave for thy service; may my son Duthaliyas rule the house of Ishtar. (78) I (am) the servant of the goddess; let him also be the servant of the goddess. (79) And whatever (birth-)house I have dedicated to the goddess, let every (child?) celebrate (?) the *seyanan marnan* for the goddess.

14

(81) Now, whoever in the future takes a descendant of Hattusilis (and) Puduhepas away from the service of Ishtar (or) covets the food (?) of the *garupahis* house, the possessions, (or) the granary of Ishtar of Samuhas, let him be an opponent at law of Ishtar of Samuhas. (85) Let no one assess feudal services (or) taxes upon them.

15

(86) In the future whatever son, grandson, (or) future descendant of Hattusilis (and) Puduhepas ascends the throne, let him be reverent toward Ishtar of Samuhas among the gods.

COMMENTARY

Hattusilis, the Third, was the youngest son of Mursilis, the Second, who ruled in Ḫattusas from about 1353 to about 1325 B.C. Mursilis was succeeded by Muwattallis (ca.1325–1303), who died without leaving a legitimate son. There is little doubt that Hattusilis would have seized the throne at this time if it had not been for the strict regulation of the succession by the decree of Telipinus (below, pp. 175–200), according to which a son by a secondary wife must become king in default of a prince of the first rank. So Hattusilis established his nephew, Urhitesupas, on the throne. The latter, however, was jealous of the influence of Hattusilis, and perhaps justly afraid that he would some day contrive to get the throne of Hattusas for himself. At any rate Urhitesupas deprived Hattusilis of his authority bit by bit, until finally he tried to take from him the last remnant of his lawful power, the kingship over the cities of Hakpissas and Nerikkas. Then Hattusilis declared war upon his titular suzerain, deposed and banished him, and established himself in his place.

Such action was, to say the least, of doubtful legality in what was, after all, a limited monarchy, and it required justification before the *pankus*, the council of the nobility, which we elsewhere call the senate. While the document before us is not ostensibly addressed to this body, it is hard to see what other purpose it could have had.

Our text is virtually that of Götze, Hatt. and NBr. We have omitted a few hopelessly defective passages, and have ventured a few variations from Götze's text. These are noted below unless Götze's critical apparatus sufficiently justifies our reading.

1.1 ff.: Many Hittite texts have an introductory sentence composed wholly in Akkadian. The proper names, even if they are elsewhere declined in the Hittite fashion, are here treated as indeclinables, as is usual with Akkadian proper names. In most transliterated Hittite texts all names are printed as Hittite, but we print as Akkadian all those that lack case endings.

Götze, Hatt. 77 f., regards the introductory formulae as Hittite written with a large proportion of ideograms. For him *UMMA* in our text stands for a Hittite word meaning 'words', and he would call ^{I}*Tabarna* ^{I}*Hattusili* genitives without case ending. He holds that proper names, being in the main not Hittite, employed the stem form in genitive and dative; and it is true that inflected genitives from proper names scarcely occur in the later language. (Datives identical with the stem form are common from other substantive *a*-stems and *i*-stems also.) But if the use of the bare stem as genitive is a trace of foreign origin, it is strange that precisely the archaic texts show inflected genitives from proper names; see on ^{URU}*Ḫal-pa-aš* (T 1.28). See also Sommer, BoSt. 10.1; Sturtevant, Lang. 5.145 f.

1.1. ^{I}*TA-BA-AR-NA*: the determinative ^{I} (properly the numeral for 'one') marks a following word as a man's name [20]. Here it is used before the title *Tabarnas*; cf. the capitalization in Eng. phrases like *King George*. *Tabarnas* is a foreign, probably Luwian, word meaning 'ruler', which serves as a standing title of the Hittite kings. For the etymology, see on T 1.2. For the use of the stem instead of a case form in Akkadian passages or phrases, see [24f.]. I construe the word as subject of the sentence. — ^{I}*ḪA-AT-TU-ŠI-LI*: Hattusilis, the Third, ruled about 1298–1260 B.C. He maintained the state at the summit of its power throughout his reign, and he cemented a treaty of peace with Egypt by giving a Hittite princess in marriage to Ramses, the Second.— KUR ^{URU}*ḪA-AT-TI*, the usual designation of the Hittite empire, as well as of the central kingdom about the capital Hattusas. The name Hatti belongs properly to the pre-Hittite population [3]. Presumably the Hittite form of the name was *Hattis* or *Hattus* (cf. the derivative *Hattusas*); but it does not occur, and so we have to use in English the Akkadian form *Hatti*. It is the name of a country; but the scribes frequently use the determinative URU 'city' in such a context, e.g. KUR ^{URU}*MI-IṢ-RI-I* 'the land of Egypt' (2.69). Construe KUR according to Sumerian syntax [21].

1.2. ^{I}*MUR-ŠI-LI*: Mursilis, the Second, ruled about 1353–1325 B.C.

1.3. DUMU.DUMU-*ŠÚ ŠA* 'grandson of'. This tautological use of -*ŠU* is common in Akkadian. — ^{I}*ŠU-UP-PÍ-LU-LI-U-MA*: Suppiluliumas ruled about 1395–1355 B.C.

1.4. ^{I}*ḪA-AT-TU-ŠI-LI*: Hattusilis, the First, son of Labarnas, ruled in the first half of the eighteenth century. — ^{URU}*KU-UŠ-ŠAR*: Kussaras was the seat of the Hittite monarchy before the conquest of Hattusas. The town probably lay somewhere within the great bend of the Halys River.

1.5. *ŠA* ^{D}*IŠTAR* 'of Ishtar'. For the determinative, see [20]. This Akkadian phrase [24b] almost certainly stands for a Hittite genitive, but we do not know what the Hittite name of the goddess is. — *pa-ra-a ḫa-an-da-an-da-tar*: from the participle *parā handanza* (1.47) 'ruled (by a god)' probably comes the denominative verb *parā handanda(e)-* [310–2], whence this verbal noun [156f.]. On the meaning, cf. Sommer, BoSt. 10.30 f.; Götze, Kulturgeschichte 138. The latter scholar holds that the supernatural power denoted by the noun is always exerted in the interest of the worshipper, who is temporarily endowed with it. Hence he interprets the verb as 'favor, bless, endow with miraculous power' or the like. I prefer the translation 'rule, control (by supernatural power)' as being nearer to the ordinary meaning of *handa(e)-* (see Additions and Corrections).

1.6. *na-at*: with certain exceptions to be mentioned hereafter, every sentence in connected discourse must be introduced by a sentence connective. The commonest of these is *nu* 'and' (often not to be translated into English). The combination of *nu* with *-as* 'is', neut. *-at*, is written *na-aš*, *na-at* [246f.]. Of course an initial sentence does not require a connective, and neither does the first sentence after an introductory passage; e.g. 1.5, 1.9. — DUMU.NAM.LÚ.GÀL.LU-*aš*: DUMU. NAM.LÚ.GÀL.LU is a Sumerian ideogram meaning 'man, mankind'; the Hittite phonetic complement *aš* represents the end of some Hittite nominative [23, 25.6]. — *iš-ta-ma-aš-du*: for the non-phonetic initial vowel, see [30–3]. — *zi-la-du-wa*: on the 'glossenkeil', see [19a].

1.7. *ŠA* ᴰUTU-*ŠI*: in Hittite texts ᴰUTU-*ŠI* = *ŠAMŠĪ* 'my sun' (*ŠAMŠU* 'sun' + *-I* 'my') is a standing designation of the reigning Hittite king; cf. Eng. *His Majesty*. The underlying Hittite phrase ended in *-mes* 'my', as is shown by the phonetic complement in KUB 25.23.4.48: ᴰUTU-*ŠI-me-iš* (?), KBo.5.3.4.29: ᴰUTU-*ŠI-in*, VBoT 1.13: ᴰUTU-*mi*; cf. Friedrich, Vert. 2.139. — DINGIR.MEŠ: for the plural sign, see the Sign List. — *-kan* need not be represented in the translation; see on 1.22.

1.8. *na-aḫ-ḫa-an*: see [154].

1.9. *A-BU-YA-an-na-aš-za* = *attas-mes-nas-za*. There is a tendency to give enclitics after ideograms and Akkadian words the orthography that is appropriate after a vowel. Here the sign *an* is non-phonetic; see Götze, Hatt. 55f. (but cf. Sommer, BoSt. 7.6 fn. 1); see also [23]. The particle *-za* is usually reflexive in force; here it combines with *ḫa-aš-ta* (1.11) to mean 'sibi genuit'. See Götze-Pedersen, MS 38–40, 80–83. It is often impossible to represent the force of the particle in idiomatic English.

1.10. ᴵNIR.GÀL-*in* = *Muwattallin*. Sumerian NIR.GÀL 'strong, mighty' sometimes stands for the equivalent Akkadian *MUṬALLU*, and hence, by a punning etymology, it is used for the Hittite name

Mu(wa)ttallis; see Weidner, BoSt. 8.127 fn. 11; but cf. Meriggi, RHA 2.16. The real etymology is quite different; the element *muwa-* occurs in a number of Hittite personal names and also in later personal names of southern Asia Minor (Friedrich, KlF 1.359–78). — SALDINGIR.MEŠ. IR-*in-na*: the accusative of the daughter's name ended in *in*; *-a* is the enclitic conjunction.

1.11. *ḫa-aš-tạ*: for the form, see [391]. — *nu-za*: the reflexive force of *-za* is often so far weakened that the particle merely makes the verb perfective. Here *-za . . . e-šu-un* properly means 'I turned out to be'; but such a phrase would be grotesque in English. — *ḫu-u-ma-an-da-aš-be* = *humandas-be*.

1.12. DUMU-*aš*: in addition to *uwas* 'son', Hittite has an unknown word for 'child, son' that is sometimes written DUMU-*la-aš*. — *ŠA* KUŠ.KA.TAB.ANŠU 'groom' is an honorary title, whose Hittite form is unknown. The lack of a sentence connective here indicates that the clause is virtually a repetition of the previous one. It would seem, then, that Hittite princes were customarily made 'groom' for some definite period of years. — *nu*: the situation of this word at the end of a line is altogether exceptional. In KUB 1.1.1.12 it was omitted by oversight, along with the two following words, and then added by way of correction.

1.13. *A-NA* I*MUR-ŠI-LI*: on the use of *ANA* as a sign of the Hittite dat., see [24b]. — *A-BI-YA* = *atte-me* (dat.) 'my father'. When a noun in an oblique case and its appositive are written ideographically, the Akkadian preposition is written only once, but it governs both nouns; hence *ABI* stands in the gen. after *ANA*.

1.14. *A-NA* I*ḪA-AT-TU-ŠI-LI-wa*: the first sentence of a direct quotation requires no sentence connective; cf. on *na-at* (1.6). Every quoted sentence, on the other hand, normally requires the particle *-wa*.

1.15. *Ú-UL-wa-ra-aš*: the lack of a sentence connective is due to the fact that this sentence merely repeats what was said in the previous sentence; tautological sentences regularly have no connective. — TI-*an-na-aš* is gen. of the verbal noun *hweswatar* [156, 188].

1.17. *ša-ra-a da-a-aš*: this merely introductory use of *sarā dā-* is very common.

1.19. BAL-*aḫ-ḫu-un* = *ši-pa-an-da-aḫ-ḫu-un*.

1.20. *u-uḫ-ḫu-un*: for the form, see [363].

1.21. ŠU-*za*: for the case, see [190]. — *pa-ra-a ḫa-an-ta-an-te-eš-ta*: from *parā hantanta(e)-* (see on *pa-ra-a ḫa-an-da-an-da-tar* — 1.5) by analogy with the second class of the *hi*-conjugation (*memanzi* : *memesta* = *parā hantantanzi* : *parā hantantesta*).

1.22–27: Since Hittite subordinate clauses are attached to main clauses by the same connectives that connect coordinate clauses and independent sentences, it is often difficult to determine the relative subordination. Here the clause introduced by *mahhan* is certainly subordinate, and I have coupled the next two with it because (1) all three are introduced by *-ma-za* and (2) that yields an excellent sense. Others may prefer to take the second clause as the main clause, and to couple the third with it (so Götze).

1.22. *ma-aḫ-ḫa-an-ma-za*: *-ma* 'but, however' is, after *nu*, the most frequent sentence connective; cf. on *na-at* (1.6). — DINGIR-*LIM-iš*: the Akkadian word for 'god' is *ILU*, gen. *ILI* or *ILIM* [24a]. The gen. is here used illogically for the nom., as is clearly shown by the Hittite phonetic complement, which marks the nom. sg. of an *i*-stem noun. DINGIR-*LIM-iš kisat* (or *kesat*) 'he became a god' is a frequent expression for the death of a Hittite king.

1.23. ŠEŠ-*YA-ma-za-kán* . . . *e-ša-at* 'and my brother seated himself': *-ma* points the contrast between this clause and the preceding one, but English idiom requires 'and' rather than 'but'. For the reflexive particle *-za*, see on 1.9. *-kan* normally suggests motion to or into, as here; see Götze, AOr. 5.16–30. Frequently, however, no actual motion is to be thought of, so in 1.7, 20, 21. Usually it is impossible to represent the particle by a separate English word.

1.25. GAL-*ME-ŠE-DI-UT-TIM*: the Akkadian word *MEŠEDI* designates some high official at court, and GAL *MEŠEDI* (also GAL $^{\text{LÚ.MEŠ}}$*MEŠEDI*) means 'chief of the *Mešedi*'. Our abstract noun seems to be derived from the phrase rather than from the word *ME-ŠEDI*. — *ti-it-ta-nu-ut*: for the formation, see [289, 326].

1.26. KUR UGU = *udne sarāzzi* 'the Upper Country'. The phrase is used almost as a proper name; cf. KUR *ŠAP-LI-TI* (1.76) and note. It designates the mountainous region to the east of the plain in which Hattusas stood.

1.27. KUR UGU-*TI* = *MĀTI ELĪTI*, gen. sg. of *MĀTU ELĪTU*. This use of an Akkadian gen. with the verb *tapar-* cannot, however, be considered proof that the verb governs the gen. Elsewhere (1.65, 2.61, 2.74) it takes the acc., and so the Akkadian gen. is probably used inexactly for the acc.; cf. on DINGIR-*LIM-iš* (1.22). — *ta-pár-ḫa*: for the form, see [426]. — *pí-ra-an-ma-at-mu* = *peran-ma-at-mu* 'it, however, before me'; *peran* is an adverb and *-mu* a dative of reference. — $^{\text{I D}}$*SIN*-^{D}U-*aš* = *Armadattas*: the phonetic value of ^{D}*SIN* is established by the variant spelling of this name in KUB 19.67.1.6: ^{I}*AR-MA*-^{D}U (see Götze, NBr. 18). The phonetic interpretation of DU is uncertain; but one god's name represented by the ideogram is *Da-at-ta-aš* (see Götze, KlH 17 fn. 2), and the phonetic complement *aš* offers some support for the assumption of that name here.

1.28. *ma-ni-ya-aḫ-ḫi-eš-ki-it*: for the formation, see [333–8].

1.29. ŠEŠ-*YA-ya*: the enclitic *-a/-ya* 'and' connects sentences or clauses that are semantically parallel. For the other sentence connectives, see on *na-at* (1.6) and on *ma-aḫ-ḫa-an-ma-za* (1.22). For asyndeton between sentences, see on 1.14 and 1.15. — *ka-ni-eš-ša-an ḫar-ta*: the present tense of *har*(*k*)- 'have' combines with the participle in *-anza* (which in this use always appears in the form of the neut. sg.) to form a periphrastic perfect. The preterit tense of *har*(*k*)- similarly forms a periphrastic pluperfect.

1.31. *ka-ni-eš-šu-u-wa-ar*: see [161].

1.32. *aš-šu-la-an* = *assulan* seems to be virtually equivalent to *assu* (30); for the suffix, see [152].

1.33. *nam-ma-ya*: *-ya*, the by-form of *-a*, probably got its consonant from combination with words in final *e* or *i*; cf. *li-e-ya-aš* = *le* + *as* (I 3.20), *ták-ku-wa-aš* = *takku* + *as* (I 3.31), etc. Sometimes *-a* is written for *-ya* after final *e* or *i*; e.g. C 1.5,7,9, etc. — *da-ma-a-uš* UKÙ.MEŠ-*uš*: for the use of plural case forms, see [182].

1.34. *ú-wa-a-i-ti-iš-ki-u-wa-an ti-i-e-ir*: for the form and meaning of the supine, see [161b,c,d]. The noun *uwai* probably means 'invidia', and it may be connected with the stem *uwa-* 'appear, be seen'. Quite possibly it had a magical or supernatural connotation. The word is known only in stereotyped phrases with the verb stems *uda-* 'bring', *peda-* 'take with one, carry', *tiya-*, and *teske-*. Since the first two verbs are transitive the others must be also, and it follows that in the phrase *uwai tiyet* (*ti-ya-at*) we have a *mi*-conjugation preterit of *dai-* 'place'. The stem *teske-* in our phrase must also come from *dai-* 'place' [304]. — *ḫu-u-wa-ap-pí-ir*: the verb *huwapp-* and the adjective *huwappas* (1.40) apparently suggest the supernatural (cf. OLZ 35.471). The meaning given the verb is only an approximation.

1.35. ⸓*ar-pa-ša-at-ta* seems to be a Luwian preterit [10, 19a]. The verb is related to *arpas* 'bad luck'; for the formative *s*, cf. [315–319].

1.36. *A-NA* GIŠDUBBIN *lam-ni-ya-at* 'named . . . for the wheel (?)'. Line 40 suggests that this is a juridical phrase; perhaps it means 'indict, bring action against', or the like. — Ù-*at* = *teshanattat*? Cf. the durative *te-eš-ḫa-ni-iš-kit₉-ta-ri* (KUB 16.55.4.8).

1.37f. DINGIR-*LIM-ni* . . . *tar-na-aḫ-ḫi*: if DINGIR-*LIM-ni* means 'god', the context requires a question equivalent to a negative statement. Hittite has no formal mark of interrogation. (The adjective 'hostile' is implied by the context, and is expressed in 1.40.) Götze suggests that DINGIR-*LIM-ni* may stand for DINGIR-*LIM-an-ni*, from DINGIR-*LIM-atar* 'divinity', and that the sentence may mean, 'I will put you under (my) divine protection'.

1.38. *li-e na-aḫ-ti*: for the negative command, see [378].

1.40. *ḫu-u-wa-ap-pí*: see on *ḫu-u-wa-ap-pí-ir* (34). — DINGIR-*LIM-ni* . . . *ḫa-an-ne-eš-ni*: since a god inevitably determines the action of a court the two words are interchangeable in such a context as this one; *hannesni* is virtually in apposition with DINGIR-*LIM-ni*.

1.41. *-ma*: it is often impossible to express in idiomatic English the contrast implied by this particle. Here and in l. 54 it points the antithesis between judicial and military enemies.

1.42. *še-ir wa-aḫ-nu-ut* does not elsewhere mean 'overthrow'. Götze suggests that LÚ KÚR may be the subject (inversion due to introductory *natta* ?) and that the verb may mean 'brandish over'.

1.43. *ḫu-u-ma-an-da-za-be*: see [196a fn. 80].

1.44. *iš-tar-ak-zi* is historical present [379].

1.46. DINGIR-*LUM* = *ILUM* = *ILU* [24a]. — *am-mu-uk-ma-za*: *-ma* here contrasts Hattusilis' obedience with Ishtar's graciousness.

1.47. *pa-ra-a ḫa-an-da-a-an-za*: literally 'controlled, governed'; see on *pa-ra-a ḫa-an-da-an-da-tar* (1.5).

1.49. DUMU.NAM.LÚ.GÀL.LU-*UT-TI* = *AMĒLŪTI*, gen. sg. of *AMĒLŪTU* 'humanity, mankind'.

1.51. *Ú-UL e-eš-ta*: for the interpretation as a question, see on DINGIR-*LIM-ni* . . . *tar-na-aḫ-ḫi* (37 f.). In spite of the tense of *daskisi* (1.50), Götze would prefer to translate, 'Has it not been (true that) thou didst rescue me?'. — *ku-wa-ya-mi*: the translation suggested for this Luwian (?) word is inferred from the context.

1.54. *A-NA* EN *DI-NI-YA*: EN = *BĒLU* = *eshas* 'master'; *DĪNU* = *hanessar* 'law-suit'; *-YA* = *-mes* 'my'. The phrase *BĒL DĪNI-YA* means 'my opponent at law'. Here *ANA* EN must function as a plural, since the appositive, LÚ.MEŠ*ar-ša-na-at-tal-la-aš*, is dat. pl.

1.55. INIM = *memiyas*: this word rather than *uttar* is required by the pronouns *-as* and *kwiski* (1.56).

1.56. *ku-iš-ki* is here little more than an indefinite article. The conditional clause justifies its use instead of *kwis* [255].

1.57. *pa-la-aḫ-ša-an*: the approximate meaning of this rare word can be inferred from the context; but our translation is probably too vague.

1.60. *kat-ta-an ar-ḫa*: see [278 end]. — *zi-en-na-aḫ-ḫu-un*: from *ze-* [287] and *nai-* 'lead, turn, drive', with transfer to the second class of the *hi*-conjugation [352].

1.62. *a-aš-ta*: Bechtel will demonstrate elsewhere that *aszi* and *asta* always mean 'remains, remained'.

1.63. KARAŠ ANŠU.KUR.RA.MEŠ: cf. Lat. *equīs virīsque* 'with horse and foot'. The Hittite word underlying ANŠU.KUR.RA.MEŠ must be masc. sg., since *ḫu-u-ma-an-da-an* (1.65) agrees with it. In 2.73 the word is subject of a singular verb.

1.64. KUR ^{URU}*ḪA-AT-TI*: see on KUR ^{URU}*ḪA-AT-TI* (1.1). Here as there the phrase is to be understood as Akkadian (i.e. *MĀT ḪATTI*), and the name of the country is indeclinable as proper names regularly are in Akkadian. Since the names of countries are regularly written in this Akkadian phraseology in our Hittite texts there are many of them whose Hittite names are unknown. The names of cities are more frequently given in the Hittite form.

1.67. IGI.ḪI.A: for the plural suffix, see [21].

1.69. KUR.KUR.MEŠ: the Sumerian word is marked as plural both by the reduplication and by the plural suffix. — *tar-aḫ-ḫi-iš-ki-nu-un* = *tarheskenun*: for the double writing of *h*, see [70].

1.70. *-be* 'the same, the aforementioned'.

1.76. *I-NA* KUR *ŠAP-LI-TI* = *udne kattere* (?), 'to the Lower Country'. The phrase is used almost as a proper name; cf. Eng. *The Netherlands*. Similarly KUR UGU (1.26).

2.2. EGIR-*az*: properly 'behind (him)'.

2.3. KUR ^{URU}*GA-AŠ-GA*-ḪI.A: the Gasgā peoples dwelt to the northeast of Hattusas, and they frequently raided the border region. The other places mentioned in this line and the next must have lain near the Gasgā countries; for a discussion of the geography of the region, see Götze, RHA 1.18–30. — *ḫu-u-ma-an-te-eš*: since *udne* 'country' is neuter, this masculine form must be felt as applying to the inhabitants — constructio ad sensum.

2.5. ^{ID}*Ma-ra-aš-ša-an-da-an*: they must have crossed the upper course of the Halys southeast of Hattusas. — *ar-ḫa da-a-ir*: the etymological meaning, given in the translation, is obviously too general for this context; it is uncertain, however, whether the insurgents plundered or won over the localities named in this sentence.

2.6. The name of one country has been lost.

2.7. KUR ^{URU}*KA-NI-EŠ*: the city of Kanes was the seat of an important Assyrian merchant colony about 2000 B.C. It has been identified with the mound Kül Tepe, about twelve miles northeast of Kaisariyeh and a hundred miles southeast of Boghazköi (Hrozný, Syria 8.1–12).

2.7b. The end of the line is preserved, and it is equivalent to the end of line 2.7. The lost sentence must have been a close parallel to the preceding one.

2.8. The name of one city has been lost. — URU*Ku-ru-uš-ta-ma-aš*: the names of cities, unlike the names of countries, are often written with case endings, especially in nom. and acc. For the other cases, see on 1.1. — URU*Gaz-zi-ú-ra-aš*: Götze, RHA 1.25 f., identifies this with Strabo's Gaziura, the modern Turchal, some fifty miles northeast of Boghazköi.

2.9. URU.DU$_6$.ḪI.A URU*ḪA-AT-TI*: it is not clear why the enemy should attack ruined cities. Perhaps this was the current designation of a district that had lain in ruin for many years, but had been occupied again.

2.12. *dan-na-at-ta-an*: for the formation, see [169].

2.13. *pa-ra-a . . . a-ar-aš-ki-it*: the durative *arske-* seems here to belong to *artari* 'rise, start, stand'.

2.14. *2-e-el* must be an adverb, but the precise meaning is uncertain. The form suggests a gen. of the pronominal declension [261]. — *iš-pár-zi-ir* [126 fn. 92].

2.15. *iš-tap-pa-an e-eš-ta*: a singular predicate with a neuter plural subject is frequent; see [380].

2.16. *I-NA* MU 10.KAM 'for ten years'; cf. Lat. *diem iam quintum cibo caruerat.* For the use of a singular noun with a numeral, see [183].

2.21. *I-NA . . . da-a-iš*: the three tablets that preserve this sentence or part of it agree in placing it before *nu-mu* ŠEŠ-*YA* (20); it clearly stood there in the archetype. I have nevertheless transferred it to this position, since that appears to be the only way to extract a meaning from it. Götze's translation assumes that the subject of *da-a-iš* is the same as that of *ḫar-ga-nu-ir* (19) in spite of the difference in number. He translates *kat-ta-an da-a-iš* 'setzte sich . . . fest', although there is no parallel for such a meaning. Furthermore, if the enemy had established himself in Pattiyarigas, it is strange to learn three lines below that Hattusilis found him in Hahhas. Perhaps knowledge of the geography of the region will some day show which reading is correct. Götze modified the translation in NBr. 10f., but without removing the difficulty (see Sommer, AU 211). Götze would now regard the meaning of *kat-ta-an da-a-iš* as quite unknown; he does not approve of the transposition.

2.24. *pí-ra-an ḫu-u-wa-a-iš*: others prefer to translate more prosaically, 'helped'.

2.25. ŠU-*an ú-e-da-aḫ-ḫu-un*: on the meaning, see Sommer, AU 26 and fn.1; Götze, NBr. 26 f.

2.26. *pí-e ḫar-ta*: this compound verb regularly implies motion, as in T 1.31; see [76].

2.28. LÚ.MEŠ *pí-ra-an ḫu-u-i-ya-tal-lu-uš*: 'marchers before'.

2.29. LÚ-*tar-mi-it*: correct [223] as follows. In line 5, for archaic read: archaizing. The last sentence should begin: These words occur in later texts chiefly in prepositional phrases, etc.

2.30. IGI-*zi* = *hantezzi*. — BAL-*ši*: the Hittite word for 'time, occasion' is unknown.

2.31. *ú-it-ma . . . a-ar-aš*: the verbs *uwa-* 'come' and *pai-* 'go' are frequently used thus without a following sentence connective to introduce another verb that agrees with the same subject. See Friedrich, Vert. 1.162 and fn.2. — URU*Pí-iš-ḫu-ru-uš*: cf. URU*Ḫa-at-tu-ša-an* (2.26).

2.32. URU*Taq-qa-aš-ta-aš*: the only text that preserves this name (KBo. 3.6.2.17) has KUR before it, but the same text reads URU*Tal-ma-li-ya-aš* in the next clause. Since (1) names of countries are usually written without case endings, (2) a city is a better mark of a boundary than a country, and (3) a city Takkastas is known from KBo. 4.13.1.31, it seems probable that KUR in our passage is an error.

2.34. 800 *ṢI-IM-TUM* : for the sing. with a numeral, see [183].

2.37. ERÍN.MEŠ-*az* represents the nom. sg. of a collective noun in -*z* (cf. ERIN.MEŠ-*za* — T 2.18) meaning 'infantry'; 1 LÚ stands in partitive apposition.

2.39. LÚ-*LUM* = *AMĒLUM*.

2.40. *e-eš-ta na-an-kán*: this is the reading of KBo.3.6.2.23. The other text available for this line (KUB 1.1.2.40 + KUB 19.61) has another clause after *e-eš-ta*; but it is incompletely preserved and it is not clear what the correct reading is.

2.44. URU*Ú-I-IŠ-TA-U-WA-AN-DA*: this is a town whose Hittite name is not citable.

2.46. *ḫa-li-iš-ši-ya-nu-un*: for the meaning, see Ehelolf ap. Sommer, AU 186.

2.48–51. I understand this passage as saying, in effect: 'While I was waging a successful war with my own resources, Muwattallis took the field with the main body of the Hittite army; but he did not give me any real assistance, and presently retired with his army.' Götze understands, however, that Muwattallis, in preparation for the war against

Egypt (2.69 ff.), deprived Hattusilis of all or part of his troops and sent them away to Hattusas. On this interpretation I find no force for the first clause in 2.50.

2.49. *ú-e-te-it*: the word usually means 'build'.

2.51. [*ku-it*]-*ma-an*: the supplement is Götze's.

2.52. *pí-di ni-ni-ik-ta*: otherwise Sommer, BoSt. 7.38 f.

2.54. [URU]*Dur-mi-it-ta*, [URU]*Ku-ru-uš-ta-ma*: for the dat. in *a* of *a*-stems, see [195a]. The words may, however, be interpreted as acc. [57, 131].

2.61. *ḫu-u-ma-an-da-an*: the gender is doubtless due to the last substantive in the list; the number is illogical; cf. [182, 183].

2.65. [LÚ]KÚR.MEŠ is used loosely to correspond to *ku-e ki-e* KUR. KUR.MEŠ (63).

2.66. GAM-*an ti-ya-at*: Götze translates 'kam herab'; but cf. *IŠTU ŠA* [D]UTU-*ŠI ti-an-zi*, which Friedrich, Vert. 1.145.17, translates 'auf Seiten der Sonne treten'; where *IŠTU ŠA* must stand for the instrumental.

2.68. *na-at*: for neut. sg. pronouns referring to plural antecedents, see Friedrich, ZA NF 2.290–6.

2.70–74. These lines refer to the campaign against Ramses of Egypt which culminated in the famous battle of Kadesh (ca. 1308 B.C.). See Götze, OLZ 32.832–8.

2.73. ANŠU.KUR.RA.MEŠ . . . *e-eš-ta*: for the agreement, see on 1.63.

2.75. *Ù ŠA* ŠEŠ-*YA-ya*: the Akkadian conjunction *U* must stand for the Hittite enclitic *-ya*, which is nevertheless written phonetically in its proper position.

2.76. [*na-aḫ-ta*] is an altogether uncertain supplement.

2.77. *nu-mu*; *-mu* is direct object of *e-ip-pir*. — *al-wa-an-za-aḫ-ḫu-u-wa-an-zi*: see [162, 436].

2.81. *A-NA* DINGIR-*LIM* *ši-pa-an-tu-u-wa-an-zi*: both datives depend directly upon the verb, the former as end of motion, the latter as dat. of purpose.

2.82. DINGIR-*LUM* *i-ya-nu-un*: *iya-* 'make' frequently has this pregnant meaning.

3.5. É-*TI* = *BĪTI*, gen. sg. of *BĪTU* 'house'.

3.8–10. Remnants of the text indicate that line 8 recorded the granting of the goddess' favor and that line 9 began the account of a new campaign.

3.12. KUR [URU]*ḪA-AK-PIŠ*: this phrase is equivalent to KUR

URU*ḪA-AK-PIŠ-ŠA* (2.61), and nearly equivalent to URU*Ḫa-ak-piš-ša-aš* (3.10).

3.14. *ú-it* 'came (and)' is omitted in the translation.

3.16. *ḫa-an-ni-iš-na-an-za*: the ablative in *anz* occurs in consonant stem nouns as well as in *a*-stems [196a].

3.17. *A-NA* I*AR-MA*-DU: the stem *arma-* 'moon' is Hittite; but the Akkadian preposition proves that the scribe intended to write the name in its Akkadian form here and in 3.30.

3.18. *na-at-ši-ya-at* is *natse* 'and it to him', with *-at* repeated at the end of the complex. The forms of *-as* 'is' are frequently repeated after *-se* 'sibi, ei' and after the reflexive particle *-za*. See Götze, NBr. 19 f., AOr. 5.3, and note on I 4.72.

3.23. One would like to read [*ni-wa-al-la*]*-an* 'innocent' at the beginning of the line, but the traces in KUB 19.67.1.14 forbid.

3.25. The surviving end of the lost word indicates that it was a genitive. The meaning suggested in the translation is Götze's conjecture.

3.27. *naš* = *nu* + *aš* must be acc. pl., since there are no clear instances of enclitic *-as* in other cases than nom. and acc.; see [246].

3.28. DUMU-*ŠU-ya* = *uwan-sen-a*: *-ya* is written instead of *-a* after ideograms and Akkadian words, even if the underlying Hittite word ends in a consonant and therefore requires *-a*; see Sommer, BoSt. 10.28 f., and cf. on 1.9. — [*A-N*]*A* URU*A-LA-ŠI-YA*: Hittite inflection of the name occurs in KBo.4.1.1.39: URU*A-la-ši-ya-az*.

3.29. [*nu* A.ŠA(G).ḪI.A *ták-ša-a*]*n*: the supplement is Götze's, and he cites paragraph 53 of the Code to show that the Hittite word underlying A.ŠA(G).ḪI.A is masculine singular.

3.31–38. These lines seem to have contained a summary of Hattusilis' relations with Muwattallis during the reign of the latter.

3.38 f. *ŠA* ŠEŠ-*YA* . . . *i-ya-nu-un*: the phrase occurs also in 3.61 f. and in 4.29 f. The interpretation given is from Hahn, Lang. 18.105 f. and fnn. 130, 131 (1942). Cf. Sommer, AU 242–5 (1933); Pedersen, Hitt. 68–71 (1938).

3.41. SAL*E-ŠE-IR-TI*: certainly a secondary wife; probably a captive woman; see Götze, AOR. 2.155–9; Feigin, AJSL 50.228–34.

3.43. EN-*an-ni*: the use of this word instead of LUGAL-*u-e-iz-na-an-ni* is striking. Hattusilis calls Urhitesupas LUGAL.GAL in 3.70.

3.46. [I*ḪA-AN*]*-TI-LI*: the reign of Hantilis belongs to the second half of the eighteenth century B.C., and so we are to understand that Nerikkas had been in ruins for five centuries. Götze's supplement has been confirmed by KUB 25.21.3.2 ff.

3.51–54. Important new material in these lines comes from KUB 31.13 (1939). See Goetze's reconstruction in BASOR 122.22 and fn. 17 (1951).

3.51. *ar-kam-ma-na-al-li-uš*: thus in KUB 31.13.10.

3.56. [*ú*]-*wa-a-i* [*ú-da*]-*a-aš*: see on *ú-wa-a-i-ti-iš-ki-u-wa-an ti-i-e-ir* (1.34).

3.60. *A-NA* ᴰU ᵁᴿᵁ*NE-RI-IK-KA-za*: in my opinion this is tautological asyndeton; see on *Ú-UL-wa-ra-aš* (1.15). If so, it follows that when a subordinate clause precedes the main clause an introductory sentence connective belongs to the entire complex, and that the connective which introduces the main clause is in the nature of a repetition. Cf. on A 1.9 f. — *k*[*u-it*]: in KUB 1.6.3.7 there is no room for the rest of Götze's suggested supplement, namely: *I-NA* ᵁᴿᵁ*ḪA-AK-PIŠ-ŠA*.

3.65. *Ne-ri-iq-qa-an*: so KUB 19.67.2.11. Götze reads *Ne-ri-ik-ka-an*.

3.66. *ma-aḫ-ḫa-an*: KUB 19.67.2.14: *ma-a*[*ḫ*-. KUB 1.6.3.12: GIM-*an*.

3.67. *i-ya-nu-un*: so KUB 19.67.2.15. KUB 1.6.3.13: DÙ-*nu-un*.

3.69. ᴸᵁ́KÚR-*li*: tautological asyndeton; this sentence is virtually a repetition of what has gone before. — *šu-ul-li-ya-at*: KUB 19.67.2.19 contains the initial character which is lacking in the other texts.

3.70. 1-*EN*: so KUB 19.67.2.20; the word is lacking or mutilated in the other texts. It is equivalent to *IŠTĒN* 'one'. — *ḫal-zi-in*: so KUB 19.67.2.20. KUB 1.4.3.37; 1.6.3.16: *ḪAL-ṢÎ*. Perhaps rather: *ḪAL-ṢÎ-in*.

3.71. [*nu-w*]*a*: the supplement is Götze's.

3.73. *ḫ*[*a-*]-*an-ni-eš-šar*: KUB 19.67.2.23 contains traces of the character *ḫa*.

3.74. [*ḫa*]-*at-ra-a-nu-un*: KUB 19.67.2.25 records the character *at*, which is lacking or mutilated in the other texts.

3.76. *ku-u-ru-ur*: so KUB 19.66.3.76. KUB 1.10.3.10: *ku-ru-ur*. Götze prefers to read *ku-*[*ru-r*]*i-ya-aḫ-ḫu-an-zi* from KUB 1.4.3.41 + KBo.3.6.3.29.

3.78. *ḫa-an-da-a-an*: the fundamental meaning seems to be 'fixed, firm', then 'true, loyal'. Cf. 3.39, 62. Götze prefers to take this as an adverb, 'really'. — *kat-te-ir-ra-aḫ-ḫi-ir*: the subject has to be supplied from DINGIR.MEŠ in the next sentence. A substantive is frequently postponed in this way. There is another instance in 4.48. Cf. also A 1.10, 3.8 f., I 2.28, 3.24.

3.79. *na-an-mu*: Götze appends -*kán* by error.

4.2. *a-pa-a-aš-ma* = Greek ὁ δέ. For *-ma* see on 1.41.

4.4. *kat-ta-an*: KUB 1.1.4.4: GAM-*an*. KUB 26.45.48: [*kat*]-*ta-an*. — *na-an-kan . . . ú-e-ri-ya-at*: literally, 'and he appointed him for the troops of the Upper Country for gathering'.

4.6. *Ú-UL-aš-mu . . . mar-aḫ-ta*: I take this to mean that Hattusilis got more recruits in the Upper Country than Sippa-LÚ-is got.

4.9. Ù-*at*: for the phonetic interpretation, see on Ù-*at* (1.36).

4.10. ⸓*ḫu-u-i-ya-mi*: this verb is usually conjugated according to the third class of the *hi*-conjugation, and we might expect a 1 sg. **huwehi* [462]. The glossenkeil suggests that *huwiyami* is a Luwian form.

4.11. *IŠ-TU ŠA MU-DI-KA* = *antiyantit-tet* [190].

4.12 f. The reference is to the events narrated in 1.33–41.

4.15. [LÚ]SANGA-*UT-TIM*: Götze erroneously prints *-TI*.

4.16. *pa-ra-aš-ši-in*: the context suggests the meaning 'patron deity'. Puduhepas, servant of Ishtar of Lawazantiyas (KBo.6.29.1.17), is now to take Ishtar of Samuhas as her patron deity. Possibly *parassis* is the Hittite word for GAŠAN.

4.20. Ù-*at*: see on Ù-*at* (1.36) and cf. Ù-*at* (4.9). Here the actually citable verb *teshaneske-* is appropriate.

4.21. *in-na-ra-u-wa-aš-ma-aš* = *innara-wa-smas*; *-smas* is ethical dative. — [URU]*ḪA-AT-TI-ma-wa*: KUB 26.44.4.21 shows part of another character after this complex.

4.22. EGIR-*an-da*: so KBo.3.6.3.54, KUB 26.44.4.22:]*an-da-an*.

4.24. *da-me-da*: for the form, see [263]. The temporal meaning is not certain.

4.26. *ḫu-u-um-ma*: this may be interpreted as dat. ('in a sty') or as nom., subject of the verb. *am-mu-uk-ma*: *am-mu-uk* belongs with *ku-u-ru-ur* in the next line, but in order to bring out the force of *-ma*, it is necessary to put a translation of it at the head of the sentence.

4.28. EGIR-*an ti-i-e-ir*: for the meaning of the phrase, cf. EGIR-*an ti-ya-at* (4.16 f. and 4.29).

4.30. *ma-an-qa*: see on *ma-an-qa* (3.38 f.); but Sommer's interpretation is less compelling here. Cf. also 3.62.

4.33–35. *ma-a-an-kán . . . pí-en-ni-iš-ta*: our interpretation was suggested by Friedrich, KlF 1.288.

4.35. *nu*: English idiom demands 'but' here.

4.36. A.AB.BA *ta-pu-ša*: for the meaning, see Götze-Pedersen, MS 23–27.

4.39 f. [D]*IŠTAR-ma-mu-kán . . . ti-iš-ki-it*: I take the literal meaning to be 'placed me in desire after desire'. The dat. *ilani* is from *ilatar*, which is probably a verbal noun from a verb related to *ilaliya-* 'desire'. A parallel formation with suffix *esar* [160] is *ilesar*. Götze, NBr. 32 f., conjectures a meaning 'Wohlstand' or 'Machtfülle' for *ilatar*.

4.40. *ti-iš-ki-it*: *dai-* 'place' has two duratives, *zke-*(*zi-ik-ki-iz-zi*) and *teske-*; for the latter, see Sommer, AU 64 fn.1.

4.45. *BE-LU*-ḪI.A *DI-NI* = *BĒLŪ DĪNI* 'opponents at law'; see on EN *DI-NI-YA* (1.54). — *e-kir*: here and in the next line KUB 19.72.4.7 f. has *e-ki-ir*.

4.47. *zi-en-na-aḫ-ḫu-un*: KUB 19.72.4.9 reads: [*zi*]-*en-na-aḫ-ḫu-ut*. — LUGAL-*UT-TA ŠA* KUR [URU]*ḪA-AT-TI*: KUB 19.60.4.47 and 19.72.4.10 read: LUGAL-*UT ŠA* KUR *ḪA-AT*[.

4.48. *da-a-aš*: the subject is postponed to the next sentence; see on *kat-te-ir-ra-aḫ-ḫi-ir* (3.78).

4.49. *tar-ni-iš-ta*: for the reading, see Götze, NBr. 33.

4.52. *TE-ME* stands for *TĒMI*, gen. of *TĒMU* 'message'. — *up-pí-eš-šar*-ḪI.A: for the number and form, see [183a].

4.54. *up-pí-eš-ki-ir*: KUB 1.8.4.32 reads *up-pí-eš*-[. — *Ù A-NA* AB.BA.AB.BA.ḪI.A-*YA*: KUB 19.60.4.54 omits *A.NA* and -*YA*.

4.55. *ku-e-da-ni-ik-ki* stands in partitive apposition with the datives plural in the preceding line.

4.56. *ku-ru-ri*-ḪI.A: see [183a].

4.62. [*nu* DUMU ŠE]Š-[*Y*]*A*: the supplement is uncertain; see Sommer, AU 35 fn. 3. — [I] [D]KAL-*an*: on the phonetic value of this name, see Ehelolf, OLZ 37.721 f.

4.62 f. *ku-it . . . pár-na-wa-iš-ki-it*: the allusion is to the events of 2.52 f.

4.63. *pár-na-wa-iš-ki-it*: the variant *pár-na-ú-i-iš-ki-it* is equally normal in a derivative in *ske/a-* from a denominative in *a*(*e*)-. — *a-pí-ya*: the dat. *apedani* might be expected instead of this adverb.

4.64. *ma-ši-wa-an*: for the form, see Götze, NBr. 35 f. The exclamatory question is nearly equivalent to *humandaz daske-* (1.43, 50, 58).

4.67. EGIR-*an tar-na-aḫ-ḫu-un*: Götze, Hatt. 39, NBr. 71 f., interprets this as 'steuerfrei lassen', and this may be correct. I can, however, find no clear evidence for such a meaning, and so I suggest an alternative. Both Götze and I believe that the primary meaning of the compound verb is 'set back, set aside', whence, I suggest, it came to mean 'remove from human use, reserve for the gods, consecrate'.

4.69. *a-pád-da-ya* = *apāt-a-ya*: -*a* is the enclitic commonly appended to pronouns (cf. *am-mu-uq-qa* in this line, and see [226]); the following -*ya* functions as a sentence connective.

4.72. *ḫu-u-ma-an-ti-ya-be ap-pa-an*: possibly the regular position of a *huwwāsi* (= [ZÁ]ZI.KIN) was on a hill-top outside the town; cf. KBo.4. 10.1.20 f.: [URU]*Kur-wa-an-ša-aš-ma-kán* (21) EGIR UGU UR.TÚG GAL [ZÁ]*ḫu-u-wa-ši* ZAG-*aš*, 'but behind (and) above *Kurwansas* a big-dog-statue (?) (is) the boundary'. — *na-an* . . . [ZÁ]ZI.KIN 'and her . . . (as) a statue (?)'. On the [ZÁ]ZI.KIN = [ZÁ]*huwwāsi*, see Götze, Kulturgeschichte 158, who holds that a *huwwāsi* stone was not a statue. For Götze's interpretation of the passage cited above, see KlF. 1.125.

4.73. DUG *ḫar-ši-ya-li-ya-kán iš-ḫu-is-kán-zi*: or perhaps, 'they pour (i.e. empty) the libation cups'. DUG *harsiyali* properly means 'cup suitable for a sacrificer'. For adjectives in *-is*, see Sturtevant, Lang. 10.266–73.

4.75. *ḫa-aš-ti-ya-aš*: on *hastai* 'bone, bones', see Sommer, AU 181; Götze, AM 240 f.; Benveniste, BSL 33.139.

4.77. *pa-ra-a*: so KUB 1.1.4.77; Götze omits the word.

4.80. *A-NA* DINGIR-*LIM*: so KUB 1.1.4.80; Götze omits the words.

4.83. *e-iz-za-an*: perhaps a derivative of *ezza-* 'eat' [358] with suffix *an* [154], but Götze points out that this suffix is not elsewhere appended to derivative verbs.

4.85. *ša-aḫ-ḫa-ni-ya-aš* = *sahhani-ya-as*: *-as* is direct object and *sahhani* dat. of purpose.

4.86. *iš-pár-za-zi*: for the form, see [35, 126].

4.89. *na-aḫ-ḫa-an-za*: this participle is active in meaning because the verb is intransitive [170]; it governs the dative, as here.

THE RITUAL OF ANNIWIYANIS

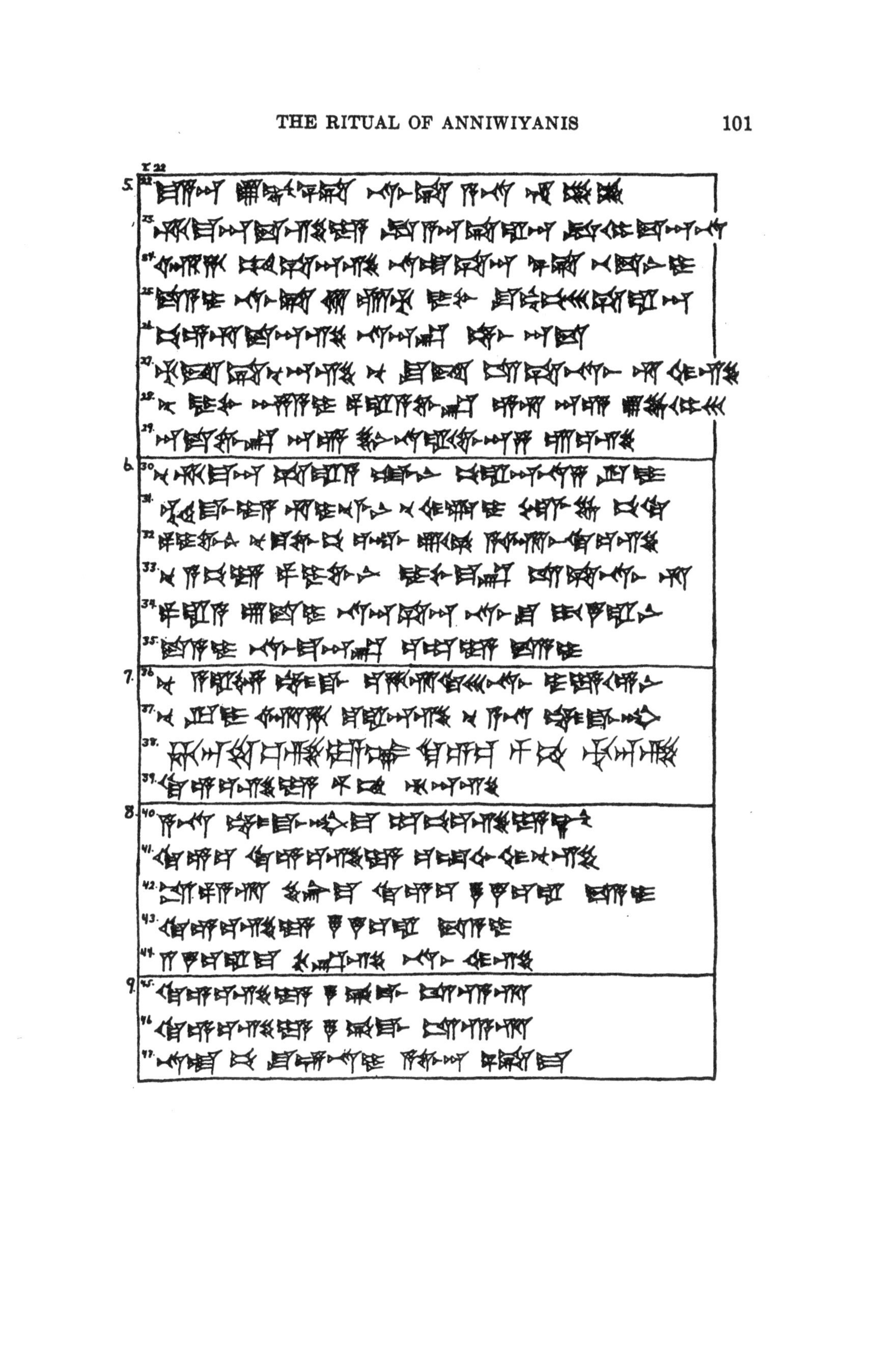

I 22

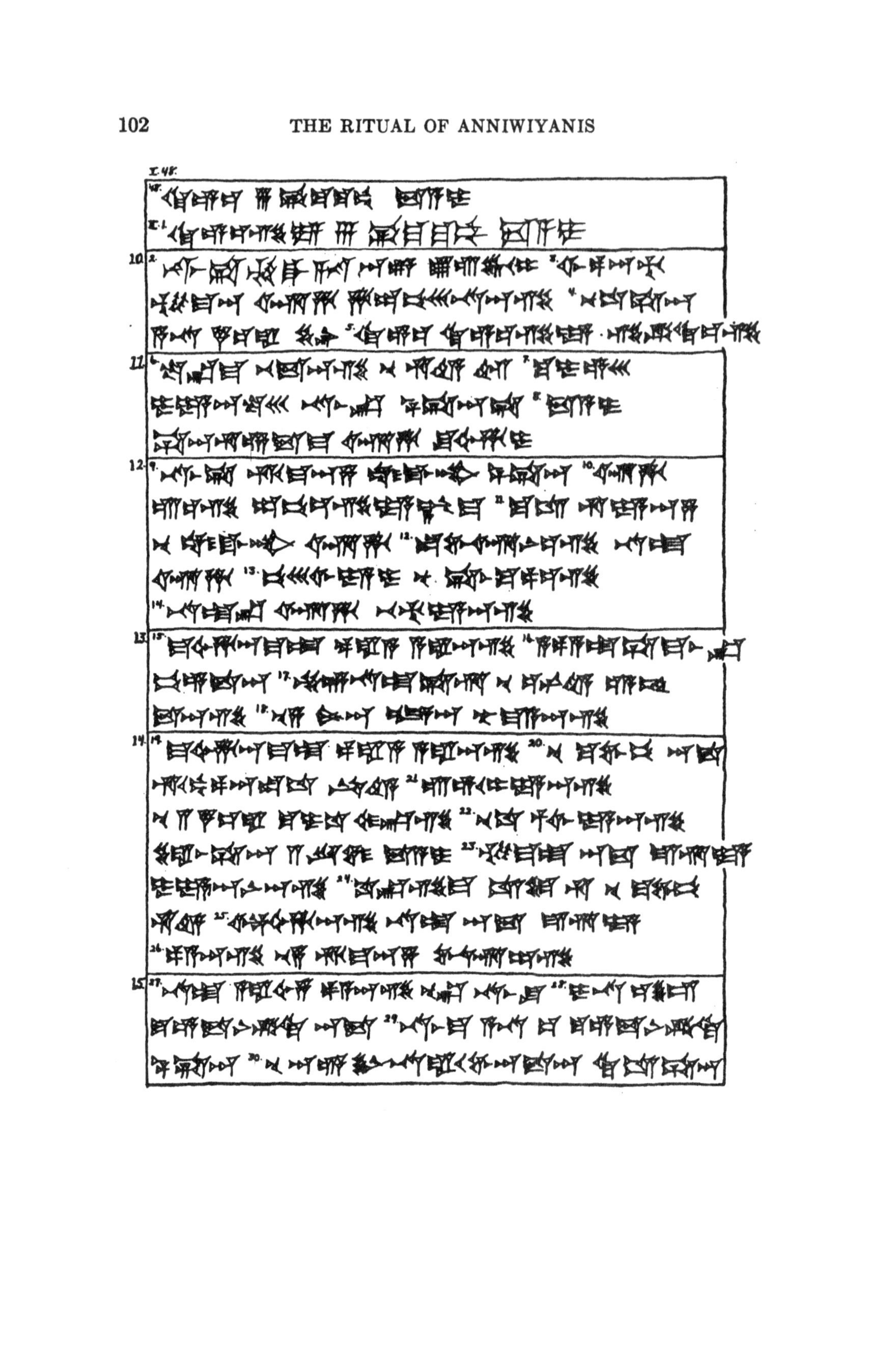

I. 48.

10

11

12

13

14

15

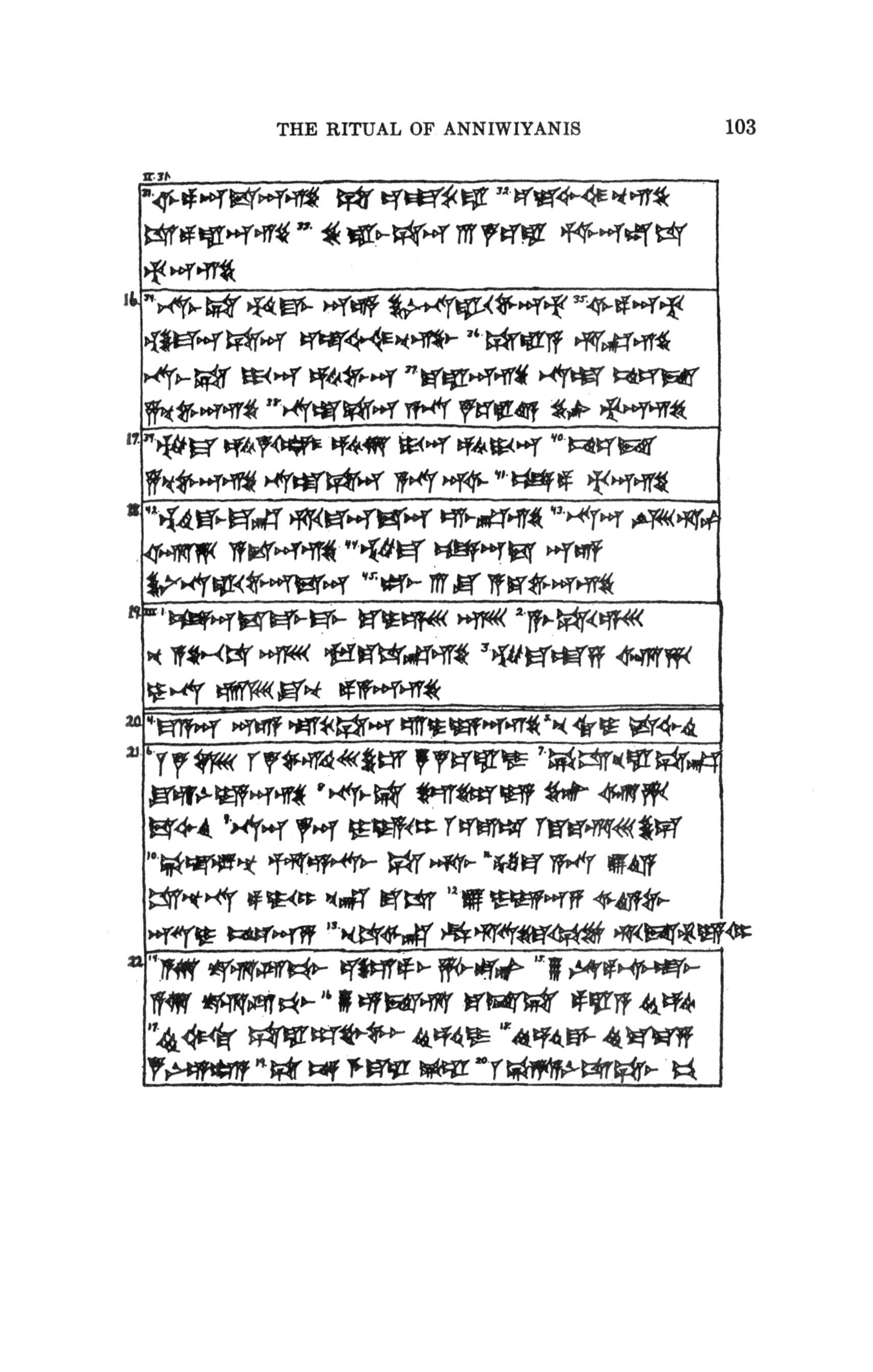

II. 31

16.

17.

18.

19.

20.

21.

22.

III. 21.

23

24

25

26

27

IV. 10.

10.

28 11. 12.

13.

29 14.

15.

16.

30 17. 18.

19.

20.

21.

31 22. 23.

24.

25.

26.

32 27. 28.

29.

30.

31.

32. 33.

34.

35.

36.

37.

38. 39.

THE RITUAL OF ANNIWIYANIS

1

(1.1) *UM-MA* ^{SAL}*A-AN-NI-Ú-I-YA-NI* AMA ^{I}*A-AR-MA-TI* ^{LÚ}MUŠEN.DÙ (1.2) ERUM ^{I}*ḪU-U-UR-LU-U* *ma-a-an* ^{D}KAL *lu-li-mi-ya-aš* (1.3) SISKUR.SISKUR *i-ya-mi nu ki-i da-aḫ-ḫi*

2

(1.4) SÍG *an-da-ra-an* SÍG *mi-ta-a-an* ŠE [K]AR-*aš* ŠE ^{LÚ}ŠAR (1.5) *da-aḫ-ḫi na-at-kán ša-an-ḫ[u]-an-zi* 1 ^{DUG}*KU-KU-UB* KAŠ 16 NINDA KUR$_4$.RA TUR (1.6) 1 MÁŠ.GAL 1 UR TUR 14 ^{GIŠ}GAG ^{GIŠ}ILDÁ[G] 2 ^{ZÁ}NUNUZ TUR-*TIM* (1.7) 14 ^{DUG}GAL TUR 12 ^{DUG}*KU-KU-UB* TUR MUŠEN.ḪI.A-*ya ḫu-u-ma-an-du-uš* (1.8) *ŠA* IM *i-en-zi ku-in ku-in* MUŠEN-*an* $^{\text{LÚ.MEŠ}}$MUŠEN.DÙ (1.9) *uš-kán-zi nu-uš-ša-an Ú-UL ku-in-ki wa-ag-ga-aš-nu-an-zi*

3

(1.10) *nu ma-aḫ-ḫa-an ne-ku-zi nu-uš-ša-an A-NA* EN SISKUR (1.11) *ḫa-an-te-iz-zi* BAL-*ši A-NA* GÌR.MEŠ-*ŠU* ŠU.MEŠ-*ŠU* (1.12) ^{UZU}GÚ-*ŠÚ iš-tar-na pí-di A-NA* ^{GIŠ}NA(D)-*ŠU* (1.13) 4 ^{GIŠ}*pa-ti-ya-al-li-e-eš ḫa-an-te-iz-zi* BAL-*ši* (1.14) SÍG *a-an-da-ra-an ḫa-ma-an-ki A-NA* ^{GIŠ}GIGIR-*ya-aš-ša-an* (1.15) ^{GIŠ}PAN.*ŠU* ^{GIŠ}MÁ.URU.ÙRU-*ŠU QA-TAM-MA-be ḫa-ma-an-ki*

4

(1.16) EGIR-*an-da-ma-aš-ša-an* SÍG *mi-da-a-an QA-TAM-MA ḫa-ma-an-ki* (1.17) *nam-ma-aš-ša-an ša-an-ḫu-un-da* NINDA KUR$_4$.RA.ḪI.A (1.18) *Ú-NU-UT* GIR$_4$ ^{GIŠ}GAG.ḪI.A-*ya* MUŠEN.ḪI.A-*ya* *ŠA* IM (1.19) ^{DUG}*KU-KU-BI*.ḪI.A [T]UR-*TIM kat-ta píd-da-ni-i* (1.20) *ḫa-an-da-a-iz-zi na-at A-NA* EN SISKUR *ŠA-PAL* ^{GIŠ}NA(D) (1.21) *da-a-i na-at-ši ŠA-PAL* ^{GIŠ}NA(D) *še-eš-zi*

5

(1.22) *ma-a-an lu-uk-kit$_9$-ta na-aš-ta A-NA* EN SISKUR.SISKUR (1.23) *ḫu-u-ma-an-da-zi-ya* SÍG *a-an-ta-ra-an* SÍG *mi-da-an-na* (1.24) *ar-ḫa túḫ-ša-an-zi na-at-ša-an kat-ta píd-da-ni-i* (1.25) *da-a-i na-aš-ta*

THE RITUAL OF ANNIWIYANIS

1

(1) Thus (speaks) Anniwiyanis, mother of Armatis, the bird-maker, slave of Hurlus. (2) When I make a sacrifice of ^{D}KAL, the effeminate (?), I take the following.

2

(4) I take blue (?) wool, red (?) wool, KAR barley, gardiner's barley (and they roast it), one pitcher of beer, sixteen small ordinary loaves, one full grown goat, one small dog, fourteen sticks of *ildaqqu*-wood, two small pearls, fourteen small bowls, (and) twelve small pitchers. (7) And they make all the birds of clay; whatever bird the bird-makers observe, they do not omit (?) any.

3

(10) And when he goes to bed, upon the sacrificer (first of all about (?) his hands, feet, and neck) and upon his bed (first of all upon the four posts?) she binds blue (?) wool; and in just the same way she binds (it?) upon (his) chariot, his bow, (and) his quiver.

4

(16) Afterwards she binds red (?) wool in the same way. (17) Then she arranges the roasted (barley), the ordinary loaves, (18) implements of asphalt, and the sticks (of *ildaqqu*-wood), and the birds of clay, (and) the small pitchers in a basket, and puts it under the sacrificer's bed; and it remains all night under his bed.

5

(22) When it grows light, then from all parts of the sacrificer they take off the blue (?) wool and the red (?) wool; and she puts it down in

ŠA(G) É-*TI* DUMU.SAL *šu-up-pí-eš-ša-ra-an* (1.26) *pí-e-ḫu-da-an-zi na-an-kán* KÁ-*aš an-da* (1.27) *ti-*[*i*]*t-ta-nu-an-zi nu* ŠU-*it iš-ša-na-aš* MUŠEN *ḫar-zi* (1.28) *nu* DUMU.SAL *ḫal-za-a-i pa-ra-a-wa-kán e-ḫu* ^{D}KAL *lu-li-mi-eš* (1.29) [*a*]*n-da-wa-kán* ^{D}KAL *in-na-ra-u-wa-an-za ú-iz-zi*

6

(1.30) *nu ḫu-u-ma-an ša-ra-a tum-me-ni pí-ra-an-na-za* UR TUR (1.31) [MÁŠ.GAL]-*ya ḫu-i-nu-me-ni nu* ḪUR.SAG-*i dam-me-li pí-di* (1.32) [*pa-i-wa-ni nu k*]*u-wa-pí* ^{GIŠ}APIN-*aš Ú-UL a-ar-aš-ki-iz-zi* (1.33) [*nu a-pí-ya*] *pa-i-wa-ni* DUMU.SAL-*ma-kán iš-ša-na-aš* MUŠEN (1.34) [*pa-ra-a ú*]*-da-i na-an-ša-an na-aš-šu* ZAG.GAR.RA-*ni* (1.35) [*da-a-i na*]*-aš-ma-an-kán* ^{GIŠ}AB-*ya da-a-i*

7

(1.36) [*nu a-ra*]*-aḫ-za* KÁ.GAL ^{GIŠ}*ḫa-tal-ki-eš-na-aš i-ya-u-e-ni* (1.37) [*nu* UR TUR] *ar-ḫa ku-ra-an-zi nu A-NA* KÁ.GAL-*TIM* (1.38) [*ḫa-an-te-iz*]*-zi-ya-az ki-e-iz* $\frac{1}{2}$-*AM ti-an-zi* (1.39) [*ki-e-iz-z*]*i-ya* $\frac{1}{2}$-*AM ti-an-zi*

8

(1.40) [*A-NA* KÁ.GAL-*T*]*IM-ma ap-pí-iz-zi-ya-az* (1.41) [*ki-e-iz ki-e*]*-iz-zi-ya* ^{GIŠ}*la-aḫ-ḫur-nu-zi* (1.42) [*iš-pa-a-ri še-ir*]*-ma ki-e-iz* 7 NINDA KUR$_4$.RA *da-a-i*(1.43) [*ki-e-iz-zi-y*]*a* 7 NINDA KUR$_4$.RA *da-a-i* (1.44) [2 NINDA KUR$_4$.RA-*m*]*a kur-kán-zi na-aš ḫar-zi*

9

(1.45) [*ki-e-iz-zi-y*]*a* 7 ^{DUG}GAL *iš-qa-a-ri* (1.46) [*ki-e-iz-zi-y*]*a* 7 ^{DUG}GAL *iš-qa-a-ri* (1.47) [*na-at* KAŠ *šu*]*-un-na-i a-wa-an kat-ta-ma* (1.48) [*ki-e-iz* 6 ^{D}]^{UG}*KU-KU-UB da-a-i* (2.1) *ki-e-iz-zi-ya* 6 ^{DUG}*KU-KU-UB da-a-i*

10

(2.2) *na-aš-ta* MÁŠ.GAL *A-NA* ^{D}KAL *lu-ú-li-mi* (2.3) *ši-pa-an-ti nam-ma-an ar-ḫa ḫa-ap-pí-eš-na-an-zi* (2.4) *nu-uš-ša-an A-NA* NINDA KUR$_4$.RA *še-ir* (2.5) *ki-e-iz ki-e-iz-zi-ya zi-ik-ki-iz-zi*

11

(2.6) *te-kán-ma be-da-an-zi nu* MUŠEN.ḪI.A IM (2.7) *ku-i-e-eš i-ya-an-te-eš na-aš-kán kat-ta-an-ta* (2.8) *da-a-i ša-an-ḫu-un-da-ma ar-ḫa šu-uḫ-ḫa-i*

the basket. Then they bring a virgin (?) into the house; and they station her within the doors. (27) She holds a bird of dough in her hand, and the girl cries: 'Go forth, ^{D}KAL, the effeminate (?); ^{D}KAL, the manly (?), will come in.'

6

(30) We pick everything up, and drive the small dog and the full grown goat before us. (31) We go to a mountain, to the second location; and we go to a place where the plough does not come. (33) The girl, however, carries forth the bird of dough, and either she puts it on an altar, or she puts it in a window.

7

(36) Outside we construct a (city) gate of twigs (?). (37) And they cut up the small dog, and before the gate they place half on this side and they place half on that side.

8

(40) Behind the gate on this side and on that she spreads a sacrificial table, and upon one she places seven ordinary loaves and upon the other she places seven ordinary loaves. (44) (They keep two ordinary loaves—she has these).

9

(45) She places seven libation bowls on one (table) and she places seven libation bowls on the other, and she fills them (with) beer; but beneath one (table) she sets away six pitchers and beneath the other she sets away six pitchers.

10

(2) Next she sacrifices the large goat to ^{D}KAL, the effeminate (?). (3) Then they cut it into bits, and she distributes it over the ordinary loaves on this (table) and on that.

11

(6) They dig (a hole in) the ground, and she (?) puts therein the birds which (have been) made. But she scatters out the roasted (barley).

12

(2.9) *na-aš-ta ḫu-u-ma-an-za* KÁ.GAL-*TIM kat-ta-an* (2.10) *ar-ḫa ú-iz-zi ap-pí-iz-zi-ya-az-ma* (2.11) *ku-iš ḫu-ya-an-za nu* KÁ.GAL-*TIM ar-ḫa* (2.12) *du-wa-ar-ni-iz-zi na-at ar-ḫa* (2.13) *pí-eš-ši-ya-i nu ta-aš-ku-pa-iz-zi* (2.14) *na-at-kán ar-ḫa pít-ti-ya-an-zi*

13

(2.15) *ma-aḫ-ḫa-an-ma-at pa-ra-a a-ra-an-zi* (2.16) *a-pa-a-at-ša-ma-aš-kán pí-e-da-an* (2.17) *mu-un-na-at-ta-ri nu* ^{GIŠ}GAG.ḪI.A ^{GIŠ}ILDÁG *da-an-zi* (2.18) *nu-za* KASKAL-*an* EGIR-*an tar-ma-a-an-zi*

14

(2.19) *ma-aḫ-ḫa-an-ma-at pa-ra-a a-ra-an-zi* (2.20) *nu ku-wa-pí an-da ḫu-u-up-pa-an-du-uš* ZÁ.ḪI.A (2.21) *ú-e-mi-ya-an-zi nu* 2 NINDA KUR$_4$.RA *ku-i-uš ḫar-kán-zi* (2.22) *nu-uš pár-ši-ya-an-zi še-ra-aš-ša-an* 2 ^{ZA}NUNUZ *da-a-i* (2.23) *nam-ma-at an-da* URU-*ri-ya i-ya-an-ni-an-zi* (2.24) *uš-kán-zi-ma IŠ-TU* MUŠEN *nu ku-wa-pí* MUŠEN.ḪI.A (2.25) SIG$_5$-*aḫ-ḫa-an-zi na-at an-da* URU-*ri-ya* (2.26) *pa-a-an-zi nu-za ḫu-u-ma-an-za wa-ar-ap-zi*

15

(2.27) *na-at a-ra-aḫ-za pa-a-an-zi nu-kán na-aš-šu* (2.28) *I-NA* ^{GIŠ}ŠAR *ku-e-da-ni-ik-ki an-da* (2.29) *na-aš-ma A-NA* GIŠ *ku-e-da-ni-ik-ki kat-ta-an* (2.30) *nu* ^{D}KAL *in-na-ra-u-wa-an-da-an ki-iš-ša-an* (2.31) *ši-pa-an-da-an-zi ŠA* ^{GIŠ}ḪAŠḪUR KUR.RA (2.32) ^{GIŠ}*la-aḫ-ḫur-nu-zi iš-pa-ra-an-zi* (2.33) *še-ra-aš-ša-an* 3 NINDA KUR$_4$.RA *pár-ši-an-du-uš ti-an-zi*

16

(2.34) *na-aš-ta* MÁŠ.GAL ^{D}KAL *in-na-ra-u-wa-an-ti* (2.35) *ši-pa-an-ti nam-ma-an-ša-an* ^{GIŠ}*la-aḫ-ḫur-nu-zi-aš* (2.36) *ša-ra-a ḫu-kán-zi na-aš-ta* ZAG-*an* ^{UZU}GEŠTUG-*an* (2.37) *ku-ra-an-zi na-at* IZI-*it za-nu-wa-an-zi* (2.38) *na-at-ša-an A-NA* NINDA KUR$_4$.RA.ḪI.A *še-ir ti-an-zi*

17

(2.39) *nam-ma* ^{UZU}NÍG.GIG ^{UZU}ŠA(G) ZAG-*an* ^{UZU}ZAG-*an* (2.40) IZI-*it za-nu-wa-an-zi na-at-ša-an A-NA* [DIN]GIR-*LIM* (2.41) EGIR-*pa ti-an-zi*

12

(9) Then every one comes away through the gate; but he who flees last breaks the gate off and throws it away. (13) He shouts, and they run away.

13

(15) When they have departed, and that spot is hidden from them, they take the sticks of *ildaqqu*-wood and blockade the road behind (them).

14

(19) When they have departed, where they find stones heaped together, they break the two ordinary loaves that they have, and place upon (them, i.e. the stones?) the two pearls. (23) Then they proceed into the city. (24) However, they take observations by means of birds, and when the birds give favorable omens, they enter the city. (26) And everyone bathes.

15

(27) They go outside; and, whether (it be) in an orchard or under a tree, they sacrifice to ^{D}KAL, the manly (?), as follows. (32) They spread a sacrificial table of pomegranate wood (?). (33) Upon (it) they place three broken ordinary loaves.

16

(34) Next she (?) sacrifices a large goat to ^{D}KAL, the manly (?). (35) Then they bless it above the sacrificial table. (36) Next they cut off the right ear, and cook it with fire, and place it on the ordinary loaves.

17

(39) Then they cook with fire the entrails (?), the heart, (and) the right leg, and set them aside for the god.

18

(2.42) MÁŠ.GAL-*ma-kán ḫu-u-ma-an-da-an mar-kán-z*[*i*] (2.43) *na-an* $^{\mathrm{LÚ.MEŠ}}$MUŠEN.DÙ *ar-ḫa a-da-an-zi* (2.44) *nam-ma* EGIR-*an-da* ^{D}KAL *in-na-ra-u-wa-a*[*n-da-an*] (2.45) GUB-*aš* 3-*ŠU a-ku-wa-an-zi*

19

(3.1) EGIR-*an-da-ma-aš-ma-*[*aš ku-i-e-eš* DINGIR.MEŠ] (3.2) *a-aš-ša-u-e-eš nu a-p*[*u-u-uš* DINGIR.MEŠ *ak-ku-uš-kán-zi*] (3.3) *nam-ma-at-za ar-ḫa I-N*[*A* É.MEŠ-*ŠU-NU pa-a-an-zi*]

20

(3.4) *ma-a-an* ^{D}KAL ^{KUŠ}*kur-ša-a*[*n ú-i-ya-an-zi*] (3.5) *nu ki-i d*[*a-aḫ-ḫi*]

21

(3.6) 1 NINDA ERÍN.MEŠ 1 NINDA *wa-gi-eš-šar* 7 NINDA KUR$_4$.RA TUR (3.7) DUG *iš-nu-ra-ša-kán šu-ú-ni-ya-an-zi* (3.8) *na-aš-ta šar-li-ya še-ir ar-ḫa da-aḫ-ḫi* (3.9) *na-an* NINDA-*an i-ya-mi* 1 ^{GIŠ}BANŠUR 1 ^{TÚG}*ku-ri-eš-šar* (3.10) *ga-la-ak-tar pár-ḫu-e-na-aš ŠA* DINGIR-*LIM* (3.11) *nam-ma A-NA* UDU.ḪI.A *iš-tar-na pa-i-mi nu-kán ku-*[*i*]*š* (3.12) UDU *i-ya-an-za* IGI.[ḪI].A-*wa* ^{D}UTU-*i ne-an-za* (3.13) *nu-uš-ši-kán* ^{SÍG}*ḫu-ut-tu-ul-li ḫu-u-it-ti-ya-mi*

22

(3.14) A.ŠA(G) *te-ri-ip-pí-aš* ^{GIŠ}*šar-pa-aš ḫa-aš-du-ir* (3.15) 9 ^{ZA}*pa-aš-ši-la-aš* A.ŠA(G) *te-ri-ip-pí-aš* (3.16) 9 *e-it-ri ku-it-ta pa-ra-a* UTÚL UZU (3.17) UTÚL *ḫar-ki ša-ra-ap-pu-wa-aš* UTÚL GÚ.TUR (3.18) [UTÚL] GÚ.GAL UTÚL BA.BA.ZA NINDA NI.E.DÉ.A (3.19) *ŠA* LÀL *me-ma-al* GA.AL (3.20) 1 ^{DUG}*ḫa-a-ni-iš-ša-aš* KAŠ

23

(3.21) *na-aš-ta* ^{GIŠ}BANŠUR *I-NA* É.ŠA(G) *an-da te-iḫ-ḫi* (3.22) *na-aš-ta* ^{TÚG}*ku-ri-eš-šar kat-ta kán-ga-aḫ-ḫi* (3.23) *še-ir-ma-aš-ša-an* NINDA ERÍN.MEŠ NINDA *wa-gi-eš-šar* (3.24) NINDA *šar-li-in-na te-iḫ-ḫi* (3.25) *pí-ra-an kat-ta-ma* GUNNI *i-ya-mi*

24

(3.26) *nu* A.ŠA(G) *te-ri-ip-pí-ya-az* 9 ^{ZA}*pa-aš-ši-la-an* (3.27) *me-ir-ra-an-da-ya ḫa-aš-du-ir ú-da-an-zi* (3.28) *nu-uš-ša-an* ^{ZA}*pa-aš-ši-lu-uš* (3.29) *A-NA* GUNNI *iš-ḫu-wa-a-i še-ra-aš-ša-an* (3.30) ^{GIŠ}*šar-pa-aš ḫa-aš-du-ir me-ir-ra-an-da* (3.31) *wa-ar-nu-zi ga-la-ak-tar-ma pár-ḫu-u-e-na-an* (3.32)

18

(42) But they cut all the large goat up, and the bird-makers eat it up. (44) Afterwards, moreover, (while) standing they offer drink to ^{D}KAL, the manly (?), three times.

19

(1) Afterwards they offer drink to whatever gods are propitious to them. (3) Then they go away to their houses.

20

(4) When they invite (?) ^{D}KAL of the shield, I take the following.

21

(6) One soldiers' loaf, one breakfast (?) loaf, seven small ordinary loaves— (7) and they fill a dough pan (?); then I take (it) out on a spoon (?), and make it into a loaf—a table, a strip of cloth, the god's *galaktar parhuwenas*. (11) Then I go among the sheep, and I shear (?) the fleece of a sheep which (is) unblemished (?) and (is) turning (its) eyes to the sun.

22

(14) Branches of brushwood of a ploughed field, 9 bits of gravel of a ploughed field, nine kinds of food, severally in order: a meat stew, a white stew, *sarppuwas*, pea stew, bean stew, gruel, porridge with honey, porridge (?), (and) cream; and one *hanissas* of beer.

23

(21) Next I set the table within the house. (22) Next I hang the strip of cloth (across it). (23) And upon (it) I set the soldiers' loaf, the breakfast (?) loaf, and the spoon (?) loaf. (25) And before (the house) near by I make a fireplace.

24

(26) They bring the nine bits of gravel and the dead branches from the ploughed field. (28) He throws the bits of gravel into the stove, and upon (them) he burns the dead branches of brushwood. (31) But

UDU *i-ya-an-da-aš* ^{SIG}*ḫu-ud-du-ul-li-it* (3.33) *an-da iš-ḫa-a-i* (3.34) *na-an* DUMU.SAL *šu-up-pí-iš-ša-ri pa-a-i* (3.35) *nu ú-i-e-eš-ki-iz-zi an-da-ma-kán* (3.36) *ki-iš-ša-an me-mi-iš-ki-iz-zi*

25

(3.37) *an-da-kán e-ḫu* ^{D}KAL ^{KUŠ}*kur-ša-aš* (3.38) *nu-un-na-aš-ša-an an-da mi-i-e-eš* (3.39) *nu-un-na-aš-ša-an an-da tal-li-i-e-eš* (3.40) *kar-pí-in-na kar-tim-mi-ya-at-ta-an* (3.41) *ša-a-u-wa-ar ar-ḫa tar-na* (3.42) *ki-e-ma-kán ḫa-aš-du-ir ma-aḫ-ḫa-an* ^{LÚ}APIN.LAL-*li* (3.43) *ar-ḫa me-ir-ta tu-ga-kán A-NA* ^{D}KAL ^{KUŠ}*kur-ša-aš* (3.44) *kar-piš kar-tim-mi-az ša-a-u-wa-ar* (3.45) *ar-ḫa QA-TAM-MA me-ir-tu*$_{4}$

26

(4.1) [*na-aš-ta*] ^{ZA}*pa-aš-ši-lu-uš IŠ-TU* KAŠ *ki-iš-ta-nu-mi* (4.2) [*nu ki-i*]*š-ša-an me-ma-aḫ-ḫi ki-e-iz ma-aḫ-ḫa-an* (4.3) [*ni-i*]*n-gir zi-ga-az* ^{D}KAL ^{KUŠ}*kur-ša-aš* (4.4) [*QA-TAM-M*]*A ni-i*[*k*] *nu-ut-ták-kán kar-pí-iš* (4.5) [*kar-tim*]*-mi-az ša-a-u-wa-ar ar-ḫa me-ir-du*

27

(4.6) [*nu* NINDA KUR$_{4}$.R]A.ḪI.A *pár-ši-ya-aḫ-ḫi na-aš-kán* EGIR-*pa* (4.7) [^{GIŠ}BANŠUR]-*i te-iḫ-ḫi nu* 9 *e-it-ri te-iḫ-ḫi* (4.8) [*nu-kán*] KAŠ *pí-ra-an kat-ta* 3-*ŠU ši-pa-an-taḫ-ḫi* (4.9) [*na-aš-t*]*a pa-ra-a ú-wa-am-mi* (4.10) [^{GIŠ}IG]-*ma-kán an-da ḫu-u-it-ti-ya-mi*

28

(4.11) *lu-uk-kit*$_{9}$*-ta-ma* NINDA KUR$_{4}$.RA.ḪI.A 9 *e-it-ri* (4.12) KAŠ-*ya ša-ra-a da-an-zi na-at ar-ḫa* (4.13) *a-da-an-zi a-ku-wa-an-zi*

29

(4.14) *nu I-NA* UD 3.KAM *ki-iš-ša-an ú-i-ya-iš-ki-mi* (4.15) NINDA KUR$_{4}$.ḪI.A-*ya* 9 *e-it-ri* KAŠ-*ya PA-NI* DINGIR-*LIM* (4.16) UD-*at* UD-*at ta-ma-i zi-ik-ki-mi*

30

(4.17) *I-NA* UD 4.KAM-*ma mu-ki-eš-šar ḫu-u-ma-an* (4.18) *ša-ra-a da-aḫ-ḫi na-at-kán pa-ra-a pí-e-da-aḫ-ḫi* (4.19) *ga-la-ak-tar-ma-aš-ša-an pár-ḫu-u-e-na-an* (4.20) UDU *i-ya-an-da-aš* ^{SIG}*ḫu-ud-du-ul-li* (4.21) EGIR-*pa A-NA* ^{D}KAL ^{KUŠ}*kur-ša-aš te-iḫ-ḫi*

the *galaktar parhuwenas* he wraps in the fleece of the unblemished (?) sheep, and gives it to a virgin (?). (35) She prays and, within (the house), speaks thus.

25

(37) Come in, [D]KAL of the shield. (38) Become gentle to us within (the house). (39) Leave us (unmolested) within (the house). (40) Remit thy anger, hate, (and) fury. (42) As these branches died for the plowman, so for thee also, [D]KAL of the shield, let anger, hate, (and) fury die.

26

(1) Next I quench (i.e. cool) the bits of gravel with beer, and I speak thus: as these have drunk their fill, so do thou, [D]KAL of the shield, drink thy fill; and let anger, hate, (and) fury die within thee.

27

(6) I break the ordinary loaves, and put them back on the table (?). (7) And I place the nine kinds of food. (8) I pour three libations of beer before (the house?) near by. (9) Next I come out and shut the door.

28

(11) The next morning, however, they take the ordinary loaves, the nine kinds of food, and the beer, and they eat and drink it up.

29

(14) And for three days I invite (? him) thus, and the ordinary loaves, the nine kinds of food, and the beer I set before the god fresh day by day.

30

(17) On the fourth day I take all the *mukessar* and carry it forth. (19) But the *galaktar parhuwenas* in the fleece of the unblemished (?) sheep I set aside for [D]KAL of the shield.

31

(4.22) *na-aš-ta* $^{\text{LÚ.MEŠ}}$MUŠEN.DÛ *A-NA* ^{D}KAL ^{KUŠ}*kur-ša-aš* (4.23) MÁŠ.GAL *ši-pa-an-da-an-zi nu ḫa-an-te-iz-zi* BAL-*ši* (4.24) ZAG-*an* ^{UZU}GEŠTUG-*an* ^{UZU}NÍG.GIG ^{UZU}ŠA(G) ZAG-*an* (4.25) ^{UZU}ZAG.DIB-*an* IZI-*az za-nu-an-zi* (4.26) *na-at-ša-an A-NA* DINGIR-*LIM* EGIR-*pa ti-an-zi*

32

(4.27) MÁŠ.GAL UTÚL.ḪI.A *i-en-zi nu-za a-da-an-zi* (4.28) *nam-ma* ^{D}KAL ^{KUŠ}*kur-ša-aš* GUB-*aš* 3-*ŠU* (4.29) *a-ku-wa-an-zi* EGIR-*an-da-ma-aš-ma-aš ku-i-e-eš* (4.30) DINGIR.MEŠ *a-aš-ša-u-e-eš nu a-pu-u-uš* DINGIR.MEŠ (4.31) *ak-ku-uš-kán-zi*

(4.32) DUB 1.KAM *A-WA-AT* ^{SAL}*A-AN-NI-WI-YA-NI* (4.33) AMA ^{I}*A-AR-MA-TI nu-uš-ša-an ki-e-da-ni* (4.34) *tup-pí* 2 SISKUR *a-ni-ya-an* [1] SISKUR (4.35) *ma-a-an* ^{D}KAL *lu-li-mi-in* [^{D}]KAL *in-ra-u-wa-an-da-an-na* (4.36) *ši-pa-an-ti* 1 SISKUR *ma-a-an* ^{D}K[A]L ^{KUŠ}*kur-ša-an* (4.37) *ú-i-ya-an-zi QA-TI* (4.38) ŠU ^{I}*ḪA-NI-IK-KU*-DINGIR-*LIM* DUMU ^{I}NU.GIŠ.ŠAR (4.39) DUMU.DUMU-*ŠÚ ŠA* ^{I}LÚGAL DUB.SAR.MEŠ

31

(22) Next the bird-makers sacrifice a large goat to ^{D}KAL of the shield. (23) And first of all they cook with fire the right ear, the entrails (?), the heart, and the right leg; and they set it aside for the god.

32

(27) They make the large goat into stews, and eat it. (28) Then three times (while) standing they offer drink to ^{D}KAL of the shield. (29) Afterwards they offer drink to whatever gods are propitious to them.

---

(32) The first tablet (of) the words of Anniwiyanis, mother of Armatis. (33) In this tablet two sacrifices (are) performed; one sacrifice when they sacrifice to ^{D}KAL, the effeminate (?), and ^{D}KAL, the manly, (and) one sacrifice when they invite (?) ^{D}KAL of the shield. (37) It is finished. (38) The hand of Hanikkuwilis, son of NU.GIŠ.ŠAR, grandson of LÚ, chief of the scribes.

COMMENTARY

The Anniwiyanis text was first published by Sturtevant in TAPA 58.5–31, where a transcription and a tentative translation were supplied. A number of corrections were made in Lang. 5.228–31. The cuneiform text was included by Götze in VBoT as No. 24.

The text contains two magic rituals, both directed toward a god who is designated ideographically as ^{D}KAL. I formerly followed Forrer, Forsch. 1.10 fn. 2, in identifying this deity with ^{D}Innaras, and I interpreted the word *innaras* as meaning 'vir'. I further understood the participle *innarawanza* (1.29) as 'ἀνδρίζων' or 'ἀνδριζόμενος' and the contrasting term *lulimis* (1.2, etc.) as 'making female' or 'effeminate'. It seemed to follow that the first ritual in our text was celebrated for the purpose of driving out the female-producing god of manhood and bringing in the male-producing god of manhood, that is, to secure the birth of sons.

Ehelolf, OLZ 37.721 f., has just now finally proved that Forrer's identification of ^{D}KAL with ^{D}*Innaras* was wrong; the Hittite name of ^{D}KAL began with the syllable *Ta-* and ended with *-ras*, with two or three still unknown signs between. This materially weakens the evidence for interpreting our ritual as designed to secure the birth of sons. Nevertheless I have, with much hesitation, retained my former interpretation of *innarawanza* and *lulimis*.

For a brief account of magic among the Hittites, see Götze, Kulturgeschichte 141–50. On ^{D}KAL and the stem *innara-*, cf. Sommer, AU 20–4, 382 f.

1.1. ^{LÚ}MUŠEN.DÙ literally means 'bird-maker'. Apparently the chief function of such persons was to observe (*uš-kán-zi* — 1.9) birds and interpret the auspices (cf. 2.24 ff.), and hence some prefer to translate the word by 'augur'. In this text, however, the birds used in the ritual are made of clay, and it therefore seems safer to keep the literal meaning.

1.4. *an-da-ra-an, mi-ta-a-an* are no doubt color adjectives; colored wool is often mentioned in the ritual texts, but usually the color is designated by ideograms. Of the four common colors for wool, white, black, blue, and red, we know Hittite words for the first two. There is, then, a certain probability that *andaras* and *mitās* mean 'blue' and 'red', but there is no indication as to which is which. I have arbitrarily translated *andaras* by 'blue' and *mitās* by 'red'. The former word occurs also KBo.5.2.3.19, and the latter KBo.4.2.1.64 and KUB 12.58.1.21, always with SÍG 'wool' or the equivalent(?) Hittite word, *asāras*.

1.5. *ša-an-ḫ[u]-an-zi*: the tablet reads *ša-an-ḫa-an-zi*, which gives no sense. The *ša-an-ḫu-un-da* of 1.17 requires the emendation here.

1.8. *ŠA* IM stands for a genitive modifying the preceding substantive.

1.9. f. *ku-in ku-in . . . wa-ag-ga-aš-nu-an-zi*: in my opinion the asyndeton is tautological (see on H 1.15). Götze does not admit tautological asyndeton when a subordinate clause precedes its main clause, as here; but cf. H 3.60. Götze takes the *kwin kwin* clause with the preceding sentence, and assumes a full stop after *uskanzi*.

1.9. *wa-ag-ga-aš-nu-an-zi*: in TAPA 58.19 I based the translation 'omit' upon an assumed connection with *wa-ag-ga-a-ri* 'is lacking', which I considered a middle with ending *-ari*; but Friedrich, Vert. 2.171 fn. 1, has shown that the stem of that word is *waggar-*. Possibly, however, our word may be connected with *waksiya-* 'be lacking' (see I 1.49 and note) and still be translated 'omit'. Equally probable is a connection with IE *aweks-* 'increase' (Gk. *αὐξάνω* 'increase', Goth. *wahsjan* 'grow'); in which case substitute 'rear' for 'omit' in the translation.

1.10. *ne-ku-zi*: the subject has to be supplied from EN SISKUR at the end of the line. See on *kat-te-ir-ra-aḫ-ḫi-ir* (H 3.78). Some consider the verb impersonal, 'it grows dark, night begins'.

1.13. ^{GIŠ}*pa-ti-ya-al-li-e-es* seems to function as dat. [182].

1.14. *ḫa-ma-an-ki*: I assume that the subject is Anniwiyanis; such shifts of the person of the verb must sometimes be assumed in Hittite rituals. Here it is possible to suppose that an assistant or even the sacrificer is the actor.

1.17. *ša-an-ḫu-un-da*: cf. 1.4 f.

1.19. *píd-da-ni-i*: for the meaning of *pittar*, cf. Friedrich, ZA NF 3.190 f.; Götze AOr. 5.34.

1.23. *ḫu-u-ma-an-da-zi-ya*: *-ya* 'and, also' is used regularly after final vowels and after ideograms, and sometimes, with an interposed *i*, after final *z*.

1.25. DUMU.SAL *šu-up-pí-eš-ša-ra-an*: this reading, rather than DUMU.SAL-*ŠU* (TAPA 58.8), is required by KUB 7.5.1.6; 7.19.1.9; 9.27.1.14. Probably the adjective is derived from the noun *suppessar* (being an adnominal genitive that came to be declined as an adjective). The meaning suggested (after Götze) in the translation is conjectural; cf. *suppis* 'sacrosanct'.

1.26. KÀ-*aš* must be dat. pl.

1.27. *iš-ša-na-aš*: Friedrich, ZA NF 3.192, suggested the meaning 'flour'; but Götze calls my attention to such phrases as *ŠA* ZÍD.DA.ŠE *iš-ni* (KUB 24.14.1.14), which prove that *ēssnas* (cf. KUB 9.34.3.26: *e-eš-ša-na-aš*) is made of flour. Since it is used to model birds, etc., and since it is put into a dough pan (see on *iš-nu-ra-ša* 3.7), it must be 'dough'. Cf. *ēssā-* 'make, prepare'.

1.28. DUMU.SAL is the subject of *harzi* (27) as well as of *halzai*, since the girl still holds the bird in 1.33 f. Cf. on 1.10. — *e-ḫu* is usually a mere introduction to another verb, like Lat. *age*; but here it seems to be a fully independent verb. — *lu-li-mi-eš*: for the vowel of the final syllable, see [191b and fn. 72].

1.30. [ḪUR.SAG-*i*]-*ya*: if the supplement is correct there seems to be no reason for the enclitic -*ya*, and so I assume the dat. in -*iya* as against the dat. in -*i* later in the line [195a, b].

1.31. [MÀŠ.GAL]-*ya*: the supplement is Götze's. — *dam-me-li pí-di*: i.e. the second location for the performance of this ritual.

1.33 ff. DUMU.SAL-*ma-kán . . . da-a-i*: apparently the girl does not accompany the others to the mountain; for she would scarcely find an altar or a window there.

1.35. ᴳᴵŠAB-*ya*: the window of the temple is often mentioned in the ritual texts as one of the sacred places where certain acts must be performed.

1.36. *a-ra-aḫ-za* 'outside', i.e. on the boundary of the second location, which has no doubt been delimited in some way all around. — KÀ.GAL: the word is marked as plural in the next line and must therefore be so understood here, no doubt because a double gate was constructed (cf. Lat. *fores*). Since all this occurs on the mountain, we must not think of real city gates; furthermore, cf. 2.10–3. — ᴳᴵŠ*ḫa-tal-ki-eš-na-aš*: the translation 'sticks' (?) is based upon the requirements of the situation in this passage and in KUB 17.28.4.46 ff.: *nu* EGIR ÍD (47) UKÙ-*an* MÀŠ.GAL UR TUR ŠAḪ TUR *iš-tar-na ar-ḫa ku-ra-an-zi* (48) *nu ki-e-iz* ½.ḪI.A *ti-ya-an-zi ki-iz-zi-ya* ½.ḪI.A *ti-an-zi* (49) *pí-ra-an-ma* ᴳᴵŠ*ḫa-at-tal-ki-iš-na-aš* KÀ.GAL-*aš i-ya-an-zi*, 'and beyond the river they cut in two a man, a large goat, a small dog, (and) a small pig; and they place halves on this side and halves on that side. But in front they construct (city) gates of sticks (?)'. Cf. KUB 12.44.3.2 ff.: *nu ŠA* GIŠŠAR GEŠTIN *ku-wa-pí* KÁ.ḪI.A-*eš nu* KÁ-*aš* (3) EGIR-*an ki-e-iz ki-e-iz-zi-ya te-e-kán be-da-aḫ-ḫi* (4) *na-aš-ta ki-e-iz ki-e-iz-zi be-te-eš-ni an-da* (5) 3 GIŠ*ḫa-tal-ki-iš-*<*šar*> *ti-it-ta-nu-um-mi* (6) *nu ki-iš-ša-an te-mi i-da-a-lu-uš-wa-aš-ša-an* (7) *an-tu-u-wa-aḫ-za i-da-a-lu-uš* EME-*aš* (8) *i-da-a-la-wa* IGI.ḪI.A-*wa* GIŠ*ḫa-tal-ki-iš-ni-it* (9) *kat-ta tar-ma-a-an e-eš-du*, 'now where the gates of the vineyard are, behind the gates, on this side and on that, I dig (holes in) the ground. Then in the hole, on this side (and) on that, I set up three sticks. And I speak thus: "Let evil man, evil tongue, evil eyes be restrained by the stick (*or* sticks)".'

1.38. [*ḫa-an-te-iz*]-*zi-ya-az*: the supplement is Götze's.

1.44. [2 NINDA KUR$_4$.RA]: after using fourteen loaves they still have two of the sixteen mentioned in 1.5. — *kur-kán-zi*: for the meaning cf. KUB 9.31.2.35 ff (= HT 1.2.10 ff.): GIŠIG-*an-na* (36) *ḫa-at-ki na-at IŠ-TU* YÀ DÙG.GA *iš-ki-ya-iz-zi* (37) *nu me-ma-i* (38) *i-da-lu-kán pa-ra-a iš-tap-du a-aš-šu-wa-kán an-da kur-ak-du* 'he shuts the door, and smears it with fine oil, and says: "Let it shut out the evil; let it keep in the good".' — *na-aš ḫar-zi*: this appears to be a sort of cross reference to 1.5.

1.45 f. 7 DUGGAL, 7 DUGGAL: this time the sum equals the number given in 1.7; so again in 1.48 and 2.1, if the supplement in 1.48 is correct.

1.47. [*na-at* KAŠ *šu*]-*un-na-i*: in Lang. 5.230 I did not supply KAŠ, but there is room for four signs in the lacuna, and we need mention of the substance with which the bowls are filled. For KAŠ instead of *IŠTU* KAŠ, cf. KUB 10.91.3.13: EGIR-*ŠU za-an-za-pu-uš-ši-in* KUBABBAR GEŠTIN *šu-un-na-an-zi*, 'next they fill a silver *zanzapussis* (with) wine'.

2.3. *ar-ḫa ḫa-ap-pí-eš-na-an-zi*: Götze will elsewhere demonstrate the correctness of the translation.

2.6. *be-da-an-zi*: for the meaning 'dig', see Götze, Kulturgeschichte 146 and fn. 10; Güterbock, ZA NF 8.225–32.

2.8. *ša-an-ḫu-un-da*: see on 1.5 and 1.17.

2.20. *an-da ḫu-u-up-pa-an-du-uš*: the verb properly means 'hold, fasten' (cf. KBo.3.21.2.16; 3.34.1.3); but the context here demands some modification of that. The verbal prefix means 'together', as in *anda aranda* and *anda appanda* 'gathered together, taken together, all together', on which see Götze, AM 252.

2.21. 2 NINDA KUR$_4$.RA: see on 1.44.

2.27. *a-ra-aḫ-za*: apparently outside the city.

2.27 ff. *nu-kán . . . kat-ta-an*: this passage is felt as a conditional clause (or perhaps two), as is shown by the use of *kwiski* and by the use of *nu* at the beginning of line 30.

2.30. ᴰKAL *in-na-ra-u-wa-an-da-an*: sections 15–18 describe a supplementary sacrifice to this deity. It is not strictly a part of the sacrifice to ᴰKAL *lulimis*, and so the three ordinary loaves required in 2.33 and the large goat of 2.34 are not included in the list of sacrificial materials in 1.4–9.

2.40. *na-at-ša-an . . . ti-an-zi*: possibly the meaning is, 'they set it behind the god'; but then we must suppose that a statue of the god has been carried out of the city for the sake of this supplementary ceremony. Similar phrases occur in 4.21 and 26.

3.1–3. These lines may mark the close of the supplementary sacrifice to ᴰKAL *innarawanza*; but it is at least equally probable that they belong to the main sacrifice to ᴰKAL *lulimis*.

3.4 ff. There is no indication that this ritual has any connection with the previous one, except that the god is the same.

3.4. ᴰKAL ᴷᵁŠ*kur-ša-an*: the god's epithet usually stands in the genitive, as in 3.43, 4.22, 4.28; but here and in 4.36 we have an equivalent adjective. — [*ú-i-ya-an-zi*]: the restoration comes from the colophon, 4.37. This verb must be distinguished from *weya-* 'send, drive' on account of the prayer in 3.37. Furthermore, the latter verb is regularly written with *u* instead of *ú*. On account of the prayer *andakan ehu* (3.37), I suggest the meaning 'invite'; but that meaning is inappropriate in the places cited by Götze, Madd. 145 fn. 1. Possibly we shall have to assume two verbs *ú-i-ya-*.

3.6. *wa-gi-eš-šar*: cf. *wāk-* 'bite'; the precise meaning is uncertain.

3.7. *iš-nu-ra-ša*: the only passage known to me where this word occurs without DUG is KBo. 6.34.1.32 (cf. Friedrich, ZA NF 1.162 f.; Götze, Madd. 73). I translate the paragraph thus: 'He puts yeast into their hands, and they smear it (about). He says: "As they take a little of this yeast which, in the present case (*ki-i*), is not yeast (i.e., it represents the persons taking the oath)—and they mix it in the dough (*iš-nu-u-ri*) and they set the dough (*iš-nu-u-ra-an*) one day and it ferments (? *pu-ut-ki-i-e-it-ta*), (just so) whoever breaks these oaths . . . , let these oaths seize him, and let him be broken into bits . . . "'. I suggest that *isnur* (i.e. *essnur*) may be derived from *essā-* 'prepare', by way of an intensive **essnā-* [353–6]. The original meaning would then be 'preparation', and DUG *isnuras* would be 'a bowl for preparing (dough)'. Like many such genitives in Hittite, *isnuras* came to be felt and declined as an adjective; hence DUG *iš-nu-u-ra-an*

(KBo. 2.3.2.7). The meaning 'dough' in KBo. 6.34.1.32 comes easily from 'preparation (of bread)'. Cf. on *iš-ša-na-aš* (1.27).

3.8. *šar-li-ya*: the meaning suggested here and in 3.24 is suggested in part by the word's apparent connection with *sarla(e)-*, *sarliya-* 'lift, raise' and in part by the requirements of the context.

3.9. *na-an*: the accusative goes with *dahhi* as well as with *iyami*; see on 1.10.

3.9 f. 1 GIŠBANŠUR . . . *pár-ḫu-e-na-aš*: we might expect these substantives to be accusatives after *dahhi*; but *parhuwenas* must be a nominative, in view of the accusative *parhuwenan* (3.31, 4.19).

3.12. *i-ya-an-za* is an epithet of a sacrificial victim in KUB 7.1.1.4. I owe the suggested translation 'unblemished' (?) to Götze. No doubt *iyanza* is the participle of *iya-* 'make'. — IGI.[ḪI].A-*wa*: accusative of specification with the intransitive participle *neyanza.*

3.13. SIG*ḫu-ut-tu-ul-li*: the determinative and the context require the meaning 'fleece'; it seems to fit in KBo.6.28.2.23 also.

3.14–20. This list, like the one in 3.9 f., seems to be in the nominative; cf. especially *ša-ra-ap-pu-wa-aš* (3.17) and *ḫa-a-ni-iš-ša-aš* (3.20).

3.14. GIŠ*šar-pa-aš ḫa-aš-du-ir*: my attempt (TAPA 58.23) to prove that *hasdwēr* means 'branches' depended upon the interpretation of GIŠŠAR-*pa-aš* as 'orchard'; but the latter word occurs in contexts where that meaning is scarcely possible. The interpretation of *sarpas hasdwēr* must be based upon a comparison of this passage with 3.26 f, 3.30 f., and 3.42 f. In 3.27 and 3.30 *hastwēr* is an acc. pl. modified by *meranda* 'dead', while in 3.42 it is the subject of *merta* 'died'. Evidently it is a neuter substantive, and therefore *sarpas* is most naturally taken as a genitive; the omission of *sarpas* in 3.27, 3.42 indicates that it is the less essential part of the phrase, and its form forbids us to consider it an adjective. Since the *hasdwēr* have died, they must once have been alive; and since the determinative GIŠ precedes the phrase, they are of wood. Furthermore the use of the determinative with *sarpas* rather than with *hasdwēr* suggests that the latter are parts of the former. Since the *sarpas hasdwēr* are employed in sympathetic magic (3.43 ff.) to produce the destruction of the god's anger, they also must be injurious, and, in view of LÚAPIN.LAL-*li* (3.42), injurious to the plowman. I infer, then, that the phrase means 'branches of brushwood'. Near the close of the second prayer to avert pestilence (Götze, KlF 1.218 = KUB 14.10.4.19 f.) Mursilis promises, in case a certain petition is granted: *nu-kán* URUDZI.KIN.BAR-*aš* (20) GIŠ*šar-pa-az ku-un-ku-u-e-ni* 'and we shall decorate (?) the statues (?) with *verbenae*'. The word *sarpan* occurs in a fragmentary line in KUB 10.92.5.13, and with determinative KUŠ 'leather' in KBo.5.2.1.31. For the etymology, cf. Lat. *sarmentum* 'brushwood' and *sarpo* 'trim, prune'.

3.16–20. There is a similar passage in KUB 17.23.1.7–10: *nu* EGIR-*an-da* 9 UTÚL.ḪI.A *i-ya-an* BA.BA.ZA UTÚL *ga-an-ga-ti* (8) UTÚL *ḫa-ra-am-ma* UTÚL *kap-pa-a-ra* UTÚL GÚ.GAL UTÚL *ḫa-pít-tu-ul-li* (9) *ŠA* GIŠ*IN-BI*-ḪI.A *me-ma-al ŠA* LÀL *me-ma-al* GA.AL (10) *ša-ri-pu-wa-aš ga-ka-aš-du-la-aš na-at ú-da-an-zi*. Here all the foods are called stews, and so it seems impossible to translate *memal* 'meal', although that seems to be its primary meaning (see Lang. 5.229). 'Porridge' (i.e. stewed meal) must be the meaning here; it must differ in some way from UTÚL BA.BA.ZA 'gruel'. Since six stews are clearly named in ll. 7–8, and since *ša-ri-pu-wa-aš* (l. 10) must be identical with *ša-ra-ap-pu-wa-aš* (l. 17) of our text (i.e. *sarppuwas*), and therefore constitute a separate item in the list, there remain only two items for l. 9; and these must be the two *memal*. Then it is necessary to connect GA.AL 'cream' either with *memal* or with *sarppuwas*, and cream seems to go better with porridge than with most other kinds of stew. Consequently the other two epithets of l. 9 probably go with the preceding substantives. In our text, on the other hand, it is necessary to count GA.AL as a separate item in the list, in order to make up the total of nine; and it is natural to include cream in a list of foods (*etri*), although not in a list of stews (UTÚL). Nevertheless the collocation of *memal* and GA.AL is scarcely accidental, and it is therefore likely that *ŠA* LÀL (3.19) goes with the preceding NINDA NI.E.DÉ.A. The question arises whether NINDA NI.E.DÉ.A *ŠA* LÀL is equivalent to *memal ŠA* LÀL and to NINDA LÀL (KUB 20.11.2.5). Götze points out that in KBo.4.2.1.10 and KUB 12.26.3.18 GÚ.TUR and GÚ.GAL are accompanied by GÚ.GAL.GAL, and he suggests that the last named ideogram may have been omitted from our list by error. In that case *sarppuwas* may be a genitive modifying UTÚL *ḫar-ki*.

3.18. [UTÚL] GÚ.GAL: the tablet has UZU instead of UTÚL; but the passage cited in the last note proves that it is an error, as we would suspect in any case.

3.20. 1 DUG*ḫa-a-ni-iš-ša-aš* KAŠ: that this is not one of the nine *etri* is shown by the separate mention of KAŠ in 4.15 and elsewhere. The word *hānissas* reminds one of the verb *han-* 'dip'; but the vessel must be of considerable size, since its contents are used below (4.1) to cool the nine bits of gravel and (4.8) to pour three libations, and the next morning (4.12 f.) there is some left to drink.

3.25. ^{TÚG}*ku-ri-eš-šar kat-ta kán-ga-aḫ-ḫi*: literally, 'I hang the strip of cloth down'; presumably the cloth was spread across the table, but was long enough for its ends to hang down.

3.23. *pí-ra-an*: the principal reason for interpreting this as 'before the house' is the repeated distinction between *anda* (3.21, 35, 4.10) and *peran* (3.25, 4.8), *parā* (4.9).

3.37. *an-da-kán e-ḫu*: cf. *parāwakan ehu* (1.28). If the latter phrase contains a full verb of motion, this one probably does also, and in 1.28 the context clearly demands that interpretation. The briefer prayer of 1.28 f. has the particle of direct quotation, but here it is omitted.

3.39. *tal-li-i-e-eš*: Götze suggests that this is probably a derivative verb in suffix *es* [323], as the syntactically parallel *mi-i-e-eš* (3.38) certainly is. He suggests, furthermore, that another derivative from the underlying adjective may be seen in *talliya-*, which Friedrich, Vert. 2.24, translates 'anrufen'. At any rate *talliya-* always has a human subject and a divine object. In our passage *tallēs* is an imperative addressed to a god, and since it must harmonize with *miēs* in meaning as well as in syntax, it is natural to translate it 'become propitious', and to infer for *talliya-* some such force as 'propitiate'.

3.40 f. *kar-pí-in-na kar-tim-mi-ya-at-ta-an ša-a-u-wa-ar*: the difference between these three synonyms is unknown; we have used three English synonyms at random.

4.6. [NINDA KUR$_4$.R]A.ḪI.A: the supplement is virtually certain, since ordinary loaves are present in the ceremony (3.6, 4.11), and since such loaves are very often broken in the rituals.

4.7. [^{GIŠ}BANŠUR]-*i*: this supplement is uncertain; we have not been told that the ordinary loaves were on the table. — 9 *e-it-ri*: those listed in 3.16–19.

4.8. f. *pí-ra-an, pa-ra-a*: see on *pí-ra-an* (3.25). Here the use of *peran* and *parā* in successive sentences is difficult; Anniwiyanis must go into the house between the two acts.

4.10. [^{GIŠ}IG]-*ma*: the supplement was suggested by Götze.

4.16. UD-*at* UD-*at*: this adverb may be a stereotyped acc. neut. that may have survived after a transfer of the noun itself to the masc. gender (see Sommer, BoSt.10.41 f.). But since the common forms of the Hittite abl. and inst. must owe their contrasting vocalism (*-az* : *-et*) to a secondary distribution, an isolated inst. in *-at* (cf. IE gen.-abl. in *-es*/*os*) would not be surprising; cf. [197d]. Neither should we be surprised to find an isolated inst. carrying an ablatival meaning [190, 196].

4.17. *mu-ki-eš-šar*: the primary meaning of this verbal noun from *muga(e)-* 'lament, implore' should be 'lamentation', but here it is used of material objects—no doubt the objects that in the ritual accompany a prayer of lamentation. Cf. the note on *galaktar* (A 3.10; page 123) in the Additions and Corrections.

4.23. MÁŠ.GAL: the lists in 3.6–20 do not include this item, no doubt because those lists are intended to cover only the first day of the main sacrifice; cf. 4.16. See also on 2.30.

4.38 f. We have already encountered Hittite names written with ideograms in H 1.10 and elsewhere. The practice is particularly common in writing the names of scribes. No doubt the use of ideograms was a mark of learning, and so the scribes took professional pride in applying that system to their own names. The last two signs of [I]*Ḫ̮A-NI-IK-KU*-DINGIR-*LIM* stand for Akkadian *ILI*, gen. of *ILU* 'god', as in the well known [I]*MUR-ŠI*-DINGIR-*LIM* = *MURŠILI* = *Mursilis* (cf. Sommer, OLZ 27.27; Friedrich, Vert. 1.151).

INSTRUCTIONS FOR TEMPLE OFFICIALS

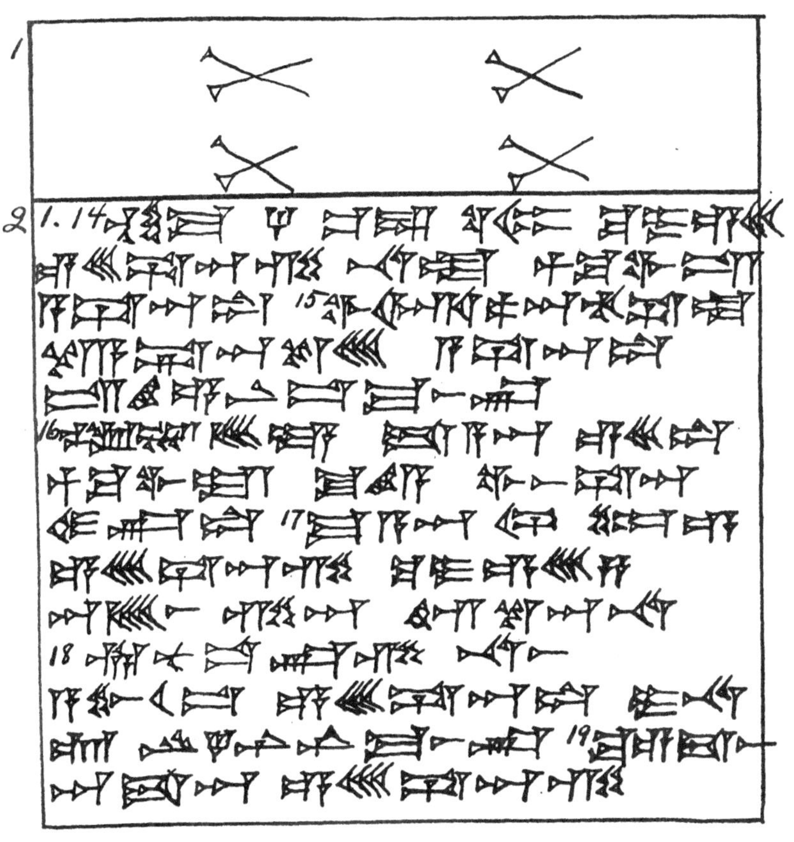

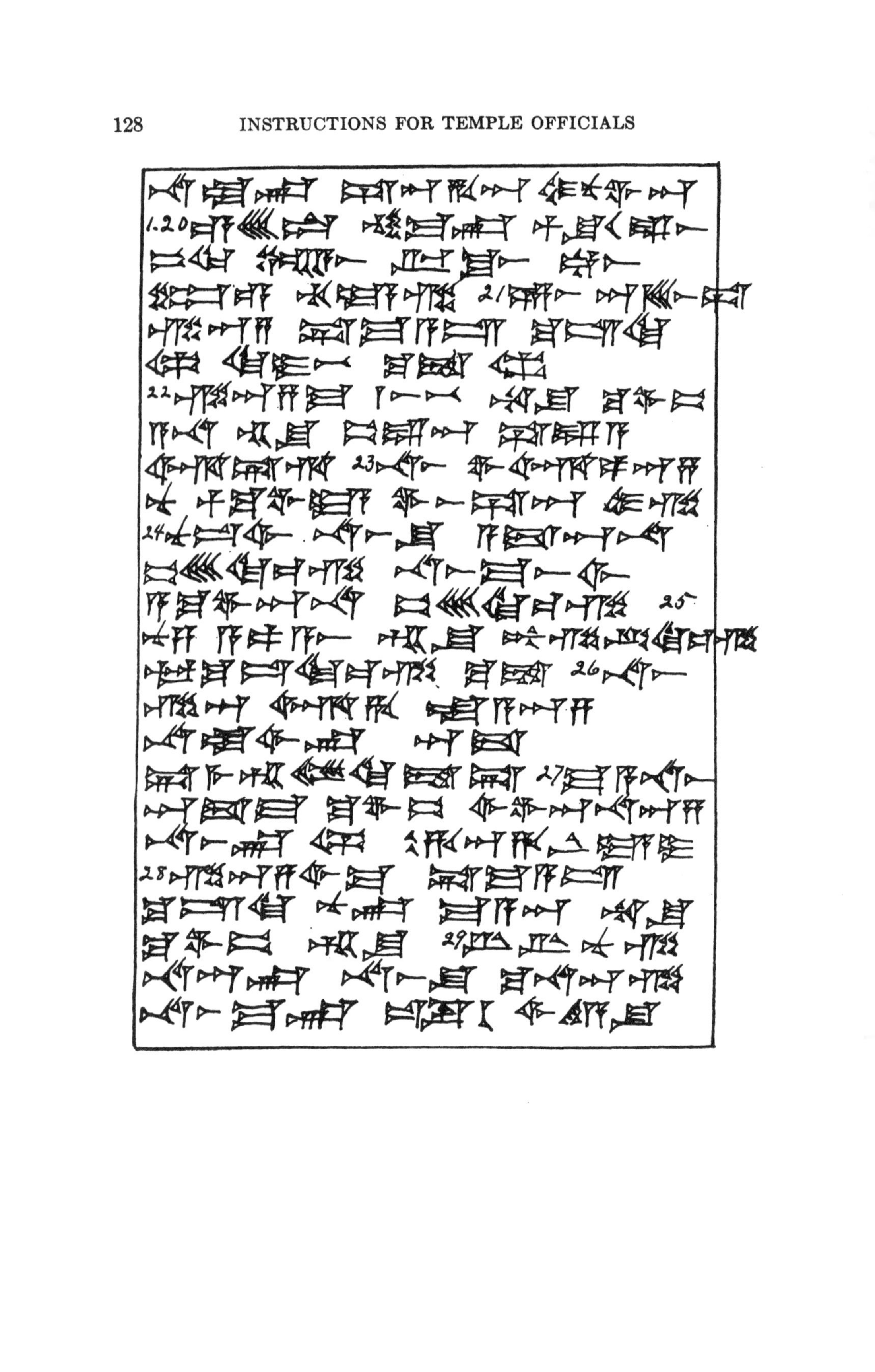

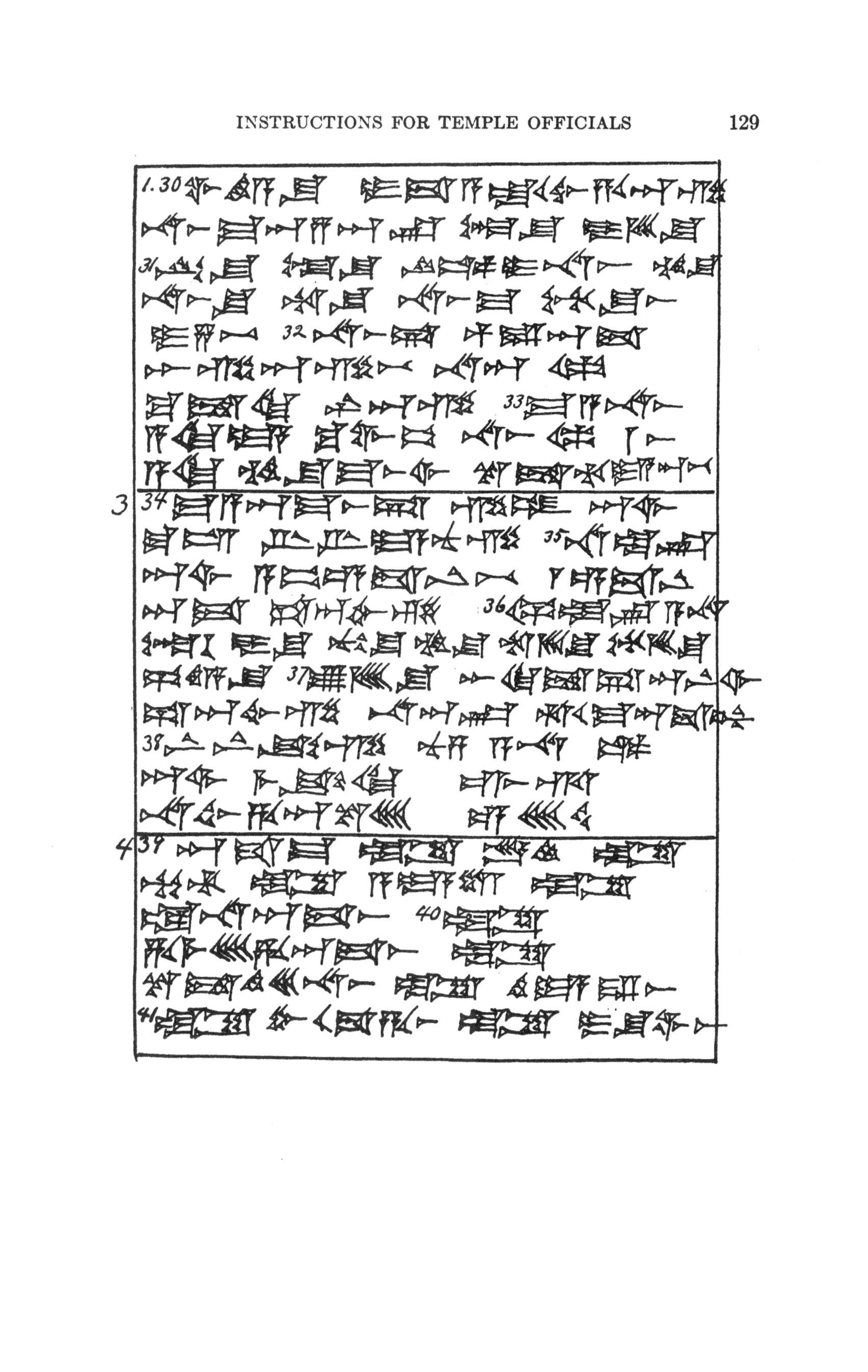

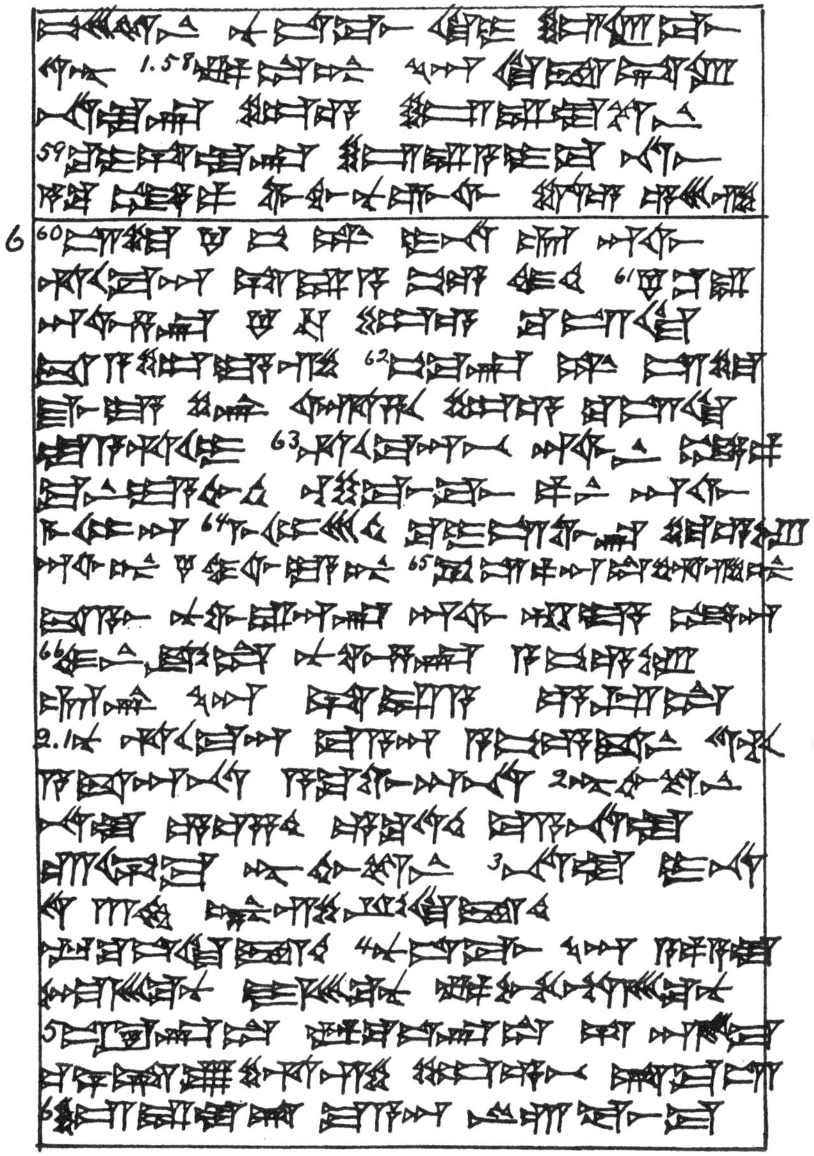

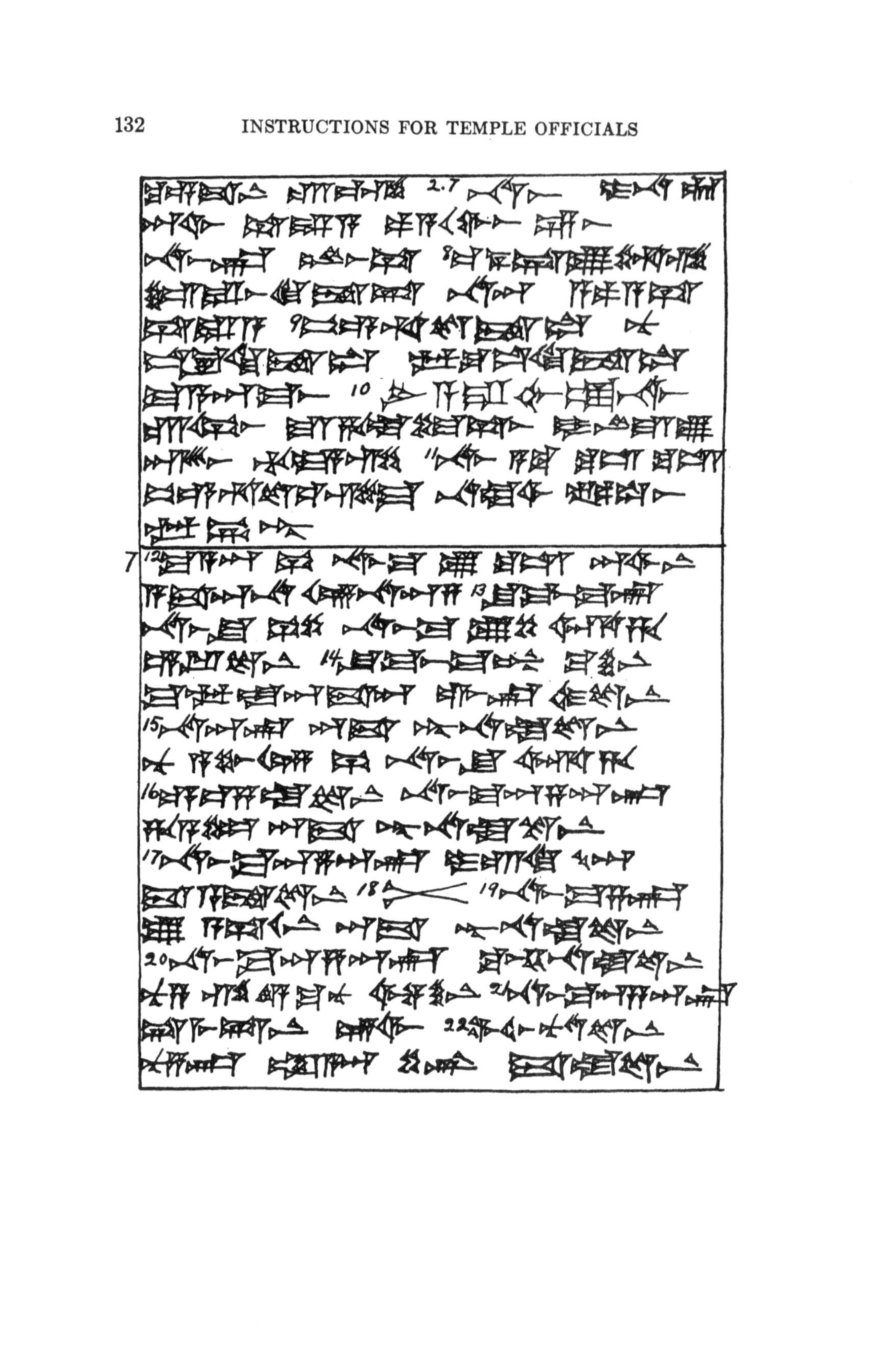

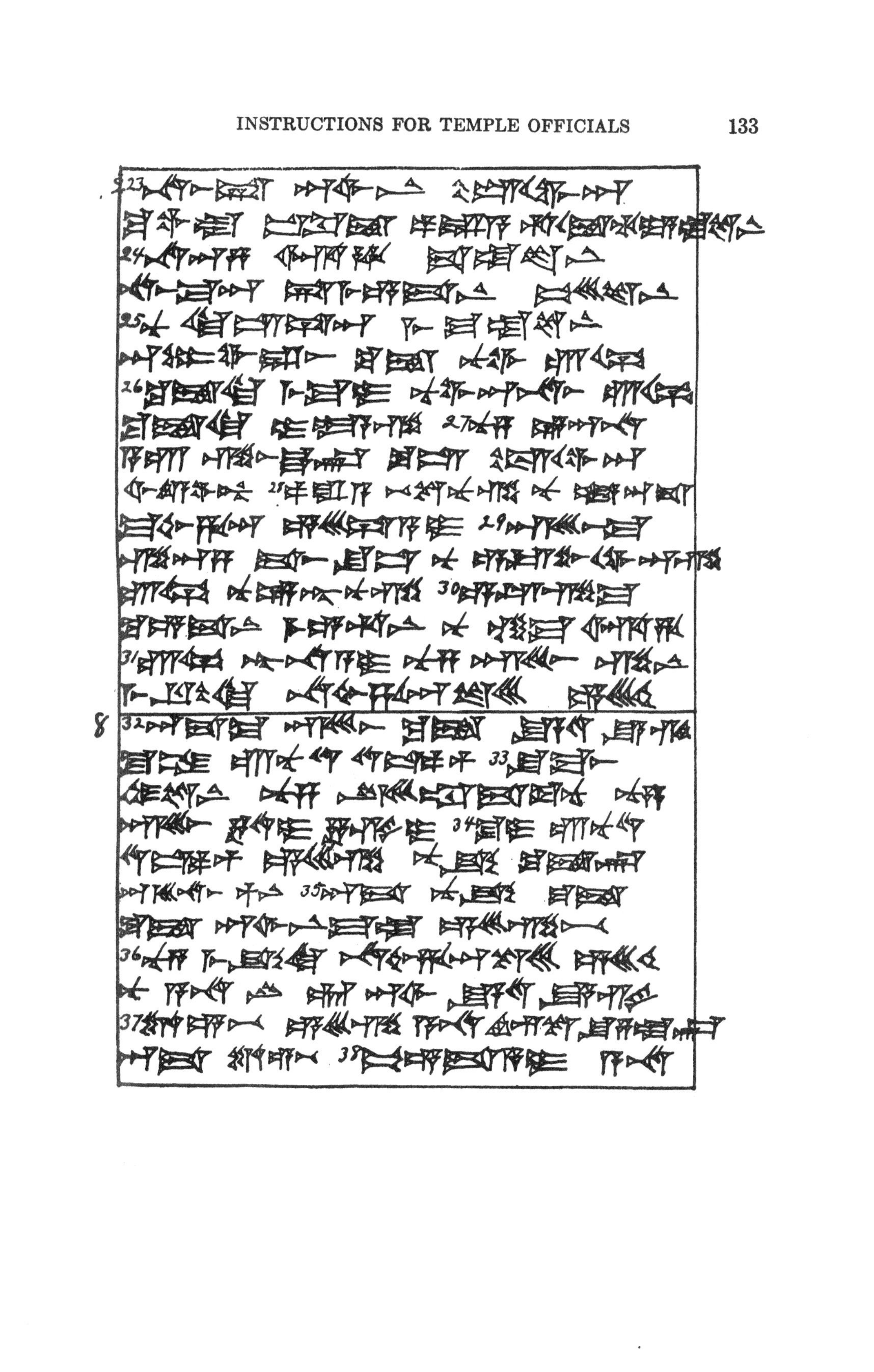

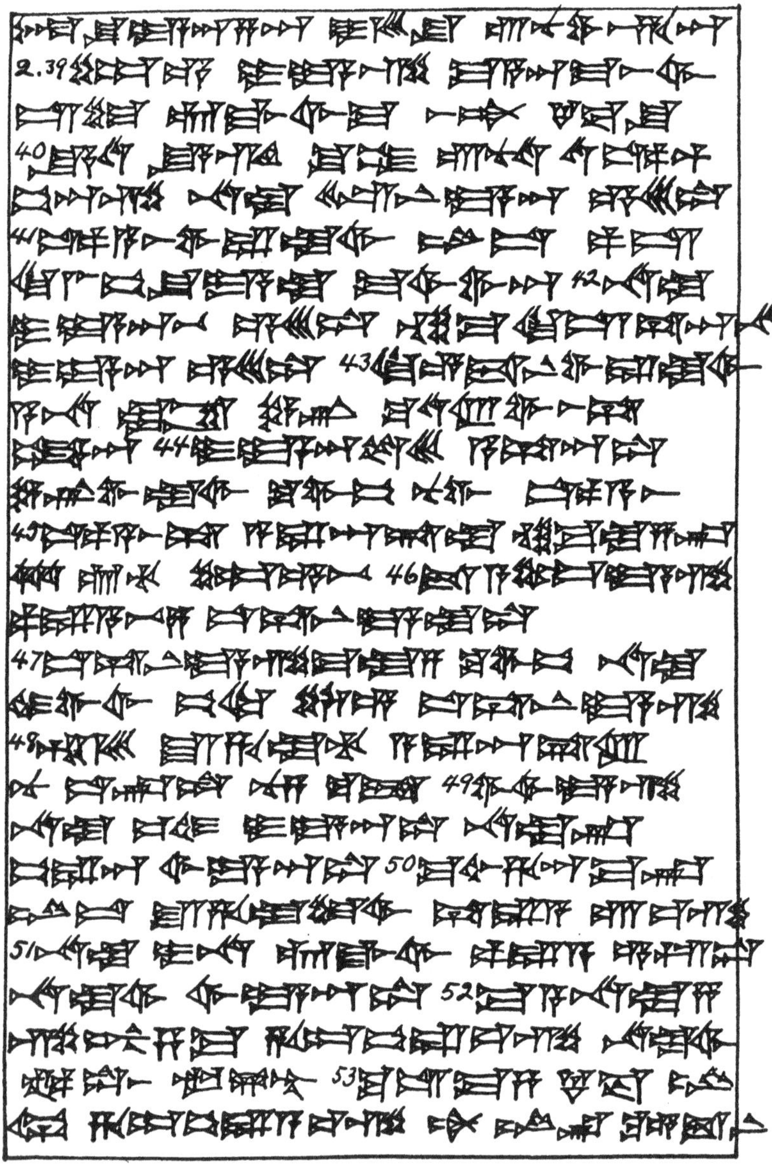

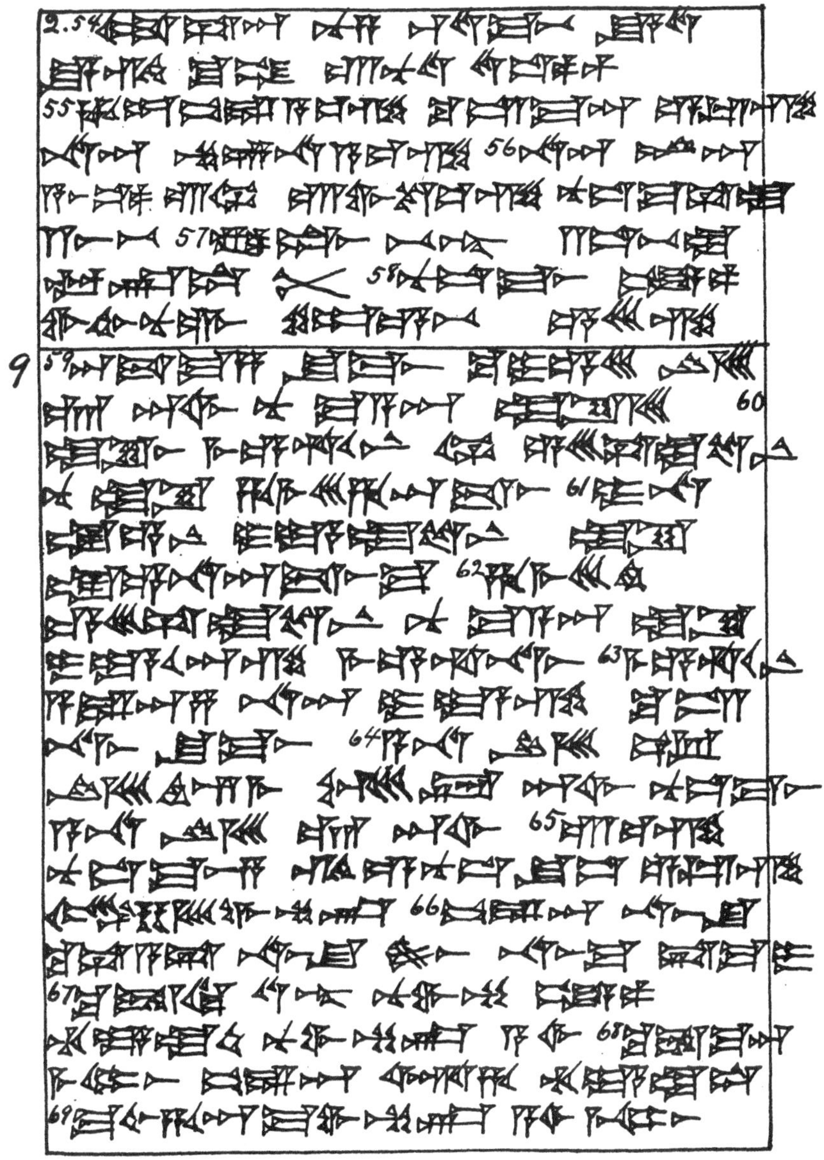

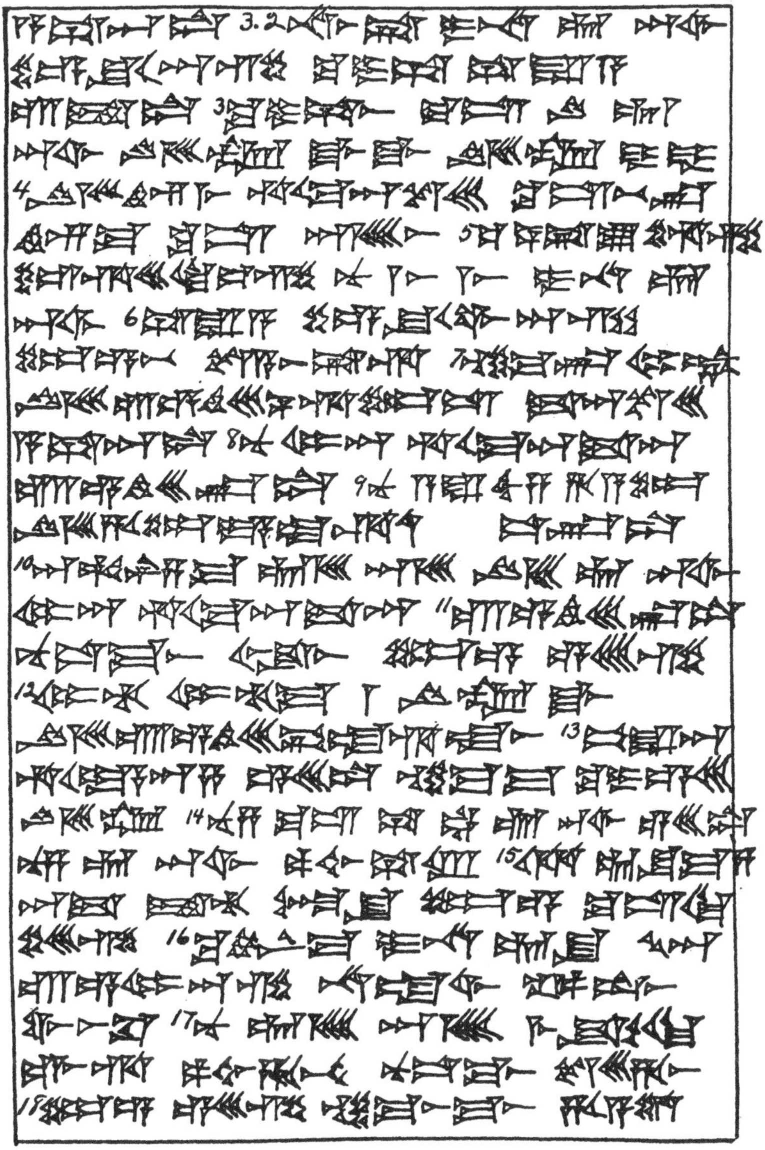

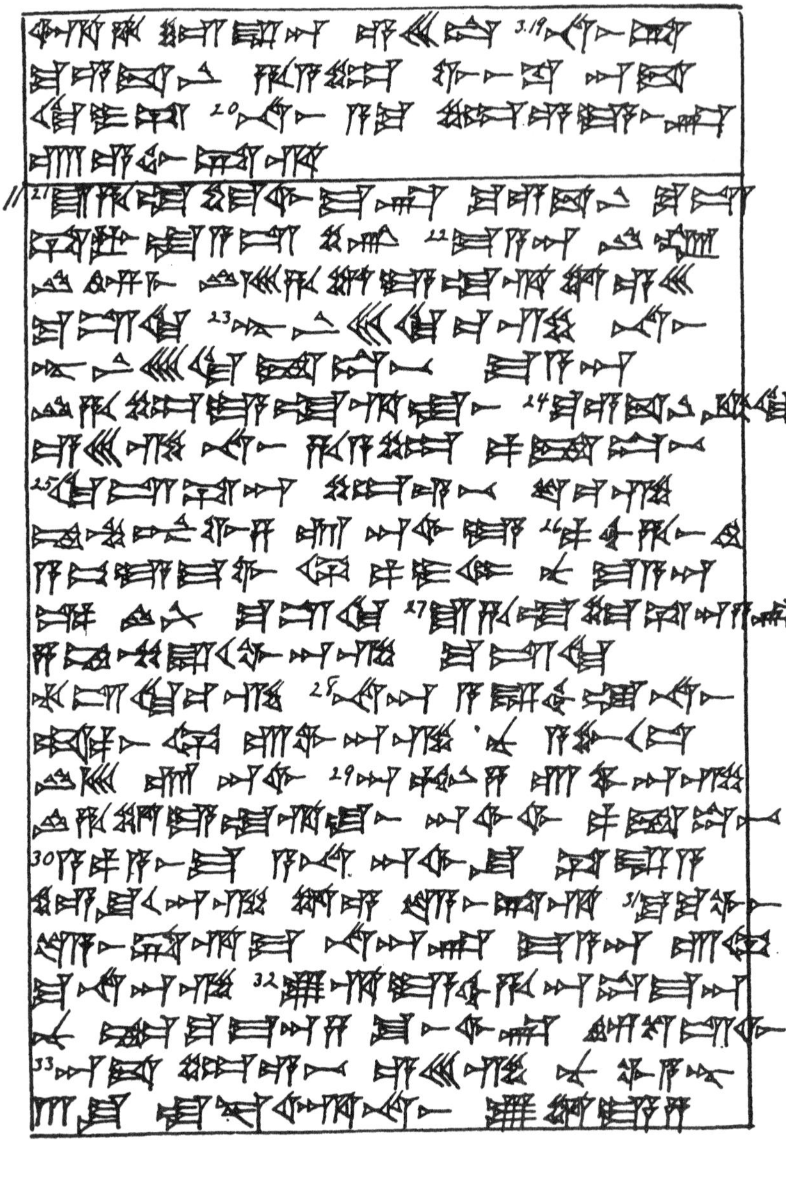

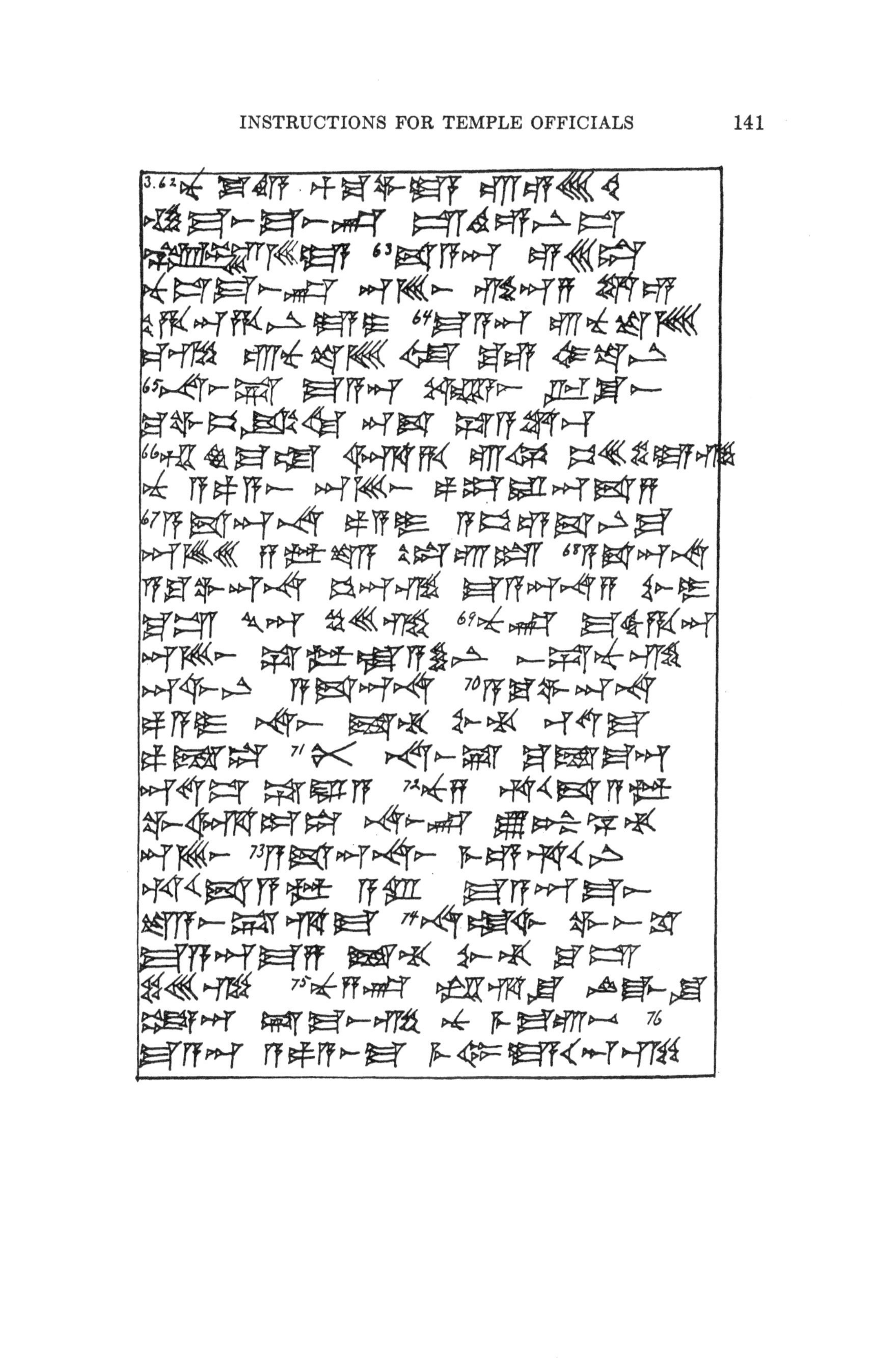

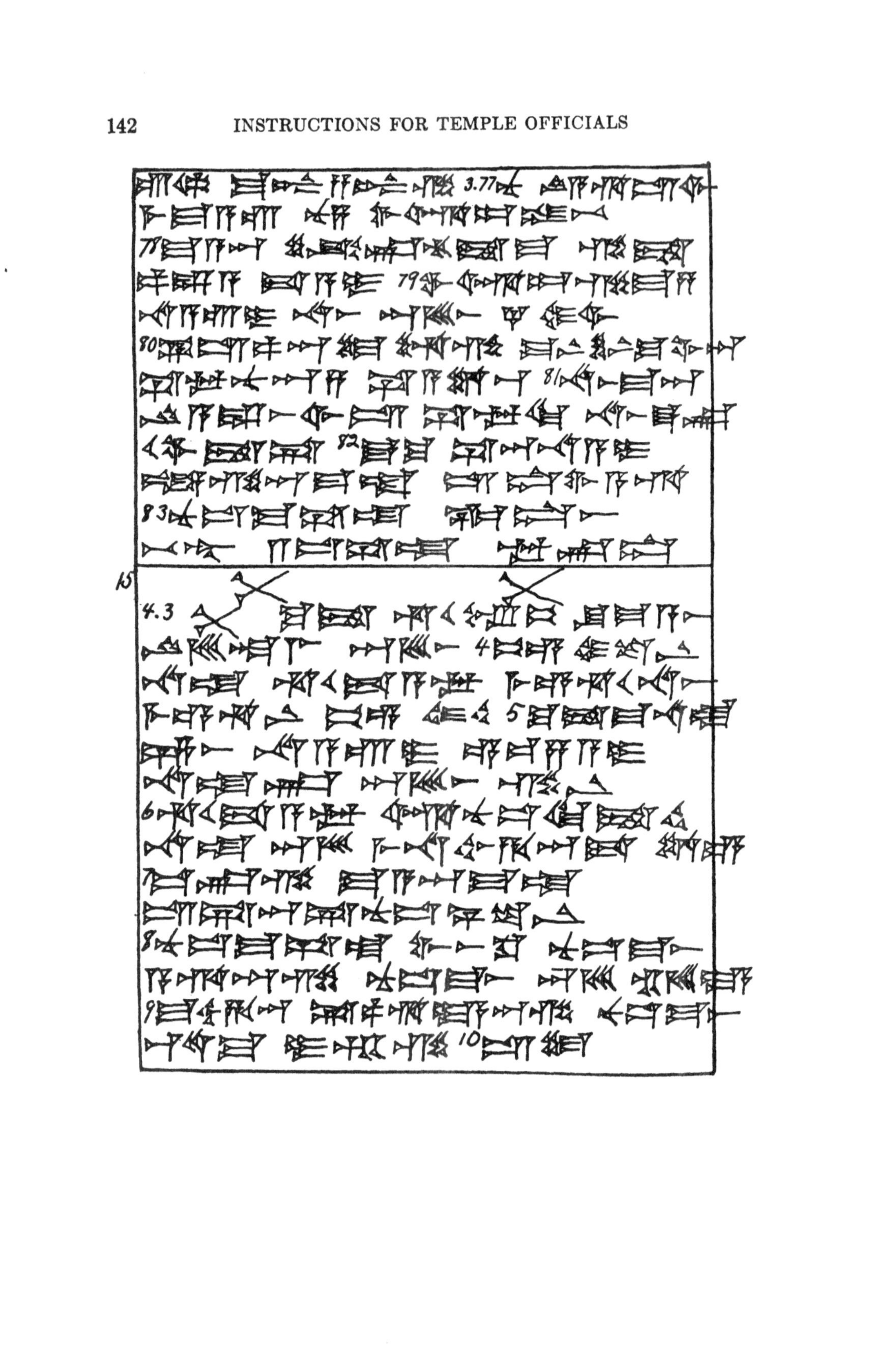

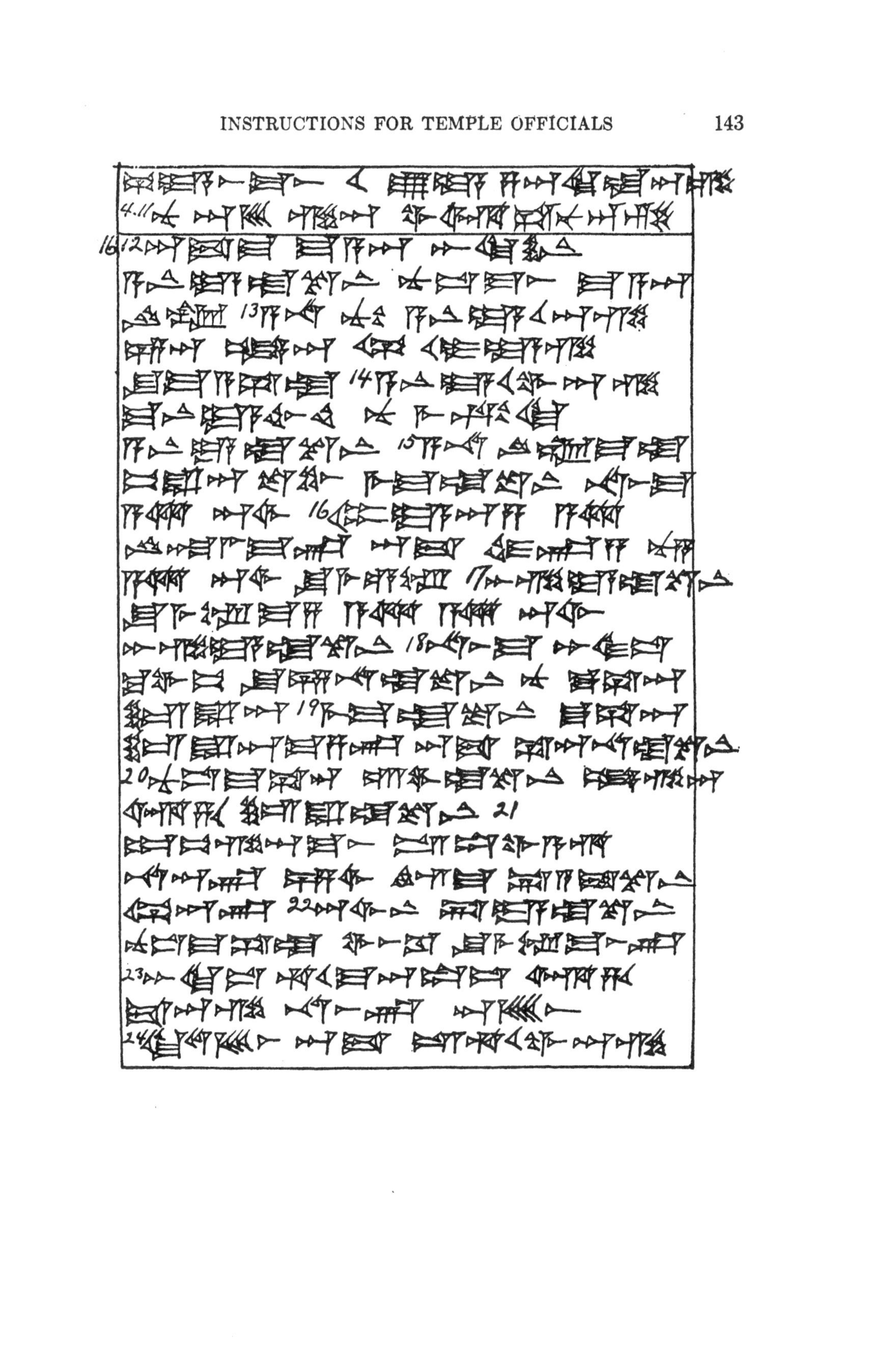

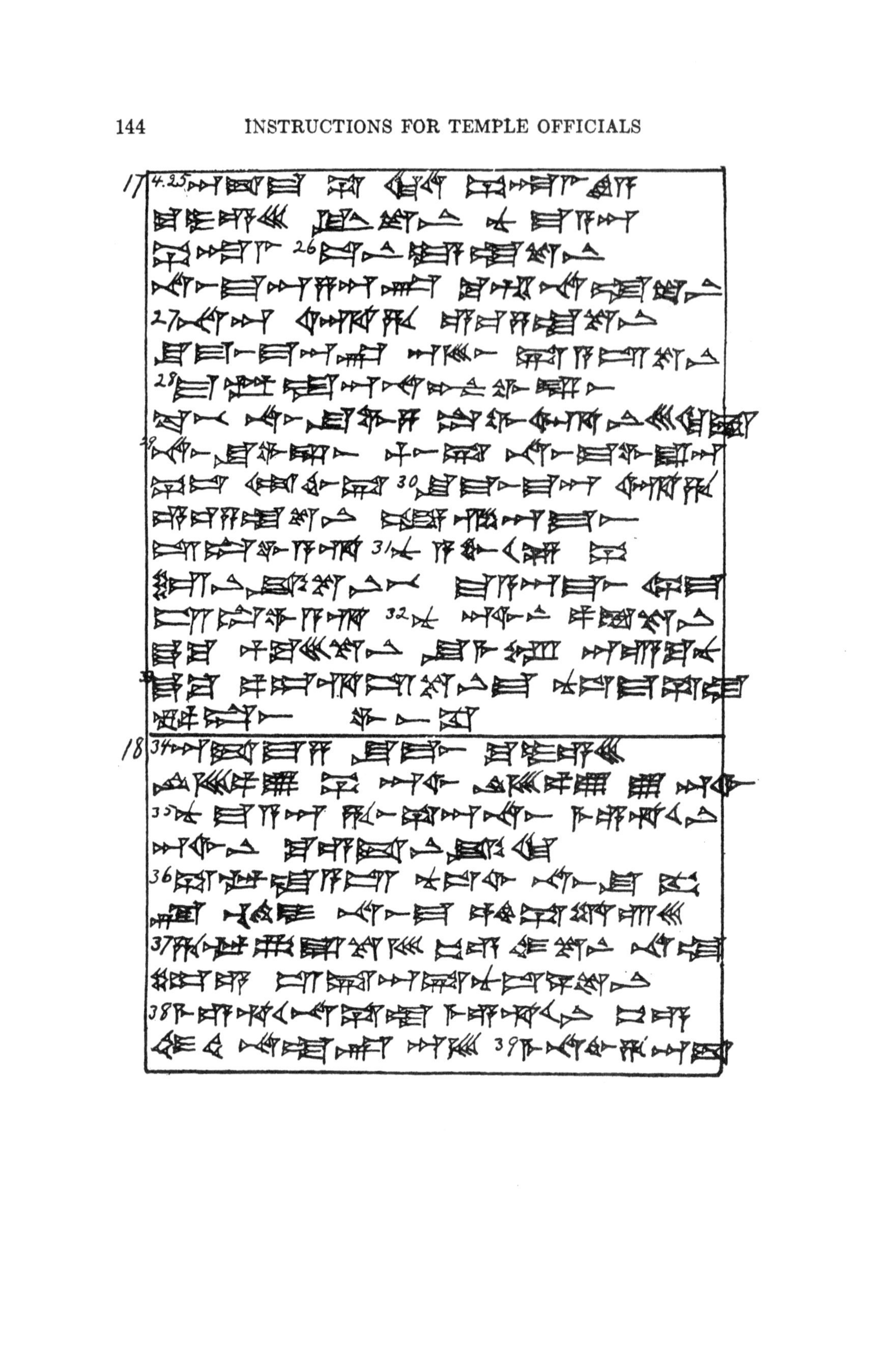

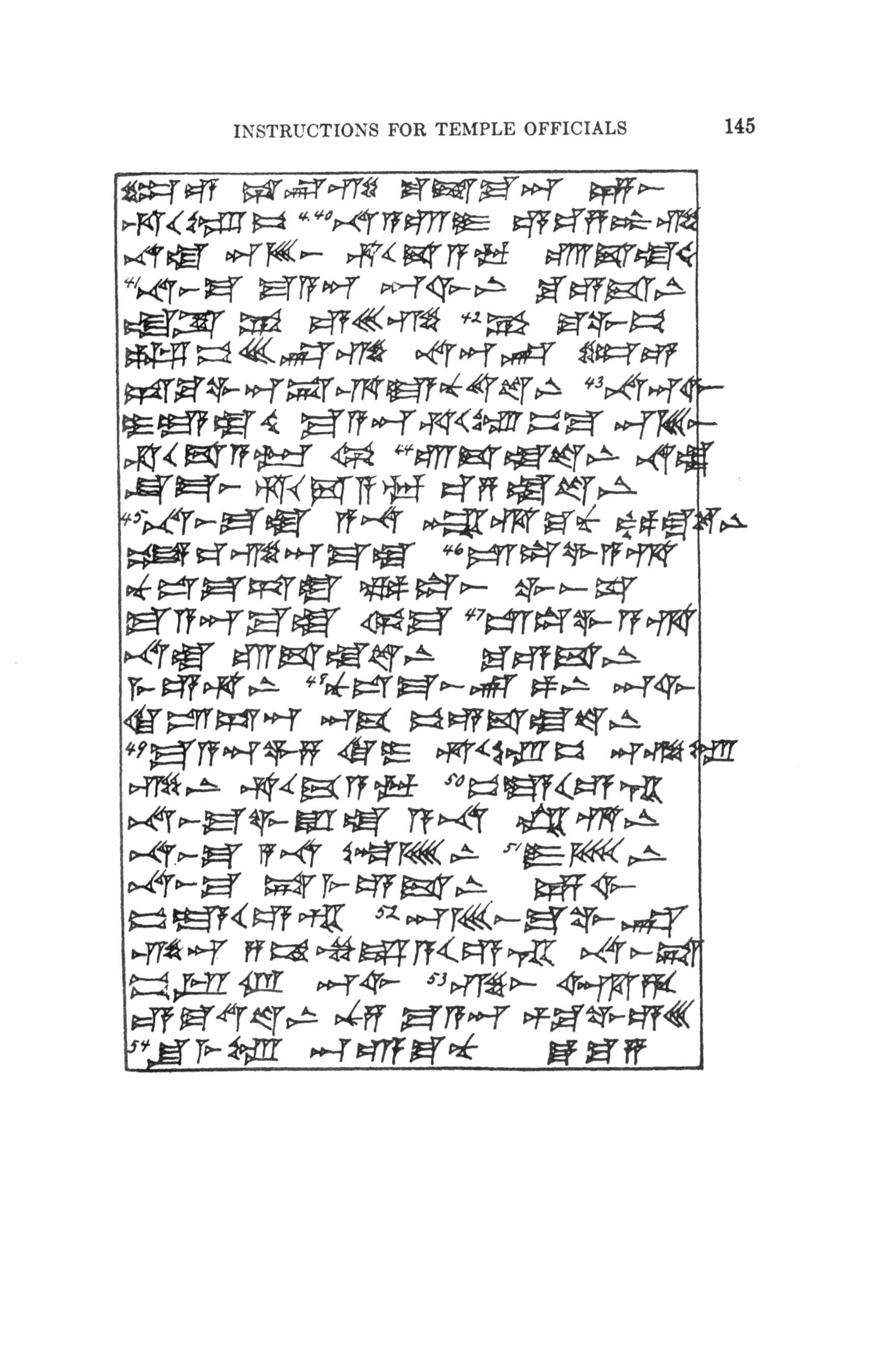

19

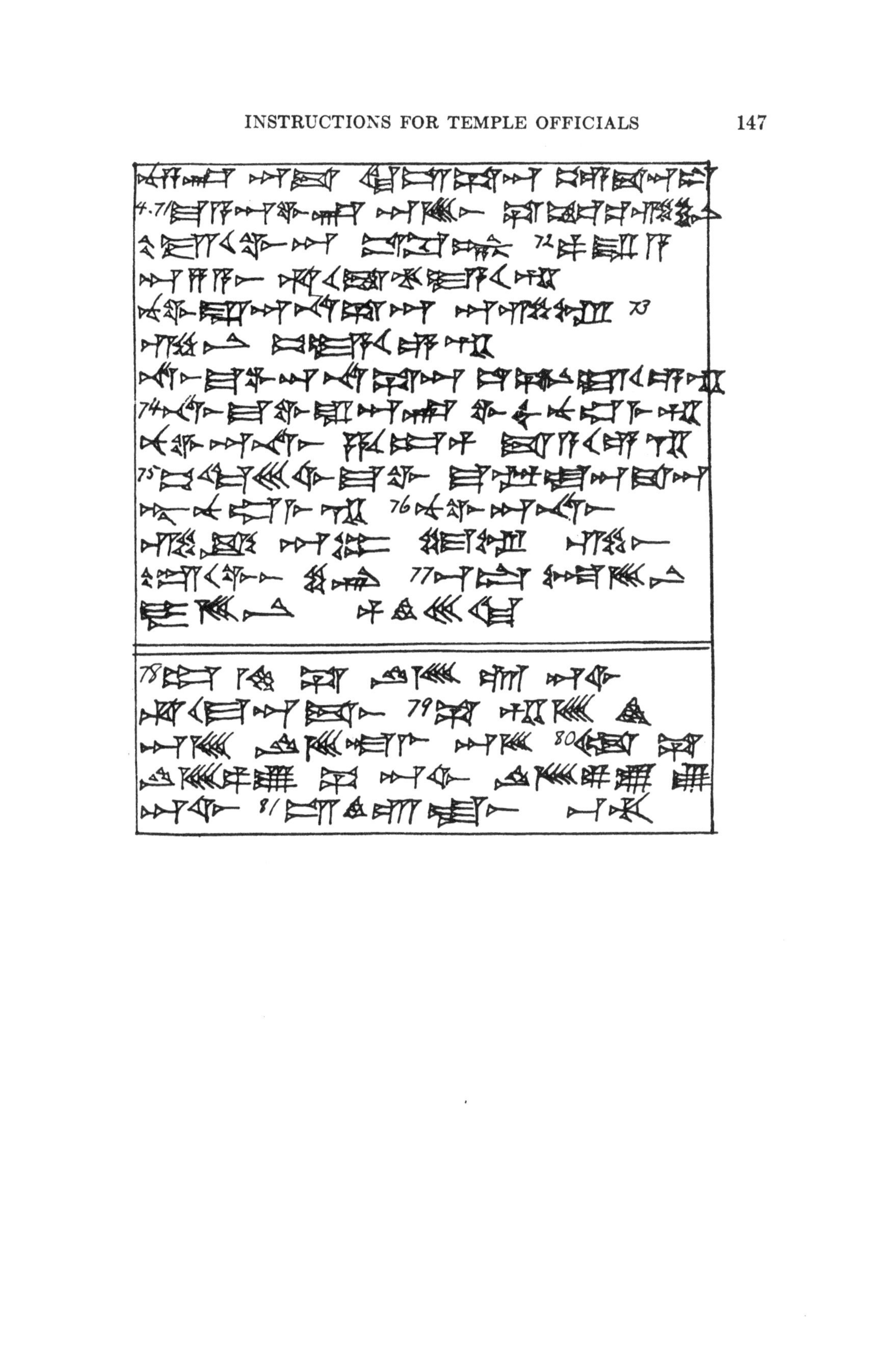

2

(1.14) *nam-ma* NINDA [KUR$_4$].RA UD-*MI* *ku-i-e-eš e-eš-ša-an-zi na-at pár-*[*k*]*u-wa-iš a-ša-an-du* (1.15) *wa-ar-*[*pa*]*-an-ti-ša-at kar-ta-an-te-eš a-ša-an-du iš-ḫi-*[*e*]*-ni-uš-ma-aš-kán* (1.16) DUB[BIN.MEŠ-*y*]*a da-a-an e-eš-du pár-ku-wa-ya* TÚG.ḪI.A *wa-aš-ša-an ḫar-kán-du* (1.17) [*ma-a-an UL*] *li-e e-eš-ša-an-zi ku-i-e-eš-za* DINGIR.MEŠ-*aš* ZI-*an* NÍ.TE-*an-na* (1.18) [ŠE$_{12}$-*nu-uš*]-*kán-zi na-aš a-pu-u-uš e-eš-ša-an-du I-NA* É L[Ú]NINDA.DÙ.DÙ-*ma-aš-kán* (1.19) *ku-e-da-aš an-da-an e-eš-ša-an-zi na-at-kán ša-*[*a*]*n-ḫa-an ḫur-nu-wa-an* (1.20) *e-eš-du nam-ma-kán pár-šu-u-ra-aš pí-di* ŠAḪ-*aš* UR.TÚG-[*aš*] KÁ-*aš li-e ti-ya-zi* (1.21) UKÙ-*aš* DINGIR.MEŠ-*aš-ša* ZI-*an-za ta-ma-a-iš ku-iš-ki UL* [*k*]*i-i-be ku-it UL* (1.22) ZI-*an-za-ma* 1-*aš-be* ERUM-*ŠU ku-wa-pí A-NA* EN-*ŠU pí-ra-an ša-ra-a ar-ta-ri* (1.23) *na-aš wa-ar-pa-an-za nu pár-ku-wa-ya wa-aš-ša-an ḫar-zi* (1.24) *nu-uš-ši na-aš-šu a-da-an-na pí-eš-ki-iz-zi na-aš-ma-aš-ši a-ku-wa-an-na pí-eš-ki-iz-zi* (1.25) *nu-za a-pa-a-aš* EN-*ŠU az-zi-ik-ki-iz-zi ak-ku-uš-ki-iz-zi ku-it* (1.26) *na-aš* ZI-*an ar-ḫa la-a-an-za na-at-ši-kán an-da* [*ta*]*-me-en-kiš-k*[*i-i*]*t-ta* (1.27) *ma-a-na-aš an-da-ma ku-wa-pí* IGI-*wa-an-na-an-za na-aš-kán UL* ⸗*ḫa-an-ḫa-ni-y*[*a*]*-i* (1.28) ZI-*an-*<*za*>*-ši-ma ta-ma-a-iš ku-iš-ki nu-kán ma-a-an* ERUM-*ŠU ku-wa-pí* EN-[*Š*]*U* (1.29) TUKU.TUKU-*nu-zi na-an-kán na-aš-šu ku-na-an-zi na-aš-ma-k*[*á*]*n* KA×GAG-*ŠÚ* IGI.ḪI.A-*ŠU* (1.30) GEŠTUG.ḪI.A-*ŠU i-da-a-la-u-aḫ-ḫa-an-zi na-aš-ma-an-za-an-kán* DAM-*ŠU* DUMU.MEŠ-[*Š*]*U* (1.31) ŠEŠ-*ŠU* NIN-*ŠU* LÚ*ka-i-na-aš* MÁŠ-*ŠU na-aš-šu* ERUM-*Š*[*U*] *na-aš-ma* GÌM-*ŠU-aš* [*I-ṢA*]*-BAT* (1.32) *na-aš-ta pár-ra-an-da ḫal-zi-an-zi-be na-an UL* [*k*]*u-it-ki* DÙ-*an-zi* (1.33) *ma-a-na-aš a-ki-ya ku-wa-pí na-aš UL* 1-*aš a-ki* MÁŠ-*ŠU-ma-aš-ši te-it-ti-ya-an-be*

3

(1.34) [*m*]*a-a-an-ma-aš-ta* ZI-*TUM* DINGIR-*LI*[*M ku-i*]*š* TUKU.TUKU-*ya-nu-zi* (1.35) *na-at-kán* DINGIR-*LIM a-pí-e-da-ni-be* [1-*e*]*-da-ni an-da š*[*a-an-aḫ*]*-zi* (1.36) *UL-at-kán A-NA* DAM-*ŠÚ* [DUMU-*ŠU* N]UMUN-*ŠU* MÁŠ-*ŠU* [ER]UM.MEŠ-*Š*[*U* GÌ]M.MEŠ-*ŠU* [GU]D.ḪI.A-*ŠU* (1.37) UDU.MEŠ-*ŠU ḫal-ki-it-ta-an-*[*ni-ši ša-a*]*n-aḫ-zi na-an-kán ḫ*[*u-u-m*]*a-an-da-az* (1.38) *n*[*i*]*-ni-*[*i*]*k-zi nu-za A-NA* INIM [DINGIR-*LIM me-i*]*k-ki mar-ri na-aḫ-*[*ḫa-an-t*]*e-eš e-eš-tin*

INSTRUCTIONS FOR TEMPLE OFFICIALS

2

(1.14) Furthermore let those who prepare the daily bread be clean; let them be washed (and) cleansed (?); let their hair (?) and finger-nails be removed, and let them have on clean clothes. (17) If not, let them not prepare (it). (17) Let those who propitiate the heart and soul of the gods prepare them (i.e. the loaves). (18) And let the baker's house in which they prepare them be swept (?) and sprinkled (?). (20) Furthermore let not a pig or a dog approach the door of the place of the broken bread (?). (21) Is the disposition of men and of the gods at all different? No! (21) Even in this (matter) somewhat (different)? No; but (their) disposition is quite the same. (22) When a slave stands before his master, he is washed and he has on clean (clothes); and either he gives him (something) to eat, or he gives him (something) to drink. (25) And he, his master, eats (and) drinks something and he is relaxed in spirit and he is favorably inclined (?) to him. (27) If, however, he (the slave) is ever dilatory (?), and is not observant (?), there is a different disposition toward him. (28) And if ever a slave vexes his master, either they kill him or they injure his nose, his eyes, (or) his ears; or he (i.e. the master) calls him to account (and also) his wife, his sons, his brother, his sister, (his) relatives by marriage, (and) his family, whether it (be) a male slave or a female slave. (32) Then they revile him in public (?), and they consider him nothing at all. (33) And if ever he dies, he does not die alone, but his family (is) included with him.

3

(34) If then, on the other hand, anyone vexes the feelings of a god, does the god punish him alone for it? (36) Does he not punish his wife, his children, his descendants, his family, his slaves male (and) female, his cattle, his sheep, (and) his harvest for it, and remove him utterly? (38) Now, of your own accord, be very much afraid of the word of a god.

4

(1.39) *an-*[*da-m*]*a* EZEN×ŠE ITU.KAM EZEN×ŠE MU-*TI* EZEN×ŠE *a-ya-li* EZEN×ŠE *zé-n*[*a-an-d*]*a-aš* (1.40) EZEN×ŠE *ḫa-me-eš-ḫa-an-da-aš* EZEN×ŠE *te-it-ḫi-eš-na-aš* [EZE]N×ŠE *ḫi-ya-r*[*a*]*-aš* (1.41) EZEN×ŠE *pu-u-da-ḫa-aš* EZEN×ŠE *i-šu-wa-aš* EZEN×ŠE [*iš-š*]*a-la-aš-ša-aš* (1.42) EZEN×ŠE *BI-IB-RI* EZEN×ŠE.MEŠ *šu-up-pa-ya-aš* LÚSANGA-*aš* (1.43) EZEN×ŠE.MEŠ LÚ.MEŠŠU.GI EZEN×ŠE.MEŠ SAL.MEŠAMA DINGIR-*L*[*IM*] EZEN×ŠE *da-ḫi-ya-aš* (1.44) EZEN×ŠE.MEŠ LÚ.MEŠ *ú-pa-ti-ya-aš* EZEN×ŠE.MEŠ *pu-u-l*[*a*]*-aš* EZEN×ŠE.MEŠ *ḫa-aḫ-ra-an-na-aš* (1.45) *na-aš-ma-aš ku-iš im-ma ku-iš* EZEN×ŠE-*aš* URU*Ḫa-*[*a*]*t-tu-ši-kán še-ir* (1.46) *na-aš ma-a-an IŠ-TU* GUD.ḪI.A UDU.ḪI.A NINDA KAŠ *Ù IŠ-TU* GEŠTIN (1.47) *ḫu-u-ma-an-da-az ša-ra-a ti-ya-an-ta-*<*aš*> *UL e-eš-ša-at-te-ni* (1.48) *na-at pí-eš-kán-zi ku-i-e-eš nu-uš-ma-aš šu-me-eš* LÚ.MEŠ É DINGIR-*LIM* (1.49) *ḫa-ap-pár da-aš-kit$_9$-te-ni* DINGIR.MEŠ-*aš-ma-at-kán* ZI-*ni wa-ak-ši-ya-nu-ut-te-ni*

5

(1.50) *na-aš-ma-at-kán ma-a-an ša-ra-a ti-ya-an-da ku-wa-pí da-at-te-ni* (1.51) *na-at* DINGIR.MEŠ-*aš* ZI-*ni pa-ra-a UL ar-nu-ut-te-ni nu-uš-ma-ša-at ar-ḫa* (1.52) *I-NA* É.MEŠ-*KU-NU pí-e ḫar-te-ni na-at šu-me-el* DAM.MEŠ-*KU-NU* DUMU.MEŠ-*KU-NU* (1.53) SAG.GÌM.ERUM.MEŠ-*KU-NU ar-ḫa e-iz-za-a-i na-aš-šu-ma-aš-ma-aš* LÚ*ka-e-na-a*[*š*] (1.54) *na-aš-ma a-aš-šu-wa-an-za ku-iš-ki* LÚ*Ú-BA-*[*RUM*] *ú-iz-zi na-at a-pí-e-*<*da*>*-ni* (1.55) *pí-eš-te-ni A-NA* ZI-*TUM* DINGIR-*LIM-ma-at-kán da-at-te-ni* (1.56) *na-at-ši pa-ra-a-be UL ar-nu-ut-te-ni na-at ták-ša-an šar-ra-aš* (1.57) *ták-ša-an šar-ra-an pi-eš-te-n*[*i*] *nu-uš-ma-aš ki-i šar-ru-ma-aš ut-tar* (1.58) SAG.DU-*az* GAM-*an ki-it-ta-ru na-at-kán li-e šar-ra-at-te-ni* (1.59) *ku-i-ša-at-kán šar-ra-a-i-*[*m*]*a na-aš a-ku* EGIR-*pa wa-aḫ-nu-mar-ši li-e e-eš-zi*

6

(1.60) *IŠ-TU* NINDA KAŠ GEŠTIN *I-NA* É DINGIR-*LIM ḫu-u-ma-an ša-ra-a pí-e ḫar-tin* (1.61) NINDA KUR$_4$.RA DINGIR-*LIM-za-kán* NINDA SIG *li-e ku-iš-ki da-a-li-ya-zi* (1.62) KAŠ-*ma-kán* GEŠTIN *IŠ-TU* GAL-*ya še-ir ar-ḫa li-e ku-iš-ki la-a-ḫu-u-i* (1.63) *ḫu-u-ma-an-be* DINGIR-*LIM-ni* EGIR-*pa ma-ni-ya-aḫ-tin nam-ma-aš-ma-aš PA-NI* DINGIR-*LIM me-mi-an* (1.64) [*me*]*-mi-eš-tin ku-i-iš-wa-kán tu-e-el* DINGIR-*LIM-az* NINDA *ḫar-ši-ya-az* (1.65) [DUG*i*]*š-p*[*a-a*]*n-du-uz-zi-az da-a-aš nu-wa-ra-an-kán* DINGIR-*LIM* EN-*YA* [E]GIR-*an* (1.66)

4

(39) Within, however, (there is) a festival of the month, a festival of the year, a festival for *ayalas* (?), a festival of the autumn, a festival of the spring, a festival of the thunder, a rain (?) festival, a festival of *pūdahas* (?), a festival of *isuwas* (?), a festival of *issalas* (?), a festival of the drinking horn (?), festivals of the pure priest, festivals of the old men, festivals of the mothers of god, a festival of *dahis*, (44) festivals of the men of the east (?), festivals of *pūlas* (?), festivals of *hahratar* (?), or whatever festival there is in behalf of Hattusas. (46) If you do not perform them set up with all the cattle, sheep, bread, beer, and wine, and you, temple officials, accept pay from those who give it (i.e. the food and drink), you will cause it (the festival) to fall short of the desire of the god.

5

(50) Or if you take it (i.e. the food and drink for the festival), when (it has been) set up, and do not bring it right to the gods themselves, and you carry it away from them to your houses, and your wives, your children, (and) your slaves eat it up, or (if), on the other hand, a relative by marriage or a good citizen comes to you, and you give it to such (a person)—(55) (if) you take it from the god himself, and do not bring it straight to him, and share by share you give it away, then let this charge of division lie against you with a capital (penalty). (58) Do not divide it (i.e. the food). (59) But whoever divides it, let him die; let there be no pardon for him.

6

(60) Of the bread, beer, (and) wine carry everything up into the temple. (61) Let no one leave the god's ordinary bread (or) thin bread. (62) And let no one dip up beer (or) wine from the libation bowl; devote every bit to the god. (63) Furthermore, in the presence of the god speak for yourselves (these) words: 'Whoever has taken (anything) from thy divine ordinary bread, (or) from the libation bowl, may the god, my

[*ḫar-ni-ik-d*]*u nu-wa-za-kán a-pí-e-el* É-*ir* GAM-*an ša-ra-a e-ip-du* (2.1) [*nu ḫu-u-ma-a*]*n ma-a-an a-pí-e-da-ni* UD-*ti a-da-an-na a-ku-wa-*[*an-na*] (2.2) [*tar-aḫ-te-ni na-a*]*t e-iz-za-tin e-ku-ut-tin ma-a-na-at Ú-UL-ma tar-aḫ-t*[*e-ni*] (2.3) [*na-at I-NA*] UD 3.KAM *az-zi-ik-ki-it-tin ak-ku-uš-ki-it-tin* (2.4) [*nu-uš-ma-aš* GAM-*an a-pa-a-at* DAM].MEŠ-[*K*]*U-NU* DUMU.MEŠ-[*K*]*U-NU* SAG.GÌM.ERUM.MEŠ-[*K*]*U*-[*NU*] (2.5) [KÙ-*kán-du ak-ku-uš-kán-du Š*]*A* DINGIR.MEŠ-*m*[*a* $^{\text{GI]Š}}$*kat-ta-lu-uz-zi li-e-be* [*ta-ma-iš*] (2.6) [*šar-ra-at-ta*] *ma-a-an* ^{LÚ}*Ú-BA-RUM-ma ku-e-da-ni ú-iz-zi* (2.7) [*na-aš I-NA*] É DINGIR-*LIM ša-ra-a pa-a-u-wa-aš* UK[Ù-*aš*] *na-aš-kán* LUGAL-*aš-ša* (2.8) [^{GIŠ}*kat-ta-lu-uz-zi*] *šar-ra-aš-ki-it-ta na-an* [*a-pa-a-š*]*a ša-ra-a* (2.9) [*pí-e-ḫu-te-id-du*] *nu* KÙ-*ki-id-du ak-ku-uš-*[*ki-id-d*]*u ma-a-an-ma-aš* (2.10) [^{LÚ}*a-ra-aḫ-zé*]-*na-aš Ú-UL-aš* ^{URU}*Ḫa-at-tu-ša-aš* DUMU.L[Ú.GÀ]L.L[U DING]IR.MEŠ-*aš t*[*i-ya*]-*zi* (2.11) [*na-aš a-ku ku-iš ku-i*]*š pí-e-ḫu-te-iz-zi-ma na-at-ši* SAG.DU-*aš ag-ga-t*[*ar*]

7

(2.12) [*ma-a-an* GUD *na-aš-ma*] UDU *ku-iš* DINGIR-*LIM-ni a-da-an-na u-un-na-an-za* (2.13) *šu-ma-aš-ma-ká*[*n n*]*a-aš-šu* GUD.ŠE *na-aš-ma* UDU.ŠE *ar-ḫa e-ip-te-ni* (2.14) *šu-ma-aš-ma-az ku-i*[*n*] *ma-ak-la-an-da-an mar-kán ḫar-te-ni* (2.15) *na-an-kán an-da tar-na-a*[*t-te-ni nu a-p*]*u-u-un* GUD *na-aš-šu ar-ḫa* (2.16) *e-iz-za-at-te-ni na-aš-ma-an-za-an-kán ḫa-a-li an-da tar-na-at-te-ni* (2.17) *na-aš-ma-an-za-an-kán i-ú-*[*k*]*i* GAM-*an da-a-it-te-ni* (2.18) . . . (2.19) *na-aš-ma-za-kán* UDU *a-ša-u-ni an-da tar-na-at-te-ni* (2.20) *na-aš-ma-an-za-an-kán ku-en-na-at-te-ni nu-za* ZI.ḪI.A-*KU-NU* SIG$_5$-*in* (2.21) . . . *na-aš-ma-an-za-an-kán ta-me-ta-ni* UKÙ-*ši* (2.22) *wa-aḫ-nu-*[*ut-te-ni*] *nu-za-kán* ŠÀM *še-ir da-at-te-ni* (2.23) *na-aš-ta* DINGIR-*LIM-ni* ⸗*zu-u-wa-an ku-wa-at* KA×U-*it pa-ra-a ḫu-u-it-ti-ya-at-te-ni* (2.24) *na-an-za* [*ar-ḫa*] *da-at-te-ni na-aš-ma-an ta-me-e-da-ni pí-eš-te-ni* (2.25) *nu ki-iš-ša-a*[*n me-ma-at-te-ni*] DINGIR-*LUM-wa-ra-aš ku-it nu-wa Ú-UL* (2.26) *ku-it-ki me-ma-i nu-wa-an-n*[*a-a*]*š Ú.UL ku-it-ki i-ya-zi* (2.27) *nu-za* UKÙ-*an-na a-ú* ZI-*aš-ták-kán ku-iš* ⸗*zu-u-wa-an* IGI.ḪI.A-*wa-az* (2.28) *pa-ra-a pít-te-nu-zi* [*nu* E]GIR-*an-da ma-aḫ-ḫa-an e-eš-ša-a-i* (2.29) DINGIR.MEŠ-*aš-ma* ZI-*an-za da-aš-šu-uš nu e-ip-pu-u-wa-an-zi Ú-UL nu-un-tar-nu-zi* (2.30) *e-ip-zi-ma ku-e-da-ni me-e-ḫu-ni nu nam-ma ar-ḫa* (2.31) *Ú-UL tar-na-a-i nu-za* DINGIR.MEŠ-*aš* ZI-*ni me-ik-ki na-aḫ-ḫa-an-te-eš e-eš-tin*

8

(2.32) *an-da-ma* DINGIR.MEŠ-*a*[*š*] *ku-it* KUBABBAR GUŠKIN TÚG-*TUM Ú-NU-UT* ZABAR (2.33) *šu-ma-aš ḫar-te-ni nu-za* LÚ.MEŠ

lord, hereafter destroy him, and turn (his) house upside down (?).' (2.1) And if you can eat (and) drink everything on that day, eat (and) drink it. (2) But if you cannot, keep on eating (and) drinking it for three days; and with you let your wives, your children, (and) your slaves eat (and) drink. (5) But let no other person open the door of the gods. (6) But if a citizen comes to anyone and he has the privilege of going up to the temple and he (habitually) opens the king's door also, let that man conduct him up (to the temple), and let him eat (and) drink. (9) But if he (is) a foreigner and he (is) not a Hittite man (and) he visits the gods, let him die; and whoever conducts him (to the temple), for him there (is) the capital penalty.

7

(12) If an ox or a sheep is brought for the god to eat, but you take for yourselves either a fat ox or a fat sheep, and put in (its place) a thin animal that you have cut up for yourselves, and (if) you either eat that ox up or put it into (your) pen, or put it under the yoke . . . or (if) you put the sheep into (your) fold, or kill it, (20) and (if) your wishes (are) gratified (?); or (if) you give it in exchange to another man, and take a price for (it); why then do you withdraw meat (?) from the mouth of the god, and take it for yourselves or give it to another, and speak as follows? (25) 'Since he is a god he will not say anything, and he will not do anything to us.' Just look at the man who takes thy choice meat (?) from (before thine) eyes! (28) Afterwards, when it operates, the will of the gods (is) strong. (29) It does not make haste to seize; but when it seizes, it does not thereafter let go. (31) Now be very much afraid of the will of the gods.

8

(32) And in (the temples) what silver, gold, clothing, (or) bronze implements of the gods you have—and your metal-workers—belongs to the

URUD.DA-*KU-NU nu-za* DINGIR.MEŠ-*aš* KUBABBAR-*i* GUŠ-KIN-*i* (2.34) TÚG-*i Ú-NU-UT* ZABAR *e-eš-zi* NU.GÁL *ku-it-kán* DINGIR.MEŠ-*na-aš pár-ni* (2.35) *an-da* NU.GÁL *ku-it ku-it* DINGIR-*LIM-ni-ma-at e-eš-zi-be* (2.36) *nu-za me-ik-ki na-aḫ-ḫa-an-te-eš e-eš-tin nu A-NA* LÚ É DINGIR-*LIM* KUBABBAR GUŠKIN (2.37) *li-e-be e-eš-zi A-NA* NÍ.TE-*ŠU-za-at-kán an-da li-e-be* (2.38) *pí-e-da-a-i A-NA* DAM-*ŠU-ya-an-za-an* DUMU.MEŠ-*ŠU ú-nu-wa-aš-ḫa-an* (2.39) *li-e i-ya-zi ma-a-an-ma-aš-ši IŠ-TU* É.GAL-*LIM-ma AŠ-ŠUM* NÍG.BA-*ŠU* (2.40) KUBABBAR GUŠKIN TÚG-*TUM Ú-NU-UT* ZABAR *pí-an-zi na-at lam-ni-ya-an e-eš-du* (2.41) *ka-a-aš-wa-ra-at-ši* LUGAL-*uš pa-iš* KI.LAL.BI-*ŠU-ya-at ma-ši-wa-an* (2.42) *na-at i-ya-an-be e-eš-du nam-ma ki-iš-ša-an-na i-ya-an e-eš-du* (2.43) *ki-e-da-ni-wa-ra-at-ši A-NA* EZEN×ŠE SUM-*ir ku-ut-ru-wa-aš-ša* EGIR-*an* (2.44) *i-ya-an-te-eš a-ša-an-du* SUM-*ir-wa-at-ši ku-wa-pi nu-wa ka-a-aš* (2.45) *ka-a-aš-ša a-ra-an-ta-at ṇam-ma-at-za-kán* ŠA(G) É-*TI li-e-be* (2.46) *da-a-li-ya-zi pa-ra-a-be-za uš-ša-ni-ya-ad-du* (2.47) *uš-ša-ni-ya-zi-ma-at-za ku-wa-pí na-at ḫar-wa-ši pí-di li-e uš-ša-ni-ya-zi* (2.48) EN.MEŠ ^{URU}*ḪA-AT-TI a-ra-an-ta-ru nu uš-kán-du nu-za ku-it* (2.49) *wa-ši-ya-zi na-at* ^{GIŠ}ḪAR *i-ya-an-du na-at-kán pí-ra-an ši-ya-an-du* (2.50) *ma-aḫ-ḫa-an-ma-kán* LUGAL-*uš* ^{URU}*Ḫa-at-tu-ši ša-ra-a ú-iz-zi* (2.51) *na-at I-NA* É.GAL-*LIM pa-ra-a e-ip-du na-at-ši ši-ya-an-du* (2.52) *ma-a-na-at-za* ZI-*az-za-ma ḫa-ap-pí-ra-iz-zi na-at-ši* SAG.DU-*aš ag-ga-tar* (2.53) *ku-iš-ma-za* NÍG.BA LUGAL *UL ḫa-ap-pí-ra-a-iz-zi ŠUM* LUGAL-*kán ku-e-da-ni* (2.54) GUL-*ša-an nu-za QA-TAM-MA-be* KUBABBAR GUŠKIN TÚG-*TUM Ú-NU-UT* ZABAR (2.55) *ḫa-ap-pí-ra-a-iz-zi ku-iš-ma-an e-ip-zi na-an mu-un-na-a-iz-zi* (2.56) *na-an* LUGAL-*an a-aš-ka Ú-UL u-wa-te-iz-zi nu-uš-[m]a-ša-at 2-aš-be* (2.57) SAG.DU-*aš* UG$_6$-*tar 2-uš-be-at ak-kán-du . . .* (2.58) *nu-uš-ma-aš* EGIR-*pa wa-aḫ-nu-mar li-e-be e-eš-zi*

9

(2.59) *an-da-ma-za šu-ma-aš ku-i-e-eš* LÚ.MEŠ É DINGIR-*LIM nu ma-a-an* EZEN×ŠE.M[EŠ] (2.60) EZEN×ŠE-*aš me-e-ḫu-u-ni UL e-eš-ša-[a]t-te-ni nu* EZEN×ŠE *ḫa-me-eš-ḫa-[an-da-aš]* (2.61) *[I-]NA ZÉ-E-NI i-ya-at-te-ni* EZEN×ŠE *zé-e-na-an-da-aš-m[a]* (2.62) *ḫa-me-eš-ḫi e-eš-ša-at-te-ni nu ma-a-an* EZEN×ŠE *i-ya-u-an-zi me-[e-ḫ]u-na-aš* (2.63) *me-e-ḫu-u-ni a-ra-an-za na-[a]n i-ya-zi ku-iš na-aš šu-ma-aš* (2.64) *A-NA* $^{\text{LÚ.MEŠ}}$SANGA $^{\text{LÚ.MEŠ}}$IM.[ME] $^{\text{SAL.MEŠ}}$AMA DINGIR-*LIM nu-uš-*<*ma-aš*> *A-NA* LÚ.MEŠ É [DINGIR-*LIM*] (2.65) *ú-iz-zi nu-uš-ma-aš-za gi-e-nu-uš-šu-uš e-ip-zi* EBUR.MEŠ-*wa-[m]u-kán* (2.66) *pí-ra-*

the silver, gold, clothing, (and) bronze implements of the gods. (34) There is none (for you). In the courtyard of the gods there is nothing (which you possess); whatever (there is) belongs to the god. (36) Now be very much afraid. (36) Let a temple official have no silver (or) gold. (37) Let him not take it into his (house); and let him not make it into an ornament for his wife (or) his children. (39) But if they give him as a present from the palace silver, gold, garments, (or) bronze implements, let them be named: 'So-and-so, the king, gave it to him.' (41) And how great its weight (is), let that be set down. (42) And furthermore let it be set down as follows: 'At such-and-such a festival they gave it to him.' (43) And after (that) let the witnesses be set down: 'When they gave it to him, so-and-so and so-and-so were present.' (45) Furthermore let him not leave it in his house; let him offer it for sale. (47) However, when he sells it, let him not sell it in a secret place; let the lords of Hatti be present, and let them observe. (48) And let them make an inventory (of) what (the purchaser) buys, and let them seal it in his presence (?). (50) Moreover, when the king comes up to Hattusas, let him take it directly to the palace, and let them seal it for him. (52) If, however, he (i.e. the recipient of the gift) exchanges it just as he pleases (i.e. without due formality), (there is) the capital penalty for him. (53) But whoever is not selling a gift of the king, for which the king's name has been stamped (upon a tablet), and he nevertheless sells silver, gold, garments, (or) bronze utensils, (and) whoever receives it and hides it, and does not bring it to the royal gate, for them both (there is) the capital penalty; let them both die. . . . (58) Let there not be pardon for them.

9

(59) Now you who are temple officials in (the temple), if you do not celebrate the festivals at the time of the festivals, if you perform the festival of the spring in the autumn but celebrate the festival of the autumn in the spring, and if at the proper time for performing the festival the man who is performing it comes and approaches you, the priests, IM.ME-priests, (and) mothers of god, and you, the temple officials, and embraces (your) knees, (saying): (65) 'The harvest (is) before me, or a

an na-aš-šu ku-ša-a-ta na-aš-šu KASKAL-*aš na-aš-ma ta-ma-i* (2.67) *ku-it-ki ut-tar nu-wa-mu* EGIR-*pa ti-ya-at-tin nu-wa-mu-kán a-ši* (2.68) *ku-it-ma-an me-mi-aš pí-ra-an ar-ḫa ti-ya-ad-du* (2.69) *ma-aḫ-ḫa-an-ma-wa-mu-kán a-ši me-mi-aš pí-ra-an ar-ḫa ti-ya-zi* (2.70) *nu-wa* EZEN×ŠE *QA-TAM-MA i-ya-mi na-aš-ta* UKÙ-*aš* ZI-*ni li-e-be* (2.71) *i-ya-at-te-ni li-e-aš-ma-aš-kán u-wa-it-ta-ri* (2.72) *nu-uš-ma-aš* DINGIR.MEŠ-*aš* ZI-*ni ḫa-ap-pár li-e da-at-te-ni* (2.73) *nu-kán šu-ma-aš* UKÙ-*aš u-wa-it-ta-ri ḫa-ap-pár-ra-aš-ma-aš da-at-te-ni* (2.74) DINGIR.MEŠ-*ma-kán šu-ma-aš I-NA* EGIR UD-*MI an-da ša-an-ḫi-eš-kán-zi* (2.75) *nu-uš-ma-ša-at A-NA* ZI.ḪI.A-*KU-NU* DAM.MEŠ-*KU-NU* DUMU.MEŠ-*KU-NU* SAG.GÌM.ERUM.MEŠ-*KU-NU* (2.76) *i-da-a-la-u-an-ni-be a-ra-an-ta-ri na-aš-ta* DINGIR.MEŠ-*aš-be* ZI-*ni* (2.77) *i-ya-at-tin nu* NINDA-*an e-iz-za-at-te-ni wa-a-tar-ma e-ku-ut-te-ni* (2.78) É-*ir-ra-za i-ya-at-te-ni* UKÙ-*aš-ma-at-kán* ZI-*ni li-e-*[*be i-y*]*a-at-te-ni* (2.79) *nu-za* UG$_6$-*tar li-e uš-ni-ya at-te-ni* UG$_6$-*tar-ma-za wa-a-ši-y*[*a-at-te*]-*ni li-e*

10

(2.80) *an-da-ma-za šu-me-eš ku-i-e-eš* LÚ.MEŠ É DINGIR-*LIM nu-za ḫa-li-y*[*a-aš*] (2.81) *ud-da-ni-i me-ik-ki pa-aḫ-ḫa-aš-ša-nu-wa-an-te-eš e-*[*e*]*š-tin* (2.82) *nu ne-ku-uz me-e-ḫu-u-ni ḫu-u-da-a-ak* GAM *pa-it-tin* (2.83) [*n*]*u e-iz-za-tin e-ku-ut-tin ma-a-an-na* SAL-*aš ut-tar ku-e-da-ni-ik-*[*ki*] (2.84) *t*[*ar-ḫu*]-*u*[*z-z*]*i na-aš-za* SAL-*ni-i* GAM-*an še-eš-du* (3.1) [*nu-u*]*š-ma-aš ku-it-ma-an* K[U]Š.ḪI.[A SIG$_5$ *nu a-ša-an*]-*du* (3.2) [*n*]*a-aš-*<*ta*> *I-NA* É DINGIR-*LIM še-e-šu-u-an-zi k*[*u-i-ša š*]*a-ra-a ú-id-du* (3.3) *ku-i-ša-aš ku-iš* LÚ É DINGIR-*LIM* $^{LÚ.MEŠ}$SANGA G[AL.GAL $^{L]Ú.MEŠ}$SANGA DUMU.DUMU (3.4) $^{LÚ.MEŠ}$IM.ME *ḫu-u-ma-an-te-eš* [*k*]*u-iš-be-kán im-ma ku-iš* DINGIR.MEŠ-*aš* (3.5) ^{GIŠ}*kat-ta-lu-uz-zi šar-ri-eš-ki-iz-zi nu* 1-*aš* 1-*aš I-NA* É DINGIR-*LIM* (3.6) *ša-ra-a še-e-šu-u-wa-an-zi li-e-be kar-aš-ta-ri* (3.7) *nam-ma-kán* MI-*az* $^{LÚ.MEŠ}$*ú-e-*<*ḫi*>-*eš-kat-tal-li-iš da-an-te-eš a-ša-an-du* (3.8) *nu* MI-*an ḫu-u-ma-an-da-an ú-e-ḫi-eš-kán-du* (3.9) *nu a-ra-aḫ-za ḫa-a-li* $^{LÚ.MEŠ}$*ḫa-li-ya-at-tal-liš uš-kán-du* (3.10) *an-*[*d*]*ur-za-ma* É.MEŠ DINGIR.MEŠ LÚ.MEŠ É DINGIR-*LIM* MI-*an ḫu-u-ma-an-*[*d*]*a-an* (3.11) *ú-e-ḫi-eš-kán-du nu-uš-ma-aš* Ù-*aš li-e e-eš-zi* (3.12) MI-*ti* MI-*ti-ma* 1 ^{LÚ}SANGA GAL $^{LÚ.MEŠ}$*ú-e-ḫi-eš-ga-at-tal-la-aš* (3.13) *pí-ra-an ḫu-u-*[*y*]*a-an-za e-eš-du nam-ma-ma ku-i-e-eš* $^{LÚ.MEŠ}$SANGA (3.14) *nu-za ku-iš ŠA* K[Á] É DINGIR-*LIM e-eš-du nu-za* É DINGIR-*LIM pa-aḫ-ša-ru* (3.15) ŠA(G) É-*ŠU-ma-za a*[*n-da*] *IT-TI* DAM-*ŠU li-e ku-iš-ki še-eš-zi* (3.16) *ku-in-ma I-NA* É-*ŠU* GAM-*an ú-e-mi-an-zi na-at-ši* SAG.DU-*aš wa-aš-túl* (3.17) *nu* É.MEŠ DINGIR.MEŠ *me-ik-ki mar-ri pa-aḫ-ḫa-aš-tin*

marriage, or a journey, or some other business; now do me a favor; let this business first be finished for me. But when this business of mine is past, I shall perform the festival just so'; (70) do not thereupon work for the pleasure of a man; let him not be pitied by you. (72) Do not accept for yourselves pay for the service of the gods, and (then) take pity (?) on a man and accept pay (from him). (74) The gods will punish you on a later day; they will persist in injuring you, (namely) yourselves, your wives, your children, (and) your slaves. (76) Hereafter work for the pleasure of the gods alone; and you shall eat bread, and drink water, and establish a household. (78) But do not do that for the pleasure of a man. (79) Do not sell a capital penalty, and do not buy a capital penalty either.

10

(80) Now you who are temple officials in (the temple), be very careful of the reputation (?) of the precinct. (82) At nightfall promptly go down (into the town); and eat (and) drink, and if thoughts of a woman overcome anyone, let him sleep with a woman. (3.1) And as long as the omens are favorable for them (?), let them stay. (2) Afterwards let each come up to the temple to spend the night, whoever (is) a temple official—great priests, small priests, and all IM.ME-priests—(and) whoever else opens the temple door. (5) Let them severally not neglect (?) to spend the night up in the temple. (7) Furthermore, at night let patrolmen be chosen, and let them patrol all night. (9) Outside in the precinct let the keepers watch; but inside in the temples let the temple officials patrol all night; and let them not sleep. (12) Now from night to night let one important priest be in command of the patrolmen. (13) And besides, (of those) who are priests, let someone be door-keeper; let him guard the temple. (15) Let no one spend the night in his (own) house with his wife; and whomsoever they find down in his (own) house, it (is) a capital offense for him. (17) Now of your

nu-uš-ma-aš te-eš-ḫa-aš (3.18) *li-e e-eš-zi nam-ma-aš-ma-aš ḫa-a-li ar-ḫa šar-ra-an e-eš-du* (3.19) *na-aš-ta ku-e-da-ni ḫa-a-li wa-aš-túl an-da ki-i-ša* (3.20) *na-aš a-ku li-e-ya-aš-kán ú-e-iḫ-ta-ri*

11

(3.21) URU*Ḫa-at-*<*tu*>*-ši-ma-kán ku-e-da-ni ku-iš ša-ak-la-a-iš še-ir* (3.22) *ma-a-an* LÚSANGA LÚIM.ME LÚ.MEŠ*ḫa-li-ya-at-tal-li-e-eš ku-i*[*š-ki*] (3.23) *tar-ni-eš-k*[*i*]*-iz-zi na-aš tar-ni-eš-ki-id-du-be ma-a-an* LÚ*ḫa-li-y*[*a-a*]*t-tal-*[*la-aš*] (3.24) *ku-e-da-ni-ik-ki e-eš-zi na-aš ḫa-a-li pa-id-du-be* (3.25) *ki-iš-š*[*a*]*-an li-e-be te-iz-zi am-mu-uk-wa-za* É DINGIR-*LIM-YA* (3.26) *pa-aḫ-ḫa-aš-ḫi a-pí-ya-ma-wa UL pa-i-mi nu ma-a-an* INIM LÚKÚR *ku-iš-ki* (3.27) URU*Ḫa-at-tu-ša-an-za-kán za-am-mu-ra-u-wa-an-zi ku-iš-ki ti-iš-ki-iz-zi* (3.28) *na-an a-ra-aḫ-zé-na-aš* BÀD-*aš UL ú-wa-an-zi nu a-pu-u-uš* LÚ.MEŠ É DINGIR-*LIM* (3.29) *an-dur-za ú-wa-an-zi* LÚ*ḫa-li-ya-at-tal-la-aš* <DINGIR-*LIM*>*-ši pa-id-du-be* (3.30) *a-pa-a-aš-ma A-NA* DINGIR-*LIM-ŠU ša-ra-a še-e-šu-u-an-zi li-e kar-aš-ta-ri* (3.31) *ták-ku-wa-aš kar-aš-ta-ri-ma na-an-kán ma-a-an Ú-UL ku-na-an-zi* (3.32) [*l*]*u-ri-ya-aḫ-ḫa-*[*a*]*n-du-ma-an nu ne-ku-ma-an-za* TÚG-*aš-ši-kán* NÍ.TE-*iš-ši* (3.33) *an-*[*d*]*a li-e-be e-eš-zi nu wa-a-tar* 3-*ŠU la-ba-ar-na-aš lu-li-ya-za* (3.34) *I-NA* É DINGIR-*LIM-ŠU pí-e-da-a-ú nu-uš-ši a-pa-a-aš lu-ú-ri-iš e-eš-du*

12

(3.35) *an-d*[*a*]*-ma-za* [*n*]*am-*[*m*]*a šu-me-eš* LÚ.MEŠSANGA LÚ.MEŠIM.ME SAL.MEŠAMA DINGIR-*LIM* (3.36) LÚ.MEŠ [É] DINGIR-*LI*[*M mar-r*]*i i*[*š-ḫ*]*al-túḫ-me-ya-an-za* ŠA(G) É DINGIR-*LIM na-aš-ma ta-me-e-da-ni* (3.37) É *ka-ri-im-me ku-iš-ki ni-ik-zi na-aš-kán ma-a-an* ŠA(G) É DINGIR-*LIM* (3.38) *ni-ni-ik-ta-ri nu ḫal-*[*lu*]*-u-wa-a-in i-ya-zi na-aš-ta* EZEN×ŠE *za-aḫ-zi* (3.39) *na-an za-ḫa-an-d*[*u nu nam-m*]*a a-pu-u-un* EZEN×ŠE *QA-DU* GUD UDU NINDA KAŠ *ša-ra-a* (3.40) *ti-ya-an-da-an i-ya-ad-du* NINDA SIG-*ya-kán li-e wa-ak-ši-ya-nu-zi* (3.41) *ku-iš-ša-an-za-an-kán m*[*u-t*]*a-a-iz-zi nu* EZEN×ŠE *ša-ra-a ti-ya-an-da-an* (3.42) *Ú-UL i-ya-zi n*[*a-a*]*t a-pí-e-da-ni* [*m*]*e-i*[*k*]*-ki wa-aš-túl e-eš-du* (3.43) *na-aš-ta* EZEN×ŠE-[*a*]*n ḫa-pu-uš-du nu-za ḫal-lu-wa-ya-za me-ik-ki na-aḫ-ḫa-an-te-eš e-eš-tin*

13

(3.44) *an-d*[*a-m*]*a-z*[*a p*]*a-aḫ-ḫ*[*u*]*-u-e-na-as-*[*š*]*a ud-da-ni-i me-ik-ki na-aḫ-ḫa-an-te-eš e-eš-tin* (3.45) *na-aš-ta* [*m*]*a-a-an* [*I-NA*] É DINGIR-*LIM* EZEN×ŠE *nu* IZI *me-ik-ki pa-aḫ-ḫa-aš-tin* (3.46) *ma-aḫ-ḫa-an-*

own accord guard the temples diligently; and do not sleep. (18) Furthermore, let the precinct be divided among you; then the one in whose (part of the) precinct sin occurs shall die; let him not be pardoned.

11

(21) If there is a rite in behalf of anyone in Hattusas, if anyone admits a priest, an IM.ME-priest, (and) keepers, let him admit (them). (23) If a keeper is assigned to anyone, let him go into the precinct. (25) Let him not speak thus: 'I am guarding the temple of my god; I will not go there.' (26) And if there is any talk of an enemy, (if) anyone is about to sack (?) Hattusas, the surrounding walls do not see him; the temple officials see such (persons) within (the precinct). (29) Let the keeper by all means go to (the temple of) his god; and let him not neglect to spend the night in (the temple of) his (own) god. (31) But if he does neglect (this), if they do not kill him, let them at least humiliate him; (while) naked—let there not be a garment on his body —let him bring water three times from the king's cistern to his temple. (34) Let that be his humiliation.

12

(35) Furthermore, you priests, IM.ME-priests, mothers of god, temple officials, some voluntary giver of a festival (?) (might) get drunk in a temple or in another sacred building (?). (37) If he gets drunk in the temple and causes a quarrel, and then injures the festival, let them injure him; let him later perform that festival set up with cattle, sheep, bread, (and) beer; let him not omit even the thin bread. (41) Whoever avoids (?) it (i.e. the festival), and does not perform the festival (fully) set up, let that be a great sin for him; thereafter let him repeat the festival. (43) Now be very much afraid of a (drunken) quarrel.

13

(44) And again in the matter of the fire in (the temple) be very much afraid. (45) If hereafter there (is) a festival in the temple, guard the fire carefully. (46) But when night comes, then quench well with water

[*m*]*a* MI-[*a*]*n-za ki-i-ša na-aš-ta pa-aḫ-ḫur ku-it A-NA* GUNNI (3.47) *a-aš-zi na-at-*[*kán*] *ú-e-da-an-da* SIG$_5$-*in ki-eš-ta-nu-ut-tin* (3.48) *ma-a-an* KA.IZI-*ma ša-an-na-pí ša-an-na-pí ku-it-ki ḫa-da-an-ma* GIŠ-*ru* (3.49) *na-at ku-iš ki*[*š-t*]*a-nu-zi na-aš-ta ku-e-da-ni* ŠA(G) É DINGIR-*LIM-ŠU* (3.50) *wa-aš-túl ki-ša-ri* [*n*]*u* É DINGIR-*LIM-m*[*a*] *im-ma* 1-*an ḫar-ak-zi* ^{URU}*Ḫa-at-tu-ša-aš-ma* (3.51) LUGAL-*wa-aš a-aš-šu UL ḫar-ak-zi nu wa-aš-túl ku-iš i-ya-zi na-aš QA-DU* NUMUN-*ŠU* (3.52) *ḫar-ak-zi-be ku-e-*[*š*]*a-at-kán ku-i-e-eš im-ma* ŠA(G) É DINGIR-*LIM nu* 1-*aš-ša* (3.53) TI-*nu-ma-aš Ú-UL e-*[*e*]*š-zi QA-DU* NUMUN-*ŠU-at ḫar-kán-zi-be* (3.54) *nu-za pa-aḫ-ḫu-u-e-na-aš ud-da-ni-i me-ik-ki-be mar-ri pa-aḫ-ša-nu-wa-an-te-eš e-eš-tin*

14

(3.55) *an-da-ma-za šu-ma-aš k*[*u-i*]*-e-eš* EN.MEŠ UTÚL DINGIR.-MEŠ-*aš ḫu-u-ma-an-da-aš* (3.56) ^{LÚ}QA.ŠU.DU$_8$.A LÚ ^{GIŠ}BANŠUR ^{LÚ}MU ^{LÚ}NINDA.DÙ.DÙ ^{LÚ}TIN.NA *nu-uš-ma-aš* DINGIR.MEŠ-*aš* (3.57) ZI-*ni me-na-aḫ-ḫa-an-da me-ik-ki na-aḫ-ḫa-an-te-eš e-eš-tin* (3.58) *na-aš-ta* DINGIR.MEŠ-*aš* NINDA *ḫar-ši* ^{DUG}*iš-pa-an-tu-uz-zi na-aḫ-ša-ra-at-ta-an* (3.59) *me-ik-ki ti-ya-an ḫar-tin nu-uš-ma-aš-kán pár-šu-u-ra-aš pí-e-da-an* (3.60) *ša-an-ḫa-an ḫur-nu-wa-an e-eš-du na-aš-ta* ŠAḪ-*aš* UR.TÚG-*aš* ^{GIŠ}*kat-ta-lu-uz-zi* (3.61) *li-e šar-ri-eš-kit$_9$-ta šu-ma-ša-za wa-ar-pa-an-te-eš e-eš-tin* (3.62) *nu* TÚG.ḪI.A *pár-ku-wa-ya ú-e-eš-tin nam-ma-aš-ma-aš-kán iš-ḫi-e-ni-uš* DUBBIN.MEŠ-*ya* (3.63) *da-a-an e-eš-du nu-uš-ma-aš-kán* DINGIR.MEŠ-*aš* ZI-*an-za li-e* ^{x}*ḫa-an-ḫa-ni-ya-i* (3.64) *ma-a-an Ú-NU-TE*.MEŠ *IṢ-ṢI Ú-NU-TE*.MEŠ GIR$_4$ *ku-e ḫar-te-ni* (3.65) *na-aš-ta ma-a-an* ŠAḪ-*aš* UR.TÚG-*aš ku-wa-pí-ik-ki an-da ša-a-li-qa* (3.66) EN UTÚL-*ma-at ar-ḫa Ú-UL pí-eš-še-ya-zi nu a-pa-a-aš* DINGIR.MEŠ-*aš pa-ap-ra-an-da-za* (3.67) *a-da-an-na pa-a-i a-pí-e-da-ni-ma* DINGIR.MEŠ-*eš za-ak-kar* ^{x}*du-ú-úr* (3.68) *a-da-an-na a-ku-wa-an-na pí-an-zi ma-a-an-na-za* SAL-*i ku-iš* GAM-*an še-eš-zi* (3.69) *nu-kán ma-aḫ-ḫa-an* DINGIR.MEŠ-*aš ša-ak-la-a-in aš-ša-nu-zi* DINGIR-*LIM-ni a-da-an-na* (3.70) *a-ku-wa-an-na pa-a-i na-aš IT-TI* SAL-*TI QA-TAM-MA pa-id-du* (3.71) . . . *na-aš-ta ku-it-ma-an* ^{D}UTU-*uš ša-ra-a* (3.72) *nu-za* [*ḫ*]*u-u-*[*d*]*a-a-*[*a*]*k wa-ar-*[*ap*]*-du na-aš-kán lu-uk-kit$_9$-ti* DINGIR.MEŠ-*aš* (3.73) *a-da-an-na-aš me-e-ḫu-u-ni ḫu-u-da-a-ak a-ru ma-a-an-ma-aš kar-aš-ta-ri-ma* (3.74) *na-at-ši wa-aš-túl ma-a-an-ma-za IT-TI* SAL-*TI ku-iš še-eš-zi* (3.75) [*nu-za*]*-kán MAḪ-RI-ŠU* ^{LÚ}GAL-*ŠU* EGIR-*an ta-ma-aš-zi nu me-ma-ú-be* (3.76) [*ma-a-an*] *a-pa-a-aš-ma me-mi-ya-u-an-zi Ú-UL ma-az-za-az-zi* (3.77) *nu* ^{LÚ}*a-ri-iš-ši me-ma-a-ú nu-za wa-ar-ap-tu$_4$-be* (3.78) *ma-a-an še-ik-kán-ti-it-ma*

whatever fire remains on the hearth. But if (there is) any flame here and there and (also) dry wood, he who quenches it (i.e. the fire) and besides the temple alone of his god in which the sin occurs are destroyed; but Hattusas and the king's estate are not destroyed. (51) He who commits the sin and his descendants are completely destroyed. (52) Of those who are in the temple not one is to be spared; with their descendants they are completely destroyed. (54) Now of your own accord be very careful in the matter of fire.

14

(55) Now all you who (are) kitchen workers of the gods, cup-bearers, waiters, cooks, bakers, vintners, be very much afraid in the presence of the gods themselves. (58) Hereafter for the ordinary bread (and) the libation bowl of the gods keep (your) fear well established. (59) Let the place of the broken bread (?) be swept (?) (and) sprinkled (?) by you; and thereafter let no pig (or) dog open the door (i.e. come in). (61) You (yourselves) be washed, and put on clean clothes. (62) Furthermore, let your hair (?) and your finger nails be removed. (63) Let the displeasure of the gods not observe you. (64) If you have any implements of wood or (any) implements of asphalt, and if then a pig (or) a dog ever causes uncleanness among (them), and the kitchen worker does not throw it (i.e. the defiled vessel) away, but causes the gods to eat from an unclean (vessel), then the gods will give him dung (and) urine to eat (and) to drink. (68) And if anyone sleeps with a woman—as he performs a rite of the gods (and) offers a god food (and) drink, just so (i.e. ritually clean) let him go to the woman. (71) . . . Then as soon as the sun (is) up, let him bathe; and in the morning, at the time when the gods eat, let him arrive promptly. (73) But if he neglects (to do so), that is a sin for him. Furthermore, if anyone sleeps with a woman, and his superiors and his chief constrain (him), let him tell (the truth); if, however, he does not dare tell (his chief), let him tell his fellow (servant), and let him bathe anyway. (78) But if he with malice

ZI-*it pa-ra-a da-a-i* (3.79) *wa-ar-ap-zi-ma-za na-a-ú-i na-aš* DINGIR.MEŠ-*aš* NINDA *ḫar-ši* (3.80) ^{DUG}*iš-pa-an-tu-uz-zi ma-ni-in-ku-wa-an ša-ak-nu-an-za ša-a-li-qa* (3.81) *na-aš-ma-an* ^{LÚ}*a-ra-aš-ši-iš ša-ak-ki na-aš-ták-kán u-wa-it-ta* (3.82) [*tá*]*k*-[*k*]*u* [*š*]*a-an-na-a-i* EGIR-*zi-an-ma-at iš-du-wa-a-ri* (3.83) [*nu-uš-ma-ša-a*]*t* SAG.DU-*aš* UG$_6$-*tar* 2-*uš-ša-at ak-kán-d*[*u*]

15

* * * * *

(4.3) . . . *ku-it ḫu-u-el-pí šu-ma-a-aš* $^{\mathrm{LÚ.MEŠ}}$APIN.LAL DINGIR.MEŠ-[*aš*] (4.4) *pí-e ḫa*[*r-t*]*e*-[*ni na-a*]*t ḫu-u-da-a-ak me-e-ḫu-u-na-aš me-e-ḫu-ni pí*-[*e*] *ḫar-tin* (4.5) *ku-it-ma-na-at* [UKÙ-*a*]*š na-a-ú-i e-iz-za-a-i na-at-kán* DINGIR.MEŠ-*a*[*š*] ZI-*n*[*i*] (4.6) *ḫu-u-da-a-ak ar-n*[*u-u*]*š-ki-it-tin na-at* DINGIR.MEŠ *me-na-aḫ-ḫa-an-da l*[*i-e*] (4.7) *uš-kán-zi ma-a-an-*[*ma-a*]*t iš-ta-an-ta-nu-uš-kit*$_9$*-te-ni* (4.8) *nu-uš-ma-ša-at wa-aš-tú*[*l*] *nu-uš-ma-aš a-ri-an-zi nu-uš-ma-aš* DINGIR.MEŠ EN.MEŠ-*Y*[*A*] (4.9) *ma-aḫ-ḫa-an ta-pa-ri-ya-an-zi nu-uš-ma-aš QA-TAM-MA i-en-zi* (4.10) *IŠ-TU* GUD-*ya-aš-ma-aš* 10 UDU-*ya za-an-ki-la-an-zi* (4.11) *nu* DINGIR.MEŠ ZI-*an wa-ar-ša-nu-an-zi*

16

(4.12) *an-da-ma ma-a-an ḫal-ki-in a-ni-ya-at-te-ni nu-uš-ma-aš ma-a-an* ^{LÚ}SANGA (4.13) *A-NA* NUMUN *a-ni-ya-u-an-zi* UKÙ-*an* EGIR-*an UL u-i-ya-zi šu-ma-a-š*[*a*]*-at* (4.14) *a-ni-ya-u-wa-an-zi ma-ni-ya-aḫ-tin nu me-ik-ki a-ni-ya-at-te-ni* (4.15) *A-NA* ^{LÚ}SANGA-*ma-at pí-ra-an te-pu me-ma-at-te-ni na-aš-ma* A.ŠA(G) DINGIR-*LIM* (4.16) *mi-ya-an-za* A.ŠA(G) ^{LÚ}APIN.LAL-*ma-kán an-da ḫar-kán-za nu-za* A.ŠA(G) DINGIR-*LIM šu-me-e-el* (4.17) *ḫal-zi-ya-at-te-ni šu-me-el-ma-za* A.ŠA(G) A.ŠA(G) DINGIR-*LIM ḫal-zi-ya-at-te-ni* (4.18) *na-aš-ma ḫal-ki-uš ku-wa-pí šu-un-na-at-te-ni nu ták-ša-an šar-ra-an* (4.19) *me-ma-at-te-ni ták-ša-an šar-ra-an-ma-za-kán an-da ša-an-na-at-te-ni* (4.20) *nu-uš-ma-ša-an ú-wa-at-te-ni* EGIR-*zi-an ar-ḫa šar-ra-at-te-ni* (4.21) *ap-*<*pí*>*-zi-an-ma-aš iš-du-wa-a-ri na-an-kán* UKÙ-*ši im-ma ta-a-it-te-ni UL-an-kán* (4.22) DINGIR-*LIM-n*[*i*] *ta-ya-at-te-ni nu-uš-ma-ša-at wa-aš-túl šu-me-el-ma-aš-kán* (4.23) *ḫal-ki-uš ḫu-u-ma-an-du-uš ar-ḫa da-an-z*[*i*] *na-aš-kán* DINGIR.MEŠ-*aš* (4.24) [KISLA]Ḫ.MEŠ-*aš an-da iš-ḫu-u-wa-an-zi*

17

(4.25) *an-da-ma ŠA* KIS[LAḪ] GUD.APIN.LAL.ḪI.A *ku-i-e-eš* [KIN-*t*]*e-ni nu ma-a-an* GUD.A[PIN].LAL (4.26) *uš-ni-ya-at-te-ni na-*

aforethought postpones (the bath), and, (when) he has not yet bathed, he defiles the ordinary bread and the libation bowl of the gods (by being) unclean near (them); or (if) his fellow (servant) knows (about) him, and thereupon feels pity, in case (the fellow servant) conceals (it), and nevertheless it afterwards becomes known, there (is) a capital penalty for them; let them both die.

15

* * * * *

(4.3) Whatever first-fruits you, farmers, bring to the gods, bring them promptly at the right time. (5) Before a man has eaten of them bring them at once to the presence of the gods. (6) Let the gods not keep looking for them. (7) But if you do delay them, that is a sin for you. (8) They consult an oracle about you; and they do to you just as the gods, my lords, direct. (10) They fine you a cow and ten sheep; and they satisfy the will of the gods.

16

(12) Now if you plant grain in (the fields of a god) and if the priest does not send you a man back to plant the seed, do you manage its planting. (14) (If) you plant much, but say before the priest (that) it (was) little; or (if) the god's field (is) productive, and the field for (you) farmers is injured, and you call the god's field yours, and call your field the god's field; (18) or (if), when you store the grain, you declare half, but make no mention of (the other) half, and afterwards you come (and) divide it among yourselves, and it is nevertheless finally discovered—you (can) actually conceal it from a man; you (can) not conceal it from the god— that is a sin for you. (22) And they take away all your grain, and put it into the barns of the gods.

17

(25) Now you who care for the plow oxen belonging to the granary on (the lands of the temple), if you sell a plow ox, or kill it and eat it,

aš-ma-an-za-an-kán k[u]-en-na-at-te-n[i] (4.27) *na-an ar-ḫa e-iz-za-at-te-ni šu-ma-aš-ma-an-kán* DINGIR.MEŠ-*aš ta-a-iš-t[e]-ni* (4.28) *ma-ak-la-an-n[a]-az-wa-ra-aš* BA.UG$_6$ *na-aš-šu-wa-za du-wa-ar-ni-eš-ki-it* (4.29) *na-aš-šu-wa-ra-aš pár-aš-ta na-aš-ma-wa-ra-an* GUD.NITA GUL-*aḫ-[t]a* (4.30) *šu-ma-aš-ma-an ar-ḫa e-iz-za-at-te-ni* EGIR-*zi-an-ma-aš iš-du-wa-[a]-ri* (4.31) *nu a-pu-u-un* GUD *š[a]r-ni-ik-te-ni-be ma-a-[an-m]a-aš* *UL-ma iš-du-wa-a-ri* (4.32) *nu* [DI]NGIR-*LI*[*M-n*]*i p[a-i]t-te-ni ták-ku pár-ku-e[š-t]e-ni šu-me-el* ^{D}KAL-*KU-NU* (4.33) *ták-ku pa-ap-ri-[iš-te-ni]-ma nu-uš-ma-ša-at* SAG.DU-*aš wa-aš-túl*

18

(4.34) *an-da-ma-z[a š]u-ma-aš ku-i-e-e[š]* $^{LÚ.MEŠ}$SIPAD GUD DINGIR-*LIM* $^{LÚ.MEŠ}$SIPAD UDU DINGIR-*LIM* (4.35) *nu ma-a-an ḫa-aš-ša-an-na-aš m[e-e]-ḫu-u-ni* DINGIR-*LIM-ni ku-e-da-ni-ik-ki* (4.36) *ša-ak-l[a]-a-iš nu-uš-ši na-aš-šu* AMAR SILÀ MÁŠ.TUR *na-aš-ma* ^{UZU}*ša-li-ú(?)-eš* (4.37) *ḫa-ag-g[a]-ra-te-(m)eš pí-e ḫar-te-ni na-at li-e iš-ta-an-ta-nu-uš-kit$_9$-te-ni* (4.38) *me-e-[ḫu]-u-na-ša-at me-e-ḫu-u-ni pí-e ḫar-tin na-at-kán* DINGIR.MEŠ (4.39) *me-na-aḫ-ḫa-an-da li-e ša-kán-zi ku-it-ma-an* UKÙ-*aš ḫu-u-el-pí* (4.40) *na-a-ú-i e-iz-za-az-zi na-at* DINGIR.MEŠ-*aš ḫu-u-da-a-ak ú-da-at-tin* (4.41) *na-aš-ma ma-a-an* DINGIR-*LIM-ni ku-e-da-ni* EZEN×ŠE D[U]G *e-eš-zi* (4.42) DUG *ku-wa-pí šap-pí-eš-kán-zi na-an-kán li-e ša-ku-wa-an-ta-ri-ya-nu-ut-te-ni* (4.43) *na-an-ši i-ya-at-tin ma-a-an ḫu-u-el-pí-ma* DINGIR.MEŠ-*aš ḫu-u-da-a-ak UL* (4.44) *ú-da-at-te-ni na-at šu-ma-aš ḫu-u-da-a-ak iz-za-at-te-ni* (4.45) *na-aš-ma-at A-NA MAḪ-RI-KU-NU up-pa-at-te-ni* EGIR-[*i*]*z-zi-an-ma-at* (4.46) *iš-du-wa-a-ri nu-uš-ma-ša-at* SAG.DU-*aš wa-aš-túl ma-a-an-ma-at UL-ma* (4.47) *iš-du-wa-a-ri na-at ú-da-at-te-ni ku-e-da-ni me-e-ḫu-ni* (4.48) *nu-uš-ma-aš-kán PA-NI* DINGIR-*LIM ki-iš-ša-an an-da pí-e-da-at-te-ni* (4.49) *ma-a-an-wa-za ki-i ḫu-u-el-pí an-zi-el* ZI-*ni ḫu-u-da-a-ak* (4.50) *pí-ya-u-e-en na-aš-ma-wa-ra-at A-NA MAḪ-RI-NI na-aš-ma A-NA* DAM.MEŠ-*NI* (4.51) DUMU.MEŠ-*NI na-aš-ma ta-me-e-da-ni* UKÙ-*ši pí-ya-u-e-en* (4.52) DINGIR.MEŠ-*aš-ma-wa-kán* ZI-*an za-am-mu-ra-a-u-e-en na-aš-ta BI-IB-RU* DINGIR-*LIM* (4.53) ZI-*aš ar-ḫa e-ku-ut-te-ni nu-za ma-a-an pár-ku-wa-e-eš* (4.54) *šu-me-el* ^{D}KAL-*KU-NU ták-ku-za pa-ap-ra-an-te-eš-ma na-aš-ta QA-DU* (4.55) DAM.MEŠ-*KU-NU* DUMU.MEŠ-*KU-NU ḫar-ak-te-ni*

19

(4.56) *an-da-ma-aš-ta ma-a-an kar-ša-at-tar ku-wa-pí kar-aš-te-ni* (4.57) *na-at* DINGIR.MEŠ-*aš A-NA* EN.MEŠ-*KU-NU u-un-na-an-zi*

and (if) you conceal it from the gods, (28) (saying): 'It died from thinness, or it had been smashing (things), or it ran away, or a bull gored it'; and you eat it up; and it nevertheless afterwards becomes known; you will replace that ox. (31) But if it does not become known, and you go before the god—if you are acquitted, (it is due to) your protecting deity; if you are convicted, it is a capital sin for you.

18

(34) You who are the gods' cow-herds (and) the gods' shepherds on (the lands of the temples), if there is a rite for any god at the time of bearing young, and you bring to him either a calf, a lamb, a kid, or *saliwes haggarates*, do not delay them; bring them at the right time; let the gods not keep looking for them. (39) Before a man eats (of the) first-fruits, bring them at once to the gods. (41) Or, if there is a festival of the cup for any god, when they clean the cup, do not neglect it; prepare it for him (i.e. the god). (43) If you do not bring the first-fruits to the gods promptly, and you first eat of them, or send them to your superiors, and nevertheless it afterwards becomes known; that is a capital sin for you. (46) But if it does not become known, at whatever time you bring them (i.e. the first-fruits), you bring them before the god with these words: (49) 'If we at first devoted these first-fruits to ourselves or gave them to our superiors, or to our wives (and) our children, or to another man, (then) we have injured the gods themselves.' (52) Thereupon you drain the cup (?) of the god of life (?). (53) And if you are innocent, (it) is (due to) your protecting deity, but if you are guilty, thereupon you are destroyed with your wives (and) your children.

19

(56) Again, if in (the temple properties) you ever castrate (animals), and they bring them (i.e. the castrated animals) to the gods, your lords,

nu kar-ša-ad-da-aš (4.58) GAM-*an* ^{LÚ}SIPAD GUD ^{LÚ}SIPAD UDU-*ya i-ya-an-ta-ru* (4.59) *na-at-ša-an ḫa-li-ya-az a-ša-u-na-az ma-aḫ-ḫa-an kar-ša-an* (4.60) *na-at-kán* DINGIR.MEŠ-*aš QA-TAM-MA an-da ar-nu-wa-an-du* (4.61) EGIR KASKAL-*NI-ma-at-kán li-e wa-aḫ-nu-uš-kán-zi ma-a-an-ma-kán* ŠA(G) KASKAL-*NI* (4.62) ^{LÚ}SIPAD GUD *na-aš-ma* ^{LÚ}SIPAD UDU *mar-ša-tar ku-iš-ki i-ya-zi* (4.63) *na-aš-ta na-aš-šu* GUD.ŠE *na-aš-ma* UDU.ŠE *wa-aḫ-nu-zi nu-za-kán ḫa-ap-pár* (4.64) *ša-ra-a da-a-i na-aš-ma-an-za-an-kán ku-en-zi na-an ar-ḫa* (4.65) *a-da-an-zi pí-di-eš-ši-ma ma-ak-la-an-ta-an tar-na-an-zi* (4.66) *na-at iš-du-wa-a-ri nu-uš-ma-ša-at* SAG.DU-*aš wa-aš-túl* (4.67) DINGIR.MEŠ-*aš-kán* ZI-*aš-ša-aš ša-ne-iz-zi-in* ⁝*zu-u-wa-an da-a-ir* (4.68) *ma-a-an-ma-at UL-ma iš-du-wa-a-ri na-at ku-e-da-ni me-e-ḫu-u-ni* (4.69) *a-ra-an-zi na-aš-ta BI-IB-RU* DINGIR-*LIM* ZI-*TI* ^{GIŠ}*iš-ta-na-na-az* GAM (4.70) *da-an-du nu-za-kán an-da ki-iš-ša-an pí-e-da-an-du* (4.71) *ma-a-an-wa-kán* DINGIR.MEŠ-*aš ša-ne-iz-zi-in* ⁝*zu-u-wa-an* KA×U-*az* (4.72) *pa-ra-a an-za-a-aš ḫu-u-it-ti-ya-u-en nu-wa-ra-an-na-ša-an an-zi-el* (4.73) ZI-*ni pí-ya-u-e-en na-aš-ma-wa-an-na-ša-an uš-ša-ni-ya-u-e-en* (4.74) *na-aš-ma-wa-ra-an-kán wa-aḫ-nu-um-me-en nu-wa-an-na-aš ḫa-ap-pár da-a-u-e-en* (4.75) *pí-di-eš-ši-ma-wa ma-ak-la-an-da-an tar-nu-u[m]-me-en* (4.76) *nu-wa-an-na-aš zi-ik* DINGIR-*LUM tu-el* ZI-*aš* ⁝*zu-u-wa-aš še-ir* (4.77) *QA-DU* DAM.MEŠ-*NI* DUMU.MEŠ-*NI pár-ḫi-eš-ki*

(4.78) DUB 1.KAM *ŠA* LÚ.MEŠ É DINGIR-*LIM ḫu-u-ma-an-da-aš* (4.79) *ŠA* EN.MEŠ UTÚL DINGIR.MEŠ $^{\text{LÚ.MEŠ}}$APIN.LAL DINGIR.MEŠ (4.80) *Ù ŠA* $^{\text{LÚ.MEŠ}}$SIPAD GUD DINGIR-*LIM* $^{\text{LÚ.MEŠ}}$SIPAD UDU DINGIR-*LIM* (4.81) *iš-ḫi-ú-la-aš QA-TI*

let the cow-herd or shepherd go with the castrated (animals); and as it (has been) castrated from the stable (or) the fold, just so let them bring it in to the gods; and let them not later, on the road, make an exchange. (61) But if any cow-herd or shepherd does wrong on the road, and then exchanges a fat ox or a fat sheep, and makes a trade, (64) or if he kills it and they eat it up, and put in its place a thin (animal), and it becomes known, that is a capital sin for them; they have taken the best meat (?) of the gods' desire. (68) But if it does not become known, whenever they arrive, thereupon let them take down from the stand (?) the cup (?) of the god of life. (70) Let them deliver (the animals) with these words: 'If we have drawn forth for ourselves the best meat (?) from the mouth of the gods, and have devoted it to ourselves, or have sold it for ourselves, (74) or have accepted pay and made a trade for ourselves and have put in its place a thin (animal), then do thou, god, pursue us, with our wives (and) our children, on account of the meat (?) of thy desire.'

---

(78) The first tablet of the duties of all the temple officials, of the kitchen workers of the gods, of the farmers of the gods, and of the cow-herds of the god, (and) the shepherds of the god, is finished.

COMMENTARY

The royal library at Hattusas included regulations for various classes of officials and public servants. Those for temple officials happen to have been unusually well preserved. The cuneiform texts containing them have been published by Ehelolf in KUB 13.4,5,6,17,18,19, and an additional fragment by Götze in KUB 26.31. A complete transliterated text with translation and commentary has been published by Sturtevant in JAOS 54.363–406. This is reproduced here, with the omission of several fragmentary passages and with a number of corrections and improvements, several of which are based upon comments kindly sent by Sommer.

1.16. *da-a-an*: Ehelolf, KlF 1.150, suggested the interpretation given above, but in JAOS 54.365 I preferred his second suggestion that the adverb *da-a-an* 'iterum' might also mean 'likewise'. Sommer and Götze have convinced me that this is impossible.

1.18. *na-aš a-pu-u-uš*: the more colorless enclitic *-as* 'eos' refers to the loaves, while *apūs*, here virtually equivalent to Lat. *hī*, points the contrast between those who are unclean and those who propitiate.

1.19. *ku-e-da-aš*, *na-at*: the first pronoun agrees with the dat. pl. *parnas* (*I-NA* É) 'aedibus', but since only one house is meant, *na-at* and its predicate are singular.

1.20. KÁ-*aš*: dat. pl. (= Lat. *foribus*) in partitive apposition with *pí-di*.

1.21. The interpretation of this line as two questions and two answers is made possible by the fact that Hittite has no formal mark of a yes-no question. It was suggested by Sommer, AU 384 f. Götze, Kulturgeschichte 137, translates: 'Was den Göttern und den Menschen erwünscht ist, ist keineswegs verschieden; was unerwünscht ist, ist dasselbe.'

1.27. IGI-*wa-an-na-an-za*: the translation is based upon the assumption that this is a partially ideographic writing for *sakwananza*; but that need not imply any genuine etymological connection with *sakwa* (IGI.ḪI.A-*wa*) 'eyes'; cf. ^{I}*Mur-ši*-DINGIR-*LIM* for Mursilis, and see on A 4.38 f. — 𒑱*ḫa-an-ḫa-ni-ya-i*: the suggested translation is an attempt to meet the requirements of the context here and in 3.63.

1.28. ZI-*an*-<*za*>-*ši-ma*: cf. ZI-*an-za-ma* (1.22).

1.31. *na-aš-šu . . .* GÌM-*ŠU-aš* is a parenthesis. — *[I-ṢA]-BAT*: the supplement is uncertain.

1.33. *te-it-ti-ya-an-ḫe*: this reading, rather than the one suggested in JAOS 54.366, is required by KUB 13.6.1.30 (cf.T 1.12). So Götze and Sommer.

1.34. *ma-a-an-ma-aš-ta* = *man-ma-sta.*

1.35. *na-at, a-pí-e-da-ni*: in several of its uses *sanh-* governs the accusative of the thing and the dative of the person; see Sommer, BoSt. 7.45–56. A close parallel to our passage is presented by KUB 14.14.1.34, on which see Götze, KlF 1.168. Cf. Lat. *poenas ab aliquo petere.*

1.38. *n[i]-ni-[i]k-zi*: KUB 13.4.1.38 requires *ni-* rather than *ḫar-*, as I formerly read. For the development of meaning: 'lift' > 'remove', cf. Lat. *tollo.*

1.39–44. Since several of these names of festivals contain genitives we have, for convenience, assumed that the unknown words ending in *as* are genitives; *ḫi-ya-ra-aš* (1.40), however, is a nominative if our interpretation is correct, and *a-ya-li* (1.39) looks like a dative (unless it is an Akkadian genitive *AYALI* 'of a ram'). Several of the nominatives here assumed for the sake of the translation are entirely uncertain.

1.40. *ḫi-ya-ra-aš*: cf. *heyus* 'rain' [43]; for the suffix *ras*, see [175].

1.46 f. *na-aš . . . ša-ra-a ti-ya-an-ta-*<*aš*>: 'to set up a festival' seems to mean 'to place within easy reach the food and drink to be employed in the festival'; cf. 3.39 f., 41. The emendation of this line suggested in JAOS 54.368 is very improbable, as both Götze and Sommer have admonished me. Neither of them is responsible for the present emendation.

1.48f. *nu-uš-ma-aš . . . ḫa-ap-pár da-aš-kit*$_9$*-te-ni:* for the meaning of *happar*, see Götze, Lang. 11, No. 3.

1.49. *wa-ak-ši-ya-nu-ut-te-ni*: the meaning of the stem *waksiya-* is not altogether certain, but Götze calls my attention to the fact that in KUB 8.28.1.5, 8.35.1.11, 23.61.1.8 it seems to mean 'be lacking, be missing'. If so the causative here and in 3.40 means something like 'cause to be lacking, cause to fall short, omit'. Perhaps we may connect *wa-ag-ga-aš-nu-an-zi* (A 1.9) and translate that also 'omit'; see the note.

1.50. *-at, ti-ya-an-da*: *-at* often refers to a plural antecedent; a plural adjective or participle with *-at* is somewhat less common.

1.51. *nu-uš-ma-ša-at*: *-smas* may as readily be interpreted 'vobis'.

1.53. *e-iz-za-a-i* agrees with its nearest subject, the collective noun represented by Sumerian SAG.GÌM.ERUM.MEŠ.

1.56f. *ták-ša-an . . . šar-ra-an*: the second phrase, *taksan sarran,* appears to be the direct object of *pesteni*, but the construction of *taksan sarras* is not clear. Our translation is based on the assumption that the whole phrase is stereotyped as an adverb. If *taksan saras* is a genitive, the meaning may be 'half of a half', i.e. 'if you give away half of (your) half'; but this seems scarcely consistent with the context.

1.62. *IŠ-TU* GAL = ^{DUG}*iš-pa-an-du-uz-zi-az* (1.65). For the enclitic *-ya*, see on *ḫu-u-ma-an-da-zi-ya* (A 1.23).

1.64. DINGIR-*LIM-az*: Götze, Lang. 11, No. 3, suggests that this word is an adjective.

2.1–6. The suggested supplements are very uncertain.

2.2. *e-iz-za-tin*: as far as orthography is concerned, this may perfectly well be interpreted as *etsātten* and derived from *etsā-* (*e-iz-za-a-*); but this word and the next (*e-ku-ut-tin*) evidently match *a-da-an-na a-ku-wa-an-na* (2.1), and so it is better to read *etsten* from *et-*; cf. [35, 69, 126].

2.7. *ša-ra-a pa-a-wa-aš* UK[Ù-*aš*]: although this supplement is not quite as close to the traces recorded in the edition as the one suggested in JAOS 54.370, it appears to be possible. It gives a far more satisfactory sense.

2.10 f. The supplements are very uncertain.

2.18. It is not certain that anything has been lost from the text here, although one tablet must have had an extra line.

2.20. SIG$_5$-*in*: this adverb frequently occurs where we might expect an adjective. A verb has been lost at the beginning of the next line.

2.23. [$^{\text{↖}}$*zu-wa-an ku-wa*]-*at*: the supplement is very uncertain. — KA×U-*it* is equivalent to KA×U-*az* (4.71). The instrumental denotes separation, in addition to the values ascribed to it in [190].

2.24 f. This reconstruction is possible if we assume that KUB 13.5.2.27 has omitted a line after *da-at-te-ni*. So Götze and Sommer. The latter would supply after *na-an-za* [DINGIR-*LIM-aš* ZI-*ni* ?].

2.27. ZI-*aš* 'of desire'.

2.28. *e-eš-ša-a-i*: for the postponement of the subject, see on *kat-te-ir-ra-aḫ-ḫi-ir* (H 3.78). Sommer prefers to take the clause *nu* . . . *e-eš-ša-a-i* with the preceding sentence.

2.37. *A-NA* NÍ.TE-*ŠU*: cf. Lat. *apud sē* 'at his house', *ad sē* 'to his house'.

2.40. *na-at*: *-at* 'they', i.e. the persons concerned in the gift.

2.42. *na-at i-ya-an-be e-eš-du*: cf. *na-at* . . . *i-ya-an-du* (2.49) and note.

2.51. *na-at-ši ši-ya-an-du*: did the nobles have to execute new impressions of their seals, in order to prove the genuineness of the seal-impressions on the tablet?

2.52. ZI-*az-za-ma* = abl. + -*a* 'also, even' + -*ma*. With -*a* contrast -*ya* (1.62), and see the note.

2.56. *a-aš-ka* must be accusative on account of the phonetic complement of LUGAL-*an*; the omission of final *n* before *natta* (*Ú-UL*) is not surprising. — 2-*aš-be*: dat. pl.

2.57. 2-*uš-be*: nom. pl.; see [128, 182]. I cannot make any sense out of the imperfectly preserved latter part of this line. To the words recorded in JAOS 54.376 Sommer adds LÚ.MEŠ SANGA(?). Götze would read DINGIR-*LIM-na-ša-at* LÚ.MEŠ KIN (disregarding *nu* as having been erased).

2.61. *I-NA ZÉ-E-NI* stands for Hittite *zēne*, but the use of the preposition shows that the scribe intended to write the phrase in Akkadian; cf. [24b, f.].

2.62. *me-[e-ḫ]u-na-aš*: Sommer assures me that the final sign can still be read in KUB 13.18.2.13.

2.65. *gi-e-nu-uš-šu-uš e-ip-zi*: the gesture of clasping the knees in making an urgent request is familiar in Greek and Latin literature. In Akkadian documents a defeated king sometimes embraces the feet of his conqueror in token of submission, but there seems to be nothing analogous to the situation described in our text. The noun seems to be acc. pl. of a masc. *s*-stem. Götze, however, Lang. 11, No. 3, interprets the phrase 'genua sua capit', which, he thinks, came to mean 'takes to his knees, falls to his knees'. My interpretation is supported by KUB 26.69.7.8 f.: *nu-wa-za* ^{I}*Na-na-ya-an gi-nu-wa e-ip-pu-un*, 'And for myself I clasped Nanayas's knees'. Here *genuwa* is in partitive apposition with *Nanayan*. Götze's interpretation gives the acc. *Nanayan* the value of a dat.

2.67. *nu-wa-mu* EGIR-*pa ti-ya-at-tin* 'withdraw for me, give way to me'.

2.71. *u-wa-it-ta-ri*: Sommer admonishes me that this word cannot come from *uwai-* 'seem, be seen', but must go with *uwai* 'invidia, injury', on which see on H 1.34. For the semantic development from 'injure' to 'be pitied', cf. German *er tut mir leid.*

2.73. *u-wa-it-ta-ri*, *da-at-te-ni*: *li-e* (2.72) goes with these two verbs as well as with *da-at-te-ni* (2.72).

2.74. *šu-ma-aš*: dat.; cf. on 1.35.

2.77. *e-iz-za-at-te-ni* here represents *etsteni* rather than *etsātteni*; see on *e-iz-za-tin* (2.2).

2.79. Perhaps this line means: 'Do not take a bribe to inflict a capital penalty, and do not risk suffering a capital penalty for the sake of some (immediate) gain'.

2.82. GAM *pa-it-tin*: some at least of the temples of Hattusas were on the citadel. In this paragraph one consistently goes up to a temple and down to the town.

2.83. SAL-*aš ut-tar*: perhaps better 'an affair with a woman' or 'woman-business'.

2.84. *t*[*ar-ḫu*]-*u*[*z-z*]*i*: *tarhzi* is thus written in KUB 17.10.1.33, and *tar-ḫu-du* occurs in KBo.4.2.1.54.

3.1. The suppletion of this line is altogether uncertain.

3.3. *ku-iš-ša-aš*: the lack of a sentence connective makes it probable that this clause goes with what precedes, although relative clauses are usually to be construed with what follows.

3.9. *ḫa-a-li, ḫa-li-ya-at-tal-liš*: the root *hal-* shows two meanings, 'enclose' and 'protect, keep' (e.g., Code 198.14: *ta ḫu-ur-ki-il ḫa-li-en-zi*, 'in that case they keep their punishment'—?). Probably the more concrete meaning is primary. Otherwise Götze, Madd. 107.

3.13. *pí-ra-an ḫu-u-ya-an-za* 'marching before'.

3.14. *ku-iš* 'aliquis' stands in partitive apposition with *ku-i-e-eš* 'qui' (3.13), or, if one prefer, with its omitted antecedent.

3.21. *ku-e-da-ni* is relative and *ku-iš* indefinite; the clause is equivalent to a condition.

3.22. *ku-i*[*š-ki*]: the supplement is uncertain.

3.23–9: Götze and Sommer have convinced me that my former interpretation of this difficult passage (JAOS 54.383) is wrong; they are not responsible for the new interpretation, except as noted below.

3.24. *ku-e-da-ni-ik-ki* . . . *ḫa-a-li*: for the omission of the substantive in the first sentence and its use in the second, cf. on *kat-te-ir-ra-aḫ-ḫi-ir* (H 3.78).

3.25. É DINGIR-*LIM-YA* might perhaps be translated 'my temple'.

3.26. *ti-iš-ki-iz-zi* I derive from *tiya-* 'stand, take one's stand'.

3.29 f. *ú-wa-an-zi* 'they see': so Sommer and Götze independently.—<DINGIR-*LIM*>*ši*: better <*A-NA* DINGIR-*LIM*>-*ši*.

3.33. *la-ba-ar-na-aš*: our translation is based upon the assumption that this form is due to secondary confusion between the personal name *Labarnas* and the noun *tabarnas* 'king'; see on T 1.2. It is less probable that there was a cistern named the Cistern of Labarnas, since Labarnas did not rule in Hattusas.

3.36. [*mar-r*]*i i*[*š-ḫ*]*al-túḫ-me-ya-an-za*: the restoration is very uncertain, and the suggested meaning entirely conjectural.

3.37 f. *ni-ik-zi, ni-ni-ik-ta-ri*: the difference in voice seems to cancel the force of the causative infix; cf. [324].

3.40. *wa-ak-ši-ya-nu-zi*: for the meaning, see on 1.49.

3.41. *ku-iš-ša-an-za-an-kán* = *kwis* + *an* + *za* + *an* + *kan*: for the repetition of forms of *-as* 'is', see on H 3.18 and I 4.72.

3.43. *ḫal-lu-wa-ya-za*: *nah-* usually takes the dative, as in 1.38, 2.31, 3.44, 58. The ablative suggests separation: 'be afraid of and avoid'.

3.48. *ša-an-na-pí*: Götze will show elsewhere that this word means 'in one place'; the distributive idea comes from the repetition.

3.49–53. The interpretation is doubtful; perhaps the condition continues to the middle of line 51. (See Additions and Corrections.)

3.53. TI-*nu-ma-aš*: see [161a, 188] and cf. H 1.15. — *Ú.UL e-eš-zi*: Sommer read *Ú-UL p[í-]* in KUB 13.6.3.4, and <*Ú-UL*> *pí-e ḫ[ar]-zi* in KUB 13.4.3.53, but I can get no meaning out of that. The reading is far from certain.

3.56. *nu-uš-ma-aš*: *-smas* 'for yourselves' can scarcely be included in an idiomatic English translation.

3.63. *da-a-an*: see on *da-a-an* (1.16). — *ḫa-an-ḫa-ni-ya-i*: see on *ḫa-an-ḫa-ni-ya-i* (1.27).

3.65. *ša-a-li-qa*: here and in 3.80 I have interpreted the word according to Friedrich, AOr. 6.359–65. Sommer suggests that the fundamental force may have been 'an etwas stossen, berühren'.

3.78. *še-ik-kán-ti-it* ZI-*it*: literally 'with knowing will'.

3.81. *u-wa-it-ta*: properly 'it arouses (his) pity'; see on *u-wa-it-ta-ri* (2.71). — The tablet is broken at the end of this line, but probably no word has been lost.

4.6 f. *me-na-aḫ-ḫa-an-da . . . uš-kán-zi*: cf. *menahanda sakanzi* (4.39).

4.8. EN.MEŠ-*Y*[*A*]: Sommer would read EN.MEŠ-*K*[*U-NU*].

4.13. *A-NA* NUMUN *a-ni-ya-u-wa-an-zi*: 'for the seed for planting'. In spite of the word order, Götze-Pedersen, MS 38, take EGIR-*an* with *ANA* NUMUN: 'mit Rücksicht auf die Aussaat'.

4.20 EGIR-*zi-an* modifies the following verb, but English idiom requires a different arrangement.

4.21. *ta-a-it-te-ni* = *tayetteni*: in 2.17 *da-a-it-te-ni* stands for *daitteni* (from *dai-* 'place').

4.27. *ta-a-iš-te-ni*: by haplology from **taistaitteni*, 2 pl. of *taistai-*'conceal'.

4.32. *nu* [DI]NGIR-*LI*[*M-n*]*i p*[*a-i*]*t-te-ni*: the supplements were suggested independently by Götze and by Sommer. The clause must refer to the ordeal somewhat more fully described in 4.52 f. and 4.69 ff. — *šu-me-el* ᴰKAL-*KU-NU*: possibly 'ᴰKAL is yours'.

4.36. *ša-li-ú*(?)-*eš*: the reading is Sommer's; Götze suggests *ŠA-LI-TE*-MEŠ.

4.39. *me-na-aḫ-ḫa-an-da* . . . *ša-kán-zi*: the parallelism of *ša-kán-zi* with *uš-kán-zi* (4.7) supports the etymological connection of Hittite *sak*- 'know' with Goth. *saiħan* 'see'; see [77, 114].

4.39 f. *ku-it-ma-an* . . . *e-iz-za-az-zi*: cf. 4.5.

4.41. D[U]G: the reading is Sommer's; it seems virtually certain.

4.42. *šap-pí-eš-kán-zi*: for the meaning, cf. Forrer, RHA 1.147.32 = KUB 1.58.1.8; see also KUB 12.58.4.3,6; 25.36.1.13, 5.13,25.

4.44. *iz-za-at-te-ni*: here again the surrounding verbs suggest *etsteni* rather than *etsātteni*; see on 2.2 and on 2.77.

4.48. *nu-uš-ma-aš*: the phrase 'for yourselves' can scarcely be included in the English sentence.

4.52 f. *na-aš-ta* . . . *e-ku-ut-te-ni*: this sentence refers to an ordeal; cf. 4.32 and 4.69 f. — DINGIR-*LIM* ZI-*aš*: the corresponding DINGIR-*LIM* ZI-*TI* (4.69) must represent Akkadian *ILI NAPIŠTI*.

4.54. *šu-me-el* ᴰKAL-*KU-NU*: see on 4.32.

4.57. *kar-ša-ad-da-aš*: dat. pl., probably from **karsaz* 'a cutting' (see Sommer, AU 227 fn. 2). The development from 'a cutting' to 'that which is cut' is not surprising.

4.67. ZI-*aš-ša-aš*: if -*ša-aš* is not mere dittography, it must be -*sas* 'of his' where the context demands -*smas* 'of their'. Cf. ZI-*aš* (4.76).

4.69 f. *na-aš-ta* . . . *da-an-du*; cf. 4.52 f. and note.

4.72. *nu-wa-ra-an-na-ša-an* = *nu-war-an-nas-an*; -*nas* 'nobis' is emphatically repeated by *anzel* ZI-*ni* 'nobis ipsis'. The enclitic -*as*, accusative -*an*, and especially the neuter -*at* are sometimes repeated after an intervening -*se* or -*za* (see on *na-at-ši-ya-at* H 3.18, and on *ku-iš-ša-an-za-an-kán* I 3.41); we cannot cite another instance after -*nas*.

4.73. *na-aš-ma-wa-an-na-ša-an* = *nasma-wa-nas-an*. It would perhaps be better to neglect -*nas* 'nobis' in the translation.

4.76. ⁎*zu-u-wa-aš*: the final sign is omitted in KUB 13.4.4.76, but Sommer writes that it is visible on the tablet.

THE PROCLAMATION OF TELIPINUS

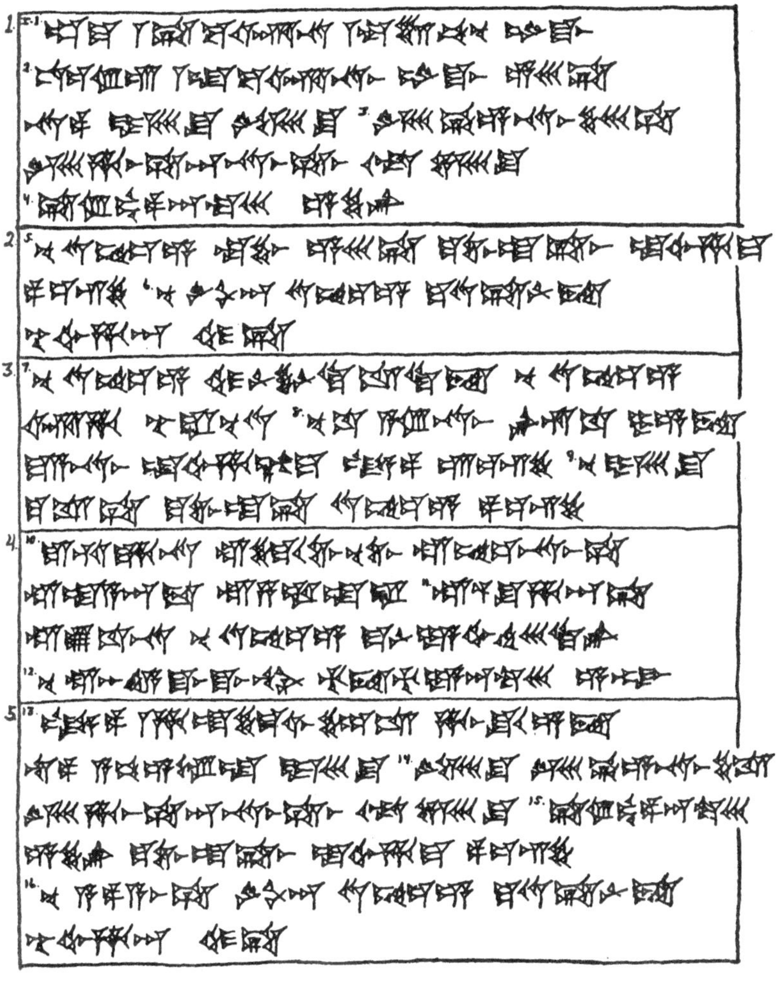

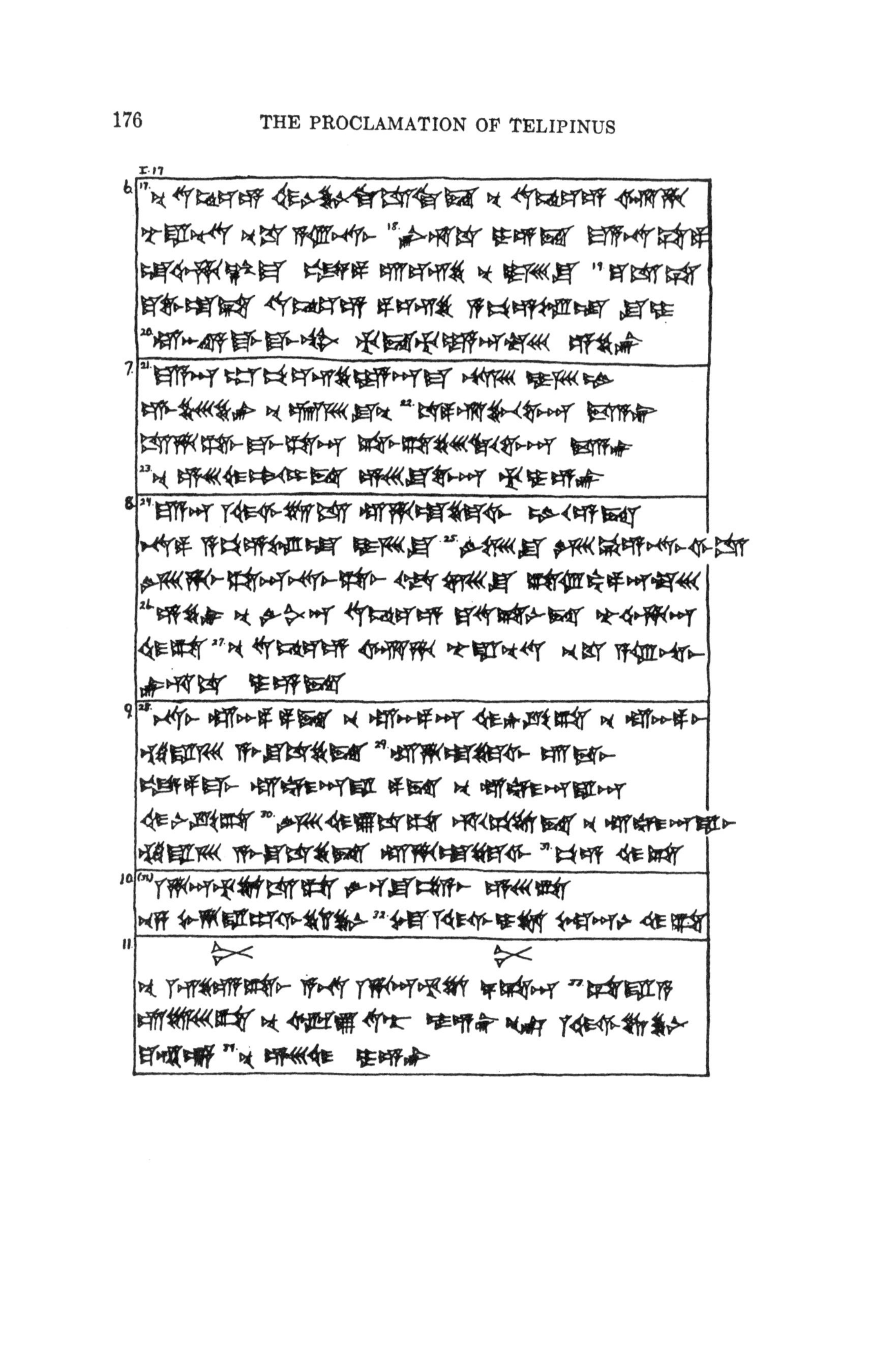

I. 17

6. 17. … 18. … 19. … 20. …

7. 21. … 22. … 23. …

8. 24. … 25. … 26. … 27. …

9. 28. … 29. … 30. … 31. …

10. (31.) … 32. …

11. … 33. … 34. …

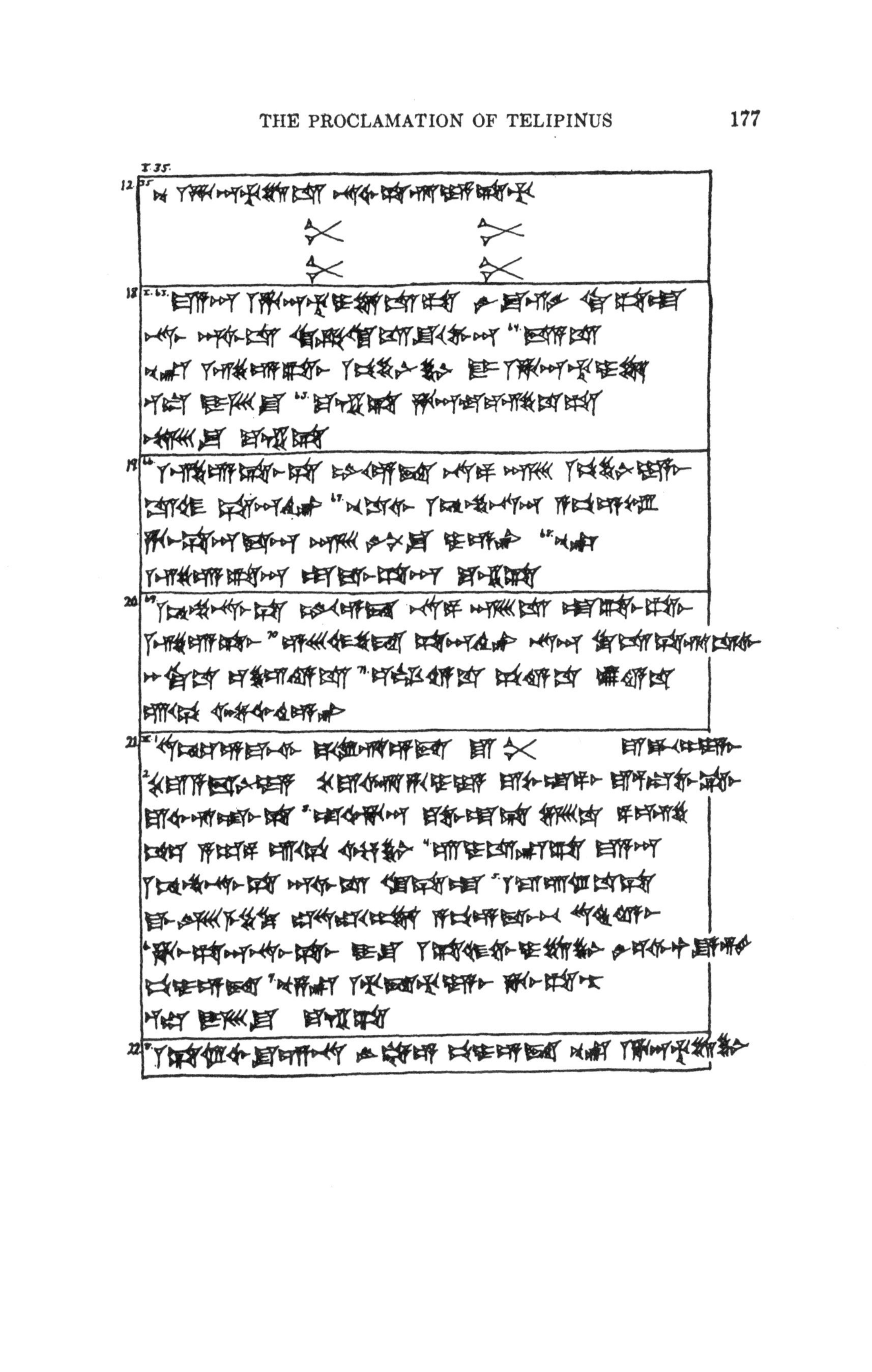

I. 35

12 35

18 I. 63 … 64 … 65

19 66 … 67 … 68

20 69 … 70 … 71

21 II. 1 … 2 … 3 … 4 … 5 … 6 … 7

22 8

II. 8.

23

24

25

26

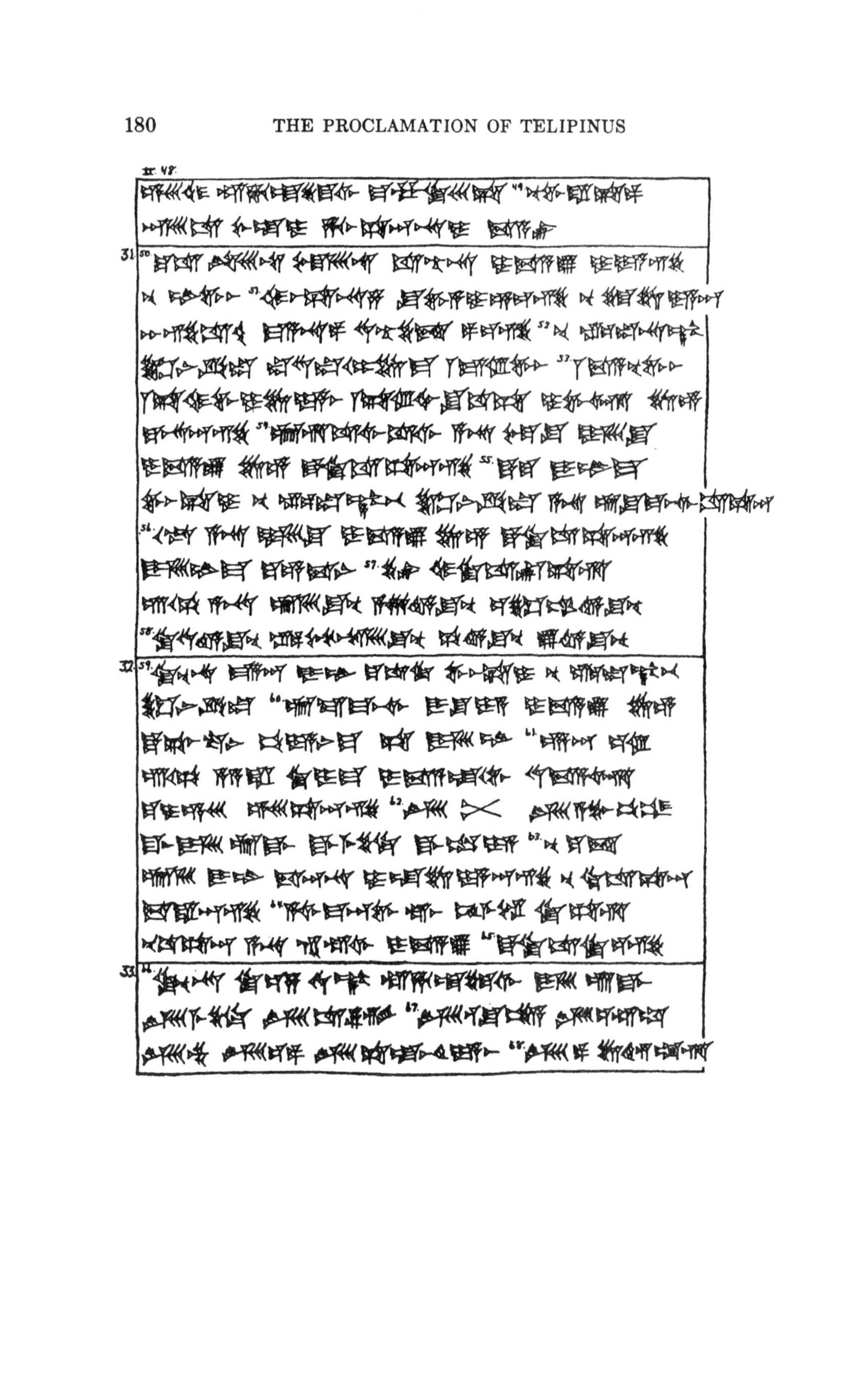

II. 48. 49.

31 50. 51. 52. 53. 54. 55. 56. 57. 58.

32 59. 60. 61. 62. 63. 64. 65.

33 66. 67. 68.

THE PROCLAMATION OF TELIPINUS

1

(1.1) [*UM-MA* ^{I}]*TA-BA-AR-NA* ^{I}*TE-LI-PÍ-NU* LUGAL.GAL (1.2) [*ka*]-*ru-ú* ^{I}*La-ba-ar-na-aš* LUGAL.GAL *e-eš-ta na-pa* [DUMU.ME]Š-*ŠU* [ŠEŠ.ME]Š-*ŠU* (1.3) $^{LÚ.MEŠ}$*ga-e-na-aš-še-eš-ša* LÚ.MEŠ *ḫa-aš-ša-an-na-aš-ša-aš* *Ù* ERÍN.MEŠ-*ŠU* (1.4) *ta-ru-up-pa-an-te-eš e-še-ir*

2

(1.5) *nu ut-ne-e te-pu e-eš-ta ku-wa-at-ta-aš la-aḫ-ḫa-ma pa-iz-zi* (1.6) *nu* ^{LÚ}KÚR-*an ut-ne-e ku-ut-ta-ni-it tar-aḫ-ḫa-an ḫar-ta*

3

(1.7) *nu ut-ne-e ḫar-ni-in-ki-iš-ki-it nu ut-ne-e ar-ḫa tar-ra-nu-ut* (1.8) *nu-uš a-ru-na-aš ir-ḫu-uš i-e-it ma-a-na-aš la-aḫ-ḫa-az-ma* EGIR-*pa ú-iz-zi* (1.9) *nu* DUMU.MEŠ-*ŠU ku-iš-ša ku-wa-at-ta ut-ne-e pa-iz-zi*

4

(1.10) ^{URU}*Ḫu-piš-na* ^{URU}*Tu-u-wa-nu-wa* ^{URU}*Ne-na-aš-ša* ^{URU}*La-a-an-da* ^{URU}*Za-al-la-ra* (1.11) ^{URU}*Pár-šu-ḫa-an-ta* ^{URU}*Lu-uš-na nu ut-ne-e ma-ni-ya-aḫ-ḫi-eš-ki-ir* (1.12) *nu* URU.AŠ.AŠ.ḪI.A GAL.GAL-*TIM ti-it-ti-ya-an-te-eš e-šir*

5

(1.13) EGIR-*pa* ^{I}*Ḫa-at-tu-ši-li-iš ḫa-aš-šu-u-e-it na-pa a-pí-e-el-la* DUMU.MEŠ-*ŠU* (1.14) ŠEŠ.MEŠ-*ŠU* $^{LÚ.MEŠ}$*ga-e-na-aš-še-iš* LÚ.MEŠ *ḫa-aš-ša-an-na-aš-ša-aš* *Ù* ERÍN.MEŠ-*ŠU* (1.15) *ta-ru-up-pa-an-te-eš e-še-ir ku-wa-at-ta-aš la-aḫ-ḫa-ma pa-iz-zi* (1.16) *nu a-pa-a-aš-ša* ^{LÚ}KÚR-*an ut-ne-e ku-ut-ta-ni-it tar-aḫ-ḫa-an ḫar-ta*

6

(1.17) *nu ut-ne-e ḫar-ni-in-ki-iš-ki-it nu ut-ne-e ar-ḫa tar-ra-nu-ut nu-uš a-ru-na-aš* (1.18) *ir-ḫu-uš i-e-it ma-a-na-*[*š*]*a-pa la-aḫ-ḫa-az-ma* EGIR-*pa ú-iz-zi nu* DUMU.MEŠ-*ŠU* (1.19) *ku-iš-ša ku-wa-at-ta ut-*[*n*]*e-e pa-iz-zi a-pí-e-el-la* ŠU-*i* (1.20) URU.AŠ.AŠ.ḪI.A GAL.GAL-*TIM ti-it-ti-ya-an-te-eš e-še-ir*

THE PROCLAMATION OF TELIPINUS

1

(1) Thus (speaks) King Telipinus, the great king. (2) Formerly Labarnas was the great king. (2) And then his sons, his brothers, and his relatives by marriage, the members of his family, and his soldiers were united.

2

(5) And the land was small; but on whatever campaign he went, by (his) strength (?) he kept the hostile country in subjection.

3

(7) And he kept devastating countries, and he made the countries tremble (?); and he made them boundaries of the sea. (8) But when he returned from the campaign, one (of) his sons went to each (of) the countries—

4

To Hupisnas, Tūwanuwas, Nenassas, Landas, Zallaras, Parsuhantas, Lusnas. They governed the countries; and the large cities were assigned (to them).

5

(13) Afterwards Hattusilis became king. (13) And then likewise his sons, his brothers, his relatives by marriage, the members of his family, and his soldiers were united. (15) And on whatever campaign he went, he also by (his) strength kept the hostile country in subjection.

6

(17) And he kept devastating countries, and he made the countries tremble (?); and he made them boundaries of the sea. (18) Moreover, when in those days he returned from the campaign, one (of) his sons went to each (of) the countries; and the large cities were put into his hands.

7

(1.21) *ma-a-an ap-pí-iz-zi-ya-an-ma* ERUM.MEŠ DUMU.MEŠ. LUGAL *mar-še-eš-še-ir nu* É.MEŠ-*ŠU-NU* (1.22) *ka-ri-pu-u-wa-an da-a-ir iš-ḫa-ša-aš-ma-aš-ša-an ta-aš-ta-še-eš-ki-u-wa-an da-a-ir* (1.23) *nu e-eš-ḫar-šum-mi-it e-eš-šu-wa-an ti-i-e-ir*

8

(1.24) *ma-a-an* ^{I}*Mur-ši-li-iš* ^{URU}*Ḫa-at-tu-ši* LUGAL-*u-e-it na-pa a-pí-e-el-la* DUMU.MEŠ-*ŠU* (1.25) ŠEŠ.MEŠ-*ŠU* $^{LÚ.MEŠ}$*ga-e-na-aš-ši-iš* LÚ.MEŠ *ḫa-aš-ša-an-na-aš-ša-aš Ù* ERÍN.MEŠ-*ŠU ta-ru-up-pa-an-te-eš* (1.26) *e-še-ir nu* ^{LÚ}KÚR-*an ut-ne-e ku-ut-ta-ni-it tar-aḫ-ḫa-an ḫar-ta* (1.27) *nu ut-ne-e ar-ḫa tar-ra-nu-ut nu-uš a-[ru-n]a-aš ir-ḫu-uš i-e-it*

9

(1.28) *[na]-aš* ^{URU}*Ḫal-pa pa-it nu* ^{URU}*Ḫal-pa-an ḫar-ni-ik-ta nu* ^{URU}*Ḫal-pa-aš* NAM.RA.MEŠ *a-aš-šu-uš-še-it* (1.29) [^{URU}]*Ḫa-at-tu-ši ú-da-aš* EGIR-*pa-ma-aš* ^{URU}KÁ.DINGIR.RA *pa-it nu* ^{URU}KÁ.DINGIR.RA-*an ḫar-ni-ik-ta* (1.30) [$^{LÚ.ME]Š}$*Ḫur-lu-uš-ša ḫu-ul-li-it nu* ^{URU}KÁ.DINGIR. RA-*aš* NAM.RA.MEŠ *a-aš-šu-uš-še-it* ^{URU}*Ḫa-at-t[u]-ši* (1.31) *pí-e ḫar-ta*

10

(1.31) ^{I}*Ḫa-an-ti-l[i-iš-š]a* ^{LÚ}QA.ŠU.DU$_8$.A-*aš e-eš-ta nu-za* ^{SAL}*Ḫa-r[a-a]p-[ši]-li-in* (1.32) [NIN] ^{I}*MUR-ŠI-I-LI* DAM-*an-ni ḫar-ta*

11

. . . . . *nu* ^{I}*[Z]i-dan-ta-a[š A]-NA* ^{I}*ḪA-AN-TI-LI [kat-t]a-an* (1.33) *ša-ra-a ú-li-eš-ta nu* ḪUL-*lu ut-t[ar i-e-i]r nu-kán* ^{I}*Mur-ši-li-in ku-en-nir* (1.34) *[nu e]-eš-ḫar i-e-ir*

12

(1.35) *[nu* ^{I}*Ḫa-an]-ti-li-iš na-aḫ-ša-ri-ya-ta-ti*

* * * * *

18

(1.63) *ma-a-an* ^{I}*Ḫa-an-ti-i-li-iš-ša* ^{LÚ}ŠU.GI *[ki-ša-a]t na-aš* DINGIR-*L[IM-iš] ki-ik-ki-iš-šu-u-wa-an* (1.64) *da-a-is nu-kán* ^{I}*Zi-dan-ta-[aš* ^{I}*Pí-še-ni-in]* DUMU ^{I}*ḪA-AN-TI-I-LI QA-DU* DUMU.MEŠ-*ŠU* (1.65) *ku-en-ta ḫa-an-te-iz-z[i-uš-ša]* ERUM.MEŠ-*ŠU ku-en-ta*

7

(21) But when afterwards the subjects of the princes became rebellious, they began to despoil their (i.e. the princes') holdings, and to conspire (against) their masters, and to shed their (i.e. the princes') blood.

8

(24) When Mursilis became king in Hattusas, then likewise his sons, his brothers, his relatives-in-law, the members of his family, and his soldiers were united. (26) And by (his) strength he kept the hostile country in subjection. (27) And he made the countries tremble (?); and he made them boundaries of the sea.

9

(28) And he went to Aleppo, and destroyed Aleppo, and brought captives and possessions of Aleppo to Hattusas. (29) Then afterwards he went to Babylon, and destroyed Babylon, and defeated the Hurrians, and carried captives and possessions of Babylon to Hattusas.

10

(31) And Hantilis was a cup-bearer, and he had Harapsilis (?), sister of Mursilis, in marriage.

11

. . . (32) And Zidantas conspired (?) with Hantilis, and they formed a traitorous plot. (33) They killed Mursilis; they shed blood.

12

(35) And Hantilis was afraid.

* * * * *

18

(63) And when Hantilis had become old and was about to become a god, Zidantas killed Pisenis, the son of Hantilis, along with his (i.e. Pisenis'?) sons, and he killed his foremost subjects.

19

(1.66) ^{I}*Zi-dan-ta-aš-ša* LUGAL-[*u-e-it na-pa* DI[NGIR.MEŠ [^{I}*P*]*í*-[*š*]*e-ni-ya-aš iš-ḫar ša-an-ḫi-ir* (1.67) *nu-uš-ši* [^{I}*Am-mu-na-an a-pí-e-el*] *ḫa-aš-ša-an-da-an* DINGIR.MEŠ ^{LÚ}KÚR-*ŠU i-e-ir* (1.68) *nu-kán* ^{I}*Zi-dan-ta-an ad-da-aš-ša-an ku-en-ta*

20

(1.69) ^{I}*Am-mu-na-aš-ša* LUGAL-*u-e-it na-pa* DINGIR.MEŠ-*iš at-ta-aš-ša-aš* ^{I}*Zi-dan-ta-aš* (1.70) *e-eš-ḫar-še-it ša-an-ḫi-ir na-an ki-iš-ša-ri-iš-ši ḫal-ki-uš* [^{GIŠ}ŠAR.ḪI.A]-*iš* (1.71) ^{GIŠ}GEŠTIN.ḪI.A-*uš* GUD.ḪI.A-*uš* UDU.ḪI.A-*uš Ú-U*[*L* SIG$_5$-*aḫ-ḫi-e-ir*]

21

(2.1) *ut-ne-e-ma-aš-ši ku-u-ru-ri-e-it* ^{URU}[ ]^{URU}*Gal-mi-ya-aš* (2.2) KUR ^{URU}*A-DA-NI-Y*[*A*] KUR ^{URU}*AR-ZA-U-I-YA* ^{URU}*Šal-la-pa-aš* ^{URU}*Pár-du-wa-ta-aš* ^{URU}*Aḫ-ḫu-la-aš-ša* (2.3) *la-aḫ-ḫa-an ku-wa-at-ta* ERÍN.MEŠ-*uš pa-iz-zi ne a-ap-pa Ú-UL* SIG$_5$-*in* (2.4) *ú-i-iš-kán-ta ma-a-an* ^{I}*Am-mu-na-aš-ša* DINGIR-*LIM-iš ki-ša-at* (2.5) ^{I}*Zu-ú-ru-uš-ša* GAL LÚ.MEŠ *ME-ŠE-DI du-ud-du-mi-li a-pí-e-da-aš-be* UD.KAM.ḪI.A-*aš* (2.6) *ḫa-aš-ša-an-na-aš-ša-aš* DUMU-*ŠU* ^{I}*Ta-ḫar-wa-i-li-in* LÚ ^{GIŠ}ŠUKUR GUŠKIN *pí-i-e-it* (2.7) *nu-za-kán* ^{I}*Ti-it-ti-ya-aš ḫa-aš-ša-tar QA-DU* DUMU.MEŠ-*ŠU ku-en-ta*

22

(2.8) ^{I}*Ta-ru-uḫ-šu-un-na* ^{LÚ}KAŠ$_4$.E *pí-i-e-it nu-kán* ^{I}*Ḫa-an-ti-li-in QA-DU* DUMU.MEŠ-*ŠU* (2.9) *ku-e*[*n-t*]*a nu* ^{I}*Ḫu-uz-zi-ya-aš* LUGAL-*u-e-it* ^{I}*Te-li-pí-nu-uš-ša-az* (2.10) ^{SAL}*Iš-ta-pa-ri-ya-an ḫa-an-te-iz-zi-ya-an* NIN-*ZU ḫar-ta* (2.11) *ma-a-nu-uš-kán* ^{I}*Ḫu-uz-zi-ya-aš ku-en-ta nu ut-tar iš-du-wa-a-ti* (2.12) *nu-uš* ^{I}*Te-li-pí-nu-uš ar-ḫa pár-aḫ-ta*

23

(2.13) 5 ŠEŠ.MEŠ-*ŠU nu-uš-ma-aš* É.MEŠ *tág-ga-aš-ta pa-a-an-du-wa-az a-ša-an-du* (2.14) *nu-wa-za az-zi-ik-kán-du ak-ku-uš-kán-du i-da-a-lu-ma-aš-ma-aš-kán li-e ku-*[*it-ki*] (2.15) *tág-ga-aš-ši nu tar-ši-ki-mi a-pí-e-wa-mu i-da-lu i-e-ir ú-ga-wa-ru-uš* ḪUL-*lu* [*Ú-UL i-ya-mi*]

24

(2.16) *ma-a-an-ša-an* ^{I}*Te-li-pí-nu-uš I-NA* ^{GIŠ}GU.ZA *A-BI-YA e-eš-ḫa-at* (2.17) *nu* ^{URU}*Ḫa-aš-šu-wa la-aḫ-ḫa pa-a-un nu* ^{URU}*Ḫa-aš-šu-wa-an ḫar-ni-in-ku-un* (2.18) ERÍN.MEŠ-*za-mi-iš-ša* ^{URU}*Zi-iz-zi-li-ip-pí e-eš-ta* (2.19) *nu* ^{URU}*Zi-iz-zi-li-ip-pí ḫu-ul-la-an-za-iš ki-ša-at*

19

(66) And Zidantas became king. (66) And then the gods avenged the blood of Pisenis. (67) And the gods made Ammunas, his (i.e. Zidantas') son, his enemy; and he killed Zidantas, his father.

20

(69) And Ammunas became king. (69) And then the gods avenged the blood of his father Zidantas; they did not prosper (?) him (or), in his hands, the grain (fields), the orchards (?), the vineyards, the cattle, (and) the sheep.

21

(1) And the (following) countries became hostile to him, ... , Galmiyas, Adaniyas, Arzawiyas, Sallapas, Parduwatas, and Ahhulas; the infantry went on campaigns everywhere. (3) And they returned unsuccessful. (4) When Ammunas too became a god, Zūrus, chief of the *Mešedi*, in those days secretly sent (one) of his family, his son Taharwailis, a man of the golden spear; and he killed the family of Tittis along with his sons.

22

(8) And he sent Taruhsus, the runner (?), and he killed Hantilis along with his sons. (9) And Huzziyas became king. (9) And Telipinus had (as wife) Istapariyas, his eldest sister. (11) Huzziyas would have killed them, but his plan became known, and Telipinus drove them away.

23

(13) His (i.e. Huzziyas') brothers (were) five; and he (i.e. Telipinus) built them houses, (saying): 'Let them go (and) dwell (there); let them eat (and) drink; and do not do them any harm. (15) And I declare: "They did me harm, and I do not do them harm".'

24

(16) When I, Telipinus, had seated myself upon the throne of my father, I went to Hassuwas on a campaign, and I destroyed Hassuwas. (18) And my infantry was in Zizzilippas, and in Zizzilippas a battle occurred.

25

(2.20) *ma-a-na-pa* LUGAL-*uš* ^{URU}*La-wa-az-za-an-ti-ya ú-wa-nu-un* ^{I}*La-aḫ-ḫa-aš-*[*mu* ^{LÚ}KÚR] (2.21) *e-eš-ta nu* ^{URU}*La-wa-za-an-ti-ya-an wa-ag-ga-ri-ya-at na-an* [DINGIR.MEŠ] (2.22) *ki-iš-ša-ri-mi da-a-ir ḫa-an-te-iz-zi-ya-aš-ša* PA LÚ.MEŠ *LI-IM* ^{ID}U-[*Ù*] (2.23) ^{I}*Kar-ru-wa-aš* PA $^{\text{LÚ.MEŠ}}$ŠA(G).TAM ^{I}*I-na-ra-aš* PA $^{\text{LÚ.MEŠ}}$QA.ŠU.DU$_8$.A ^{I}*Ki-il-l*[*a-aš Ù*] (2.24) ^{I} ^{D}U-*mi-im-ma-aš* PA LÚ.MEŠ ^{GIŠ}PA ^{I}*Zi-in-wa-še-li-iš Ù* ^{I}*Li-el-li-*[*iš*] (2.25) *me-ig-ga-e-eš nu* ^{I}*Ta-nu-u-i* LÚ ^{GIŠ}PA *du-ud-du-mi-li pí-i-e-i*[*r*]

26

(2.26) [LUG]AL-*uš Ú-UL š*[*a-ag-ga-aḫ-ḫ*]*u-un* [^{I}*Ḫu-u*]*z-zi-ya-an Ù* ŠEŠ.MEŠ-*ŠU an-da* [ ] (2.27) *ma-a-an* LUGAL-*uš iš-ta-ma-aš-šu-un nu* ^{I}*Ta-nu-wa-an* ^{I}*Ta-ḫar-wa-i-li-in* ^{I}*Ta-ru-uḫ-š*[*u-un-na*] (2.28) [*ú*]-*wa-te-ir nu-uš pa-an-ku-uš pa-ra-a ḫi-in-ga-ni ḫar-ta* LUGAL-*uš-ša me-ma-aḫ-ḫu-un* (2.29) [*ku-w*]*a-at-wa-ri ak-kán-zi nu-wa-ru-uš* IGI.ḪI.A-*wa mu-un-na-an-zi nu-uš* LUGAL-*uš kar-š*[*a-nu-un*] (2.30) [$^{\text{LÚ.M}}$]^{EŠ}APIN.LAL *i-ya-nu-un* ^{GIŠ}TUKUL.ḪI.A-*uš-šu-uš-ta* ZAG.DIB-*za da-aḫ-ḫu-un nu-uš-ma-aš* ^{GIŠ}Š[UDUN] *pí-iḫ-ḫu-un*

27

(2.31) *nu šal-la-aš-be ḫa-aš-ša-an-na-aš e-eš-ḫar pa-an-ga-ri-ya-at-ta-ti nu* ^{SAL}*Iš-ta-pa-ri-ya-aš* (2.32) SAL.LUGAL BA.UG$_6$ EGIR-*pa-ma ú-it* ^{I}*Am-mu-na-aš* DUMU.LUGAL BA.UG$_6$ *nu ši-ú-na-an an-tu-uḫ-ši-iš-ša* (2.33) *tar-ši-ik-kán-zi ka-a-ša-wa* ^{URU}*Ḫa-at-tu-ši e-eš-ḫar pa-an-ga-ri-ya-at-ta-ti* (2.34) *nu* ^{I}*Te-li-pí-nu-uš* ^{URU}*Ḫa-at-tu-ši tu-li-ya-an ḫal-zi-iḫ-ḫu-un ki-it-pa-*[*d*]*a-la-az* ^{URU}*Ḫa-at-tu-ši* (2.35) *ḫa-aš-ša-an-na-aš* DUMU-*an i-da-lu li-e ku-iš-ki i-ya-zi nu-uš-ši-ša-an* GÍR-*an ták-ki-eš-zi*

28

(2.36) LUGAL-*uš-ša-an ḫa-an-te-iz-zi-ya-aš-be* DUMU.LUGAL DUMU-*RU ki-ik-ki-i*[*t*]-*ta-ru ták-ku* DUMU.LU[GAL] (2.37) *ḫa-an-te-iz-zi-iš* NU.GÁL *nu ku-iš ta-a-an pí-e-da-aš* DUMU-*RU nu* LUGAL-*uš a-pa-a-aš* (2.38) *ki-ša-ru ma-a-an* DUMU.LUGAL-*ma* DUMU.NITA NU.GÁL *nu ku-iš* DUMU.SAL *ḫa-an-te-iz-zi-iš* (2.39) *nu-uš-ši-iš-ša-an* ^{LÚ}*an-ti-ya-an-ta-an ap-pa-a-an-du nu* LUGAL-*uš a-pa-a-aš ki-ša-r*[*u*]

29

(2.40) *UR-RA-AM ŠE-RA-AM ku-iš am-mu-uk* EGIR-*an-da* LUGAL-*uš ki-ša-ri na-pa* ŠEŠ.MEŠ-*ŠU* (2.41) DUMU.MEŠ-*ŠU* $^{\text{LÚ.MEŠ}}$*ga-e-na-*

25

(20) When at that time I, the king, came to Lawazzantiyas, Lahhas was hostile to me, and incited Lawazzantiyas to rebellion. (21) And the gods delivered it into my hand. (22) And foremost (officials were) the commanders of a thousand, . . . and Karruwas; the chief of the overseers of the treasury, Inaras; the chiefs of the cup-bearers, Killas and Dattamimmas; the chiefs of the scepter-bearers, Zinwaselis and Lellis, great (men). (25) And they secretly sent (?) to Tanuwas, the scepter-bearer.

26

(26) I, the king, did not know (it). . . . (27) When I, the king, heard, they brought Tanuwas, Taharwailis, and Taruhsus; and the senate thereafter held them for sentence (?); and I, the king, said: 'Why should they die? (29) They (i.e. the officials) shall hide their faces (?).' (29) I, the king, segregated them. (30) I made them farmers; I took their weapons from their right side, and I gave them yokes (?).

27

(31) Now blood(shed) of the royal family has become common. (31) And Istapariyas, the queen, died; and afterwards Ammunas, the king's son, died. (32) And men also are setting a stamp (?) (upon the situation): 'See there! In Hattusas blood(shed) has become common.' (34) Now I, Telipinus, have called an assembly at Hattusas. (34) From now on (?) let no one in Hattusas do harm to a son of the (royal) family, or thrust a dagger into him.

28

(36) Let a prince, a son of the first (wife), be king. (36) If there is no prince of the first rank, let one who is a son of the second rank become king. (38) If, however, there is no prince, let them take a husband for her who is a daughter of the first rank, and let him become king.

29

(40) Whoever after me through all time shall become king, in those days let his brothers, his sons, his relatives-in-law, the members of his

aš-ši-iš LÚ.MEŠ *ḫa-aš-ša-an-na-aš-ša-aš Ù* ERÍN.MEŠ-*ŠU* (2.42) *ta-ru-up-pa-an-te-eš a-ša-an-du nu-za ú-wa-ši* ^{LÚ}KÚR-*an ut-ni-e ku-ut-ta-ni-i*[*t*] (2.43) *tar-aḫ-ḫa-an ḫar-ši ki-iš-ša-an-na li-e te-e-ši ar-ḫa-wa pár-ku-nu-um-mi* (2.44) *pár-ku-nu-ši-ma-za Ú-UL ku-it nu-za an-da im-ma ḫa-at-ki-iš-nu-ši* (2.45) *ḫa-aš-ša-an-na-ša-an-za-kán li-e ku-in-ki ku-en-ti Ú-UL* SIG$_5$-*in*

30

(2.46) *nam-ma ku-i-ša* LUGAL-*uš ki-ša-ri nu* ŠEŠ-*aš* NIN-*aš i-da-a-lu ša-an-aḫ-zi* (2.47) *šu-me-eš-ša pa-an-ku-uš-ši nu-uš-ši kar-ši te-it-te-en ki-i-wa e-eš-na-aš ut-tar* (2.48) *tup-pí-az a-ú ka-ru-ú-wa e-eš-ḫar* ^{URU}*Ḫa-at-tu-ši ma-ak-ki-eš-ta* (2.49) *nu-wa-ra-ta-pa* DINGIR.MEŠ-*iš šal-la-i ḫa-aš-ša-an-na-i da-a-ir*

31

(2.50) *ku-iš* ŠEŠ.MEŠ-*na* NIN.MEŠ-*na iš-tar-na i-da-a-lu i-ya-zi nu* LUGAL-*wa-aš* (2.51) *ḫar-aš-ša-na-za šu-wa-a-i-e-iz-zi nu tu-li-ya-an ḫal-zi-iš-tin ma-a-na-pa ut-tar-š*[*e-i*]*t pa-iz-zi* (2.52) *nu* SAG.DU-*na-az šar-ni-ik-du du-ud-du-mi-li-ma* ^{I}*Zu-ru-wa-aš* (2.53) ^{I}*Da-a-nu-wa-aš* ^{I}*Ta-ḫar-wa-i-li-ya-aš* ^{I}*Ta-ru-uḫ-šu-uš-ša i-wa-ar li-e* [*k*]*u-na-an-zi* (2.54) É-*ri-iš-ši-iš-ši A-NA* DAM-*ŠU* DUMU.MEŠ-*ŠU i-da-a-lu li-e ták-ki-iš-ša-an-zi* (2.55) *ták-ku* DUMU.LUGAL-*ma wa-aš-ta-i nu* SAG.DU-*az-be šar-ni-ik-du A-NA* É-*ŠU-ma-aš-ši-iš-ša-an* (2.56) [*Ù*] *A-NA* DUMU. MEŠ-*ŠU i-da-a-lu li-e ták-ki-iš-ša-an-zi* DUMU.MEŠ.LUGAL-*ma ku-e-da-ni* (2.57) [*še-i*]*r ḫar-ki-iš-kán-ta-ri Ú-UL A-NA* É.MEŠ-*ŠU-NU* A.ŠA(G).ḪI.A-*ŠU-NU* ^{GIŠ}ŠAR GEŠTIN.ḪI.A-*ŠU-NU* (2.58) [KIS-L]AḪ.ḪI.A-*ŠU-NU* SAG.GÌM.ERUM.MEŠ-*ŠU-NU* GUD.ḪI.A-*ŠU-NU* UDU.ḪI.A-*ŠU-NU*

32

(2.59) *ki-nu-na ma-a-an* DUMU.LUGAL *ku-iš-ki wa-aš-ta-i nu* SAG.DU-*az-be šar-ni-ik-du* (2.60) É-*ZU-ma-aš-ši* DUMU-*ŠU-ya i-da-a-lu li-e tág-ga-aš-te-ni pí-ya-ni-ma ŠA* DUMU.MEŠ.LUGAL (2.61) UKÙ-*an* ^{GIŠ}ŠUB *Ú-UL a-a-ra ki-i-ma i-da-a-la-u-wa ud-da-a-ar ku-i-e-eš e-eš-ša-an-zi* (2.62) LÚ.MEŠ [ ] $^{LÚ.MEŠ}$*A-BU BI-TUM* GAL DUMU.MEŠ.É.GAL GAL *ME-ŠE-DI* GAL GEŠTIN-*ya* (2.63) [*nu ku-it*] É.MEŠ DUMU.LUGAL *da-an-na i-la-li-ya-an-zi nu ki-iš-ša-an da-ra-an-zi* (2.64) *a-ši-ma-an-wa* URU-*aš am-me-el ki-ša-ri nu-uš-ša-an A-NA* EN URU-*LIM i-da-a-lu* (2.65) *ták-ki-iš-ki-iz-zi*

family, and his soldiers be united; and you shall come (and) with (your) strength hold the hostile country in subjection. (43) But do not speak thus: 'I grant complete pardon,' (while) however, you pardon nothing and actually order (his) arrest. (45) Do not kill any member of the (royal) family; it leads to disaster.

30

(46) Whoever hereafter becomes king, and plans injury of brother or sister—you (are) his senate—speak to him frankly: 'Read in the tablet this tale of blood(shed). (48) Formerly in Hattusas blood(shed) became common; and at that time the gods exacted of the royal family the penalty for it.'

31

(50) Whatever (king) does harm among (his) brothers and sisters, risks his royal head; call the assembly. (51) If at that time he carries out his plan, let him atone with his head. (52) But let them not kill (him) secretly, in the manner of Zūrus, Tanuwas, Taharwailis, and Taruhsus. (54) Let them not contrive harm for his house, his wife, (and) his children. (55) If a prince does wrong, let him atone even with his head. (55) However, let them not contrive harm for his house and his children. (56) In whose ever behalf princes are destroyed (it does) not (apply) to their houses, their fields, their vineyards, their barns, their slaves, their cattle, (and) their sheep.

32

(59) And now when any prince does wrong, let him atone even with his head. (60) But do not contrive harm for his house and his son. (60) However, it (is) not right to give away the person (?) (or) property of the princes. (61) Whoever institute these injurious plans (whether) LÚ.MEŠ . . . , fathers of the house (?), chief of the palace servants, chief of the *Mešedi*, or chief of the cup-bearers, because they desire to take the holding of the prince, they say: 'Such and such a city would become mine', and they contrive harm for the lord of the city.

33

(2.66) *ki-nu-na ki-iz-za* UD-*az* ^{URU}*Ḫa-at-tu-ši* DUMU.MEŠ.É.GAL LÚ.MEŠ *ME-ŠE-DI* $^{\text{LÚ.MEŠ}}$IŠ.GUŠKIN (2.67) $^{\text{LÚ.MEŠ}}$QA.ŠU.DU$_8$.A LÚ.[MEŠ ^{GIŠ}B]AN[ŠU]R $^{\text{LÚ.MEŠ}}$MU LÚ.MEŠ ^{GIŠ}PA $^{\text{LÚ.MEŠ}}$*ša-la-aš-ḫi-ya-aš* (2.68) $^{\text{LÚ.MEŠ}}$PA *LI-*[*IM ṢE-RI*] *ki-i ut-tar šu-ma-a-aš* EGIR-*an še-ik-tin* ^{I}*Ta-nu-wa-aš-ma* (2.69) ^{I}*Ta-ḫar-wa-i-li-iš* ^{I}*Ta-ru-uḫ-šu-uš-ša I-NA PA-NI-KU-NU* IZKIM-*iš e-eš-d*[*u*] (2.70) *nam-ma i-da-lu m*[*a-a-an k*]*u-iš-ki i-ya-zi na-aš-šu* ^{LÚ}*A-BU BI-DU* (2.71) [*na-aš-ma* GAL DUMU.MEŠ.É.GAL GAL G]EŠTIN GAL *ME-ŠE-DI* GAL $^{\text{LÚ.MEŠ}}$PA *LI-IM ṢE-RI* (2.72) .... [ ]-*zi šu-ma-aš-ša pa-an-ku-uš an-da e-*[*ip-tin*] (2.73) *nu-uš-ma-ša-an ka-ri-ip-tin*

* * * * *

49

(4.19) *iš-ḫa-na-aš-ša ut-tar ki-iš-ša-an ku-iš e-eš-ḫar i-e-iz-zi nu ku-it e-eš-ḫa-na-aš-be* (4.20) *iš-ḫa-a-aš te-iz-zi ták-ku te-iz-zi a-ku-wa-ra-aš na-aš a-ku ták-ku te-iz-zi-ma* (4.21) *šar-ni-ik-du-wa nu šar-ni-ik-du* LUGAL-*i-ma-pa li-e ku-it-ki*

50

(4.22) ^{URU}*Ḫa-at-tu-ši al-wa-an-za-an-na-aš na-aš-ta ud-da-a-ar pár-ku-nu-uš-kit*$_9$*-tin* (4.23) *ku-iš-za ḫa-aš-ša-an-na iš-tar-na al-wa-an-za-tar ša-ak-ki šu-me-e-ša-an* (4.24) *ḫa-aš-ša-an-na-an-za e-ip-tin na-an A-NA* KÁ É.GAL *ú-wa-te-it-tin* (4.25) [*ku-i*]*-ša-an Ú-UL-ma ú-wa-te-iz-zi nu ú-iz-zi* (4.26) *a-pí-e-da-ni-be* UKÙ-*ši* É-*ri-iš-ši-be i-da-la-u-e-eš-zi*

(4.27) DUB 1.KAM (4.28) *ŠA* ^{I}*TE-LI-PÍ-NU QA-TI*

33

(66) And now from this day in Hattusas, do you, palace servants, *Mešedi*, golden grooms, cup-bearers, table-men, cooks, scepter-bearers, *salashiyas*, (and) exalted captains of a thousand, remember this matter. (68) Moreover, let Tanuwas, Taharwailis, and Taruhsus be a sign for you. (70) If hereafter anyone does wrong, either the father of the house (?), or the chief of the palace servants, (or) the chief of the cup-bearers, (or) the chief of the *Mešedi*, (or) the chief of the exalted captains of a thousand, . . . , and do you, the senate, have (him) brought before you and punish him.

* * * * *

49

(19) And a case of murder is as follows. (19) Whoever commits murder, whatever the heir himself of the murdered man says; if he says: 'Let him die', he shall die; but if he says: 'Let him make restitution', he shall make restitution. (21) At such a time, however, let no (plea be made) to the king.

50

(22) In Hattusas hereafter exorcise everything that has to do with sorcery. (23) Whoever in the (royal) family knows sorcery, do you, the (royal) family, seize him, and deliver him to the king's gate. (25) But whoever does not deliver him, he (i.e. the sorcerer?) will come (and) turn against that very man and his house.

---

(27) One tablet of Telipinus is finished.

COMMENTARY

The Telipinus text, of about the middle of the seventeenth century B.C., is our most important source for the history of the first Hittite empire. It is not, however, primarily a historical document. The author sketches the reigns of his predecessors and the events at the time of his own accession to show that harmony in the royal family and the army leads to the prosperity of the family and of the state, and that the assassination of princes must by all means be checked. We do not know whether the provisions of this edict had the desired effect; nothing further is known about the history of Hattusas for some two hundred years.

In spite of its early date the proclamation of Telipinus differs but little in language from the documents composed under the later monarchy. No doubt its great legal importance led to frequent copying and consequent modernization. Among the archaisms still remaining are the frequent use of the enclitic *-apa* 'then' and the use of the phrase *tar-aḫ-ḫa-an ḫar-ta* (1.6) in its full etymological value (see the note). An orthographic archaism is the phonetic writing of the possessive enclitics, *-še-eš*, *-ša-aš* (1.3), etc., where later texts would exhibit Akkadian *-ŠU*, etc.

The text given here is virtually that of Forrer, 2 BoTU 23. All or parts of it have been translated by Hrozný, BoSt. 3.90–129; Witzel, Hethitische Keilschrifturkunden 1.44–59; Friedrich, AO 24.3.6–9, 21 f.; Cavaignac, RHA 1.9–14. Important comments have been published by Friedrich, ZA NF 2.274–7, 282 f.; Forrer, 2 BoTU pp. 11* ff.; Götze, AO 27.2.16–21.

The line numbers printed above are based upon KBo.3.1 for the first two columns, except that each line of the first column has had to be increased by 1, and upon KUB 11.1 for the fourth column.

1.2. [I]*La-ba-ar-na-aš*, the founder of the Old Hittite empire, ruled ca. 1800 B.C. (a half-century earlier according to the chronology of Thureau-Dangin, RA 24.181-98). The scribes of a later day sometimes confused his name with the Luwian (?) title *taparnas* (see on H 1.1); but usually the two words are kept distinct, as here. Hrozný, BoSt 5.49–53, JSOR 6.63–73, traces both words to an imaginary Hattic **Tlabarna*, although there is no further evidence for his supposed Hattic sound 'between *t* and *l'*, which might be represented in cuneiform either by *t* or by *l*. Sommer, OLZ 24.316 f., expressed doubt of Hrozný's theory, and he still distinguishes between the title with initial *t* and the king's name with *L* (AU 319). A decisive argument against Hrozný is the evident etymological connection of *taparnas* with the Luwian (?) verb *tapar-* 'rule, govern'. This verb is certainly not Hattic; and even if it were, it would not be probable that the founder of the royal line was named *King*.

1.5. *la-aḫ-ḫa*: in this text the end of motion is commonly expressed by forms in *a*; see [195f.].

1.6. *tar-aḫ-ḫa-an ḫar-ta*: here the participle and *har*(*k*)- 'have, hold' retain their full meaning; phrases of this sort in the later language have perfect (or past perfect) value, as in H 1.29; see [439].

1.7. *tar-ra-nu-ut*: the meaning is very doubtful; see Friedrich, Vert. 1. 153.

1.8. *nu-uš* . . . *i-e-it*: the antecedent of *-us* must be *ut-ne-e*, but it agrees with the predicate noun. The sentence apparently means 'extended them to the sea'.

1.9. DUMU.MEŠ *ku-iš-ša*: a sort of partitive apposition.

1.10 f. URU*Ḫu-piš-na* . . . URU*Lu-uš-na*: some at least of these towns lay in the Lower Country, to the south of Hattusas. Tuwanuwas may be the later Tyana.

1.19. *a-pí-e-el-la*: *-a* 'and' is equivalent to *nu* (1.11). Contrast *-a* 'also' (1.16).

1.21. ERUM.MEŠ: these seem to be people of the subjected towns, which had been given to the princes. — É.MEŠ-*ŠU-NU*: the key to the meaning is supplied by É.MEŠ DUMU.LUGAL in 2.63, which is defined in the next line as *asi* URU-*as* 'such and such a city'.

1.22 f. *da-a-ir* . . . *da-a-ir* . . . *ti-i-e-ir*: elsewhere also supine phrases in pret. 3 pl. vary between these two forms. Usually *da-a-ir* is a form of *dā-* 'take'; but since such phrases never contain any other form that is more easily derived from *dā-* than from *dai-*, and since *da-a-ir* certainly appears elsewhere as a form of *dai-* (e.g. 2.22 below — cf. also *na-a-ir* from *nai-* 'lead, turn, drive'), probably *da-a-ir* with the supine is from *dai-*; so [161b and fn.31]. Götze, Hatt. 66 ff., takes *da-a-ir* in these phrases from *dā-*, and he tries to find a semantic difference between the supine with *dai-* and with *dā-*; but, if I understand him, he reverses the functions of the two verbs in AM 152 f. (KBo.5.8.2.4 f.). In MS 21 Götze argues that the use of *da-a-ir* and *ti-i-e-ir* in the same passage strongly opposes my view. I therefore call attention to the inconsistent forms of the supine in the passage just cited (*pi-iš-ki-u-an* from *peske/a-*

but *pa-iš-ga-u-wa-an* from *paiske/a-*), and to the use of inconsistent forms of the 1 pl. in KUB 15.32.1.50 f. (*ḫu-u-it-ti-ya-an-ni-eš-ki-u-wa-ni, ḫu-li-eš-ki-u-wa-ni mu-ki-iš-ga-u-e-ni*). — *iš-ḫa-ša-aš-ma-aš-ša-an*: *-a* 'and' is coordinate with *nu* (1.23).

1.28. URU*Ḫal-pa-aš*: in the later language inflected genitives from proper names are scarcely to be found (see on H 1.1 ff.). Other examples in this text are I*Pí-še-ni-ya-aš* (1.66), I*Ta-ḫar-wa-i-li-ya-aš* (2.53), I*Da-a-nu-wa-aš* (2.53), I*Ta-ru-uḫ-šu-uš* (2.53), I*Ti-it-ti-ya-aš* (2.7), I*Zi-dan-ta-aš* (1.69), I*Zu-ru-wa-aš* (2.52). — NAM.RA.MEŠ: properly, captive civilians. Cf. Götze, AM 217-20, and see Sommer, OLZ 38.280 f.

1.29. URUKÁ.DINGIR.RA *pa-it*: this Hittite raid is recorded also in a Babylonian chronicle, and can probably be dated ca. 1758 B.C. (ca. 1806 according to Thureau-Dangin, RA 24.181-98). It put an end to the dynasty of Hammurabi, and left the way open for the invasion of the Kassites.

1.30. [LÚ.ME]Š*Ḫur-lu-uš*: the casual way in which the Hurrians are brought into the account is striking; but there is nothing strange about a battle with this people in northern Mesopotamia during the march to or from Babylon.

1.31. I*Ḫa-an-ti-l[i-iš]*: see H 3.46 and note. — SAL*Ḫa-r[a-a]p-[ši]-li-in*: the reading is very doubtful.

1.32. [NIN]: KUB 11.1.1.31 reads DAM 'wife', but this sign and NIN are so similar that an error is easily possible.

1.32 f. *ša-ra-a ú-li-eš-ta*: the meaning given is purely conjectural.

1.33. *ut-t[ar i-e-i]r*: Götze, Ausgewählte Hethitische Texte 5, reads *ut-ta[r e-eš-še-i]r*, for which the space is insufficient. Sommer, AU 303 f., has shown that the verbs *iya-* and *essā-* correspond in use somewhat as do simplex and derivative in *ske/a-*. As to the noun we follow Forrer and Götze; but, if Figulla's copy (KBo.3.1.1.33) is correct, the restoration is improbable. Perhaps we should read *ut-t[a-ni-e-i]r*, although this verb elsewhere means 'conjure' rather than 'plot'.

1.36–62 survive only in fragments. They contained the account of Hantilis' reign.

1.63. DINGIR-*L[IM-iš] ki-ik-ki-iš-šu-u-wa-an*: for the meaning, see on H 1.22.

1.66. *ša-an-ḫi-ir*: see on I 1.35.

1.70 f. The supplements are uncertain.

2.3. *la-aḫ-ḫa-an*: so KUB 11.1.2.9. The asyndeton is tautological. — ERÍN.MEŠ-*uš*: apparently nom. sg.; but cf. ERÍN.MEŠ-*az* (H 2.37) and ERÍN.MEŠ-*za* (T 2.18). — *pa-iz-zi, ú-i-iš-kán-ta*: historical presents.

2.6. *ḫa-aš-ša-an-na-aš-ša-aš*: i.e. Taharwailis was a legitimate son.

2.7. One may infer that the family of Tittis, including his sons, were connections of the royal family.

2.8. [I]*Ḫa-an-ti-li-in*: probably not the king who was about to die in 1.64.

2.11. *ku-en-ta*: this usage reminds one of the Latin conative imperfect. It is surprising not to find the durative here.

2.12. *nu-uš*: the sequel suggests that *-us* refers to Huzziyas and his five brothers.

2.15. *tág-ga-aš-ši*: since *taks-* usually follows the *mi*-conjugation, it seems safer to regard this as 2 sg. Possibly, however, it is 3 sg. of the *hi*-conjugation; in which case read *ku-[iš-ki]* in 2.14. — *nu tar-ši-ki-mi*: perhaps not part of the quotation; but *-wa* is sometimes omitted, as in A 3.37–45, and the mythological passages listed by Friedrich, ZA NF 5.43 f. — [*Ú-UL i-ya-mi*]: the supplement is suggested by Friedrich, AO 24.3.8.15.

2.18. ERÍN.MEŠ-*za-mi-iš-ša*: since *-za* stands before the enclitic pronoun and the conjunction, it must be a phonetic complement, rather than the particle; see on ERÍN.MEŠ-*az* (H 2.37). — [URU]*Zi-iz-zi-li-ip-pí* may equally well be dat. of an *i*-stem.

2.21. Friedrich, AO 24.3.8, translates 'und empörte sich gegen Lawazzantija'. It must be admitted that the verb is elsewhere intransitive.

2.22. *da-a-ir* is normally from *dā-* 'take'; but see on 1.22 f.

2.22 ff. It is unsatisfactory to make the several names follow the corresponding titles. Götze would assume more extensive loss at the ends of certain lines, and translate about as follows: 'And the chief commander of a thousand; . . . , . . . ; (23) Karruwas, chief of the overseers of the treasury; Inaras, chief of the cup-bearers; Killas, . . . ; (24) Dattamimmas, chief of the scepter-bearers; Zinwaselis and Killas, . . . , (25) (were) great (men).'

2.24. [I D]U-*mi-im-ma-aš*: the phonetic interpretation of the ideogram is uncertain; see on H 1.27.

2.25. [I]*Ta-nu-u-i*: the situation is clearly parallel to that in 2.5 ff. and in 2.8 f. We should expect an accusative to match *Taharwailin* (2.6) and *Taruhsun* (2.8), and we want a following sentence to record the performance of Tanuwas' mission, namely the murder of Huzziyas and his brothers. Apparently the event was so recent and so well known that a mere hint was enough. Cf. Cavaignac, RHA 1.8–11.

2.26. *š[a-ag-ga-aḫ-ḫ]u-un*: the supplement is Götze's. — The rest of the line seems hopeless.

2.28. *pa-an-ku-uš*: the word properly means 'the entirety', presumably 'the whole body of nobles'. It appears again in 2.47, where this body is to intervene if the king plans to harm any of his relatives. Apparently the same body (2.51) is to call together the assembly for the trial of a member of the royal family. It reminds one of the early Roman senate as represented by Livy. Cf. Götze, AO 27.2.20. — *pa-ra-a ḫi-in-ga-ni*: the adverb suggests that *ḫenkan* is here to be taken in its etymological value as a verbal noun from *henk-* 'fix, determine' rather than in its usual meaning 'fate, death'.

2.29. IGI.ḪI.A-*wa* seems to be in partitive apposition with *-us*; but the whole sentence is obscure.

2.30. ^{GIŠ}TUKUL.ḪI.A-*uš-šu-uš-ta* = ^{GIŠ}TUKUL.ḪI.A-*us* + *sus* + *sta*; cf. Sommer, AU 89, fn. 1. — ^{GIŠ}Š[UDUN]: the supplement is unsatisfactory. Some agricultural implement is required by the context, if we have correctly inferred that; ^{GIŠ}APIN would not fit the traces on the tablet.

2.32. BA.UG$_6$: no doubt by violence. — *ú-it* . . . BA.UG$_6$: literally 'came (and) died'; cf. American Eng. *went and died.* — *ši-ú-na-an*: Götze compares *ši-ú-ni-ya-aḫ-ḫa-ti* (KUB 11.1.4.15 = 2 BoTU 23 B) and *ši-e-ú-ni-aḫ-ta* (Code § 163). In the latter passage, at least, the verb seems to mean 'put a mark of ownership upon', perhaps 'brand (cattle)'; and so the noun may mean 'a brand, a stamp, a label'. See on C 3.37. — *tar-ši-ik-kán-zi* is from *tarna-*.

2.34. The immediately preceding lines bring the narrative to an end, and this line introduces the account of Telipinus' action in the matter, the main burden of the document. At this crucial point we are told that an assembly is called, and henceforth the king is clearly addressing his subjects directly. Probably, then, the assembly was called to hear the royal proclamation which constitutes our text. — *ki-it-pa-da-la-az*: for the reading, cf. Götze, NBr. 5; on the omission of the nasal, see [57].

2.36. *ki-ik-ki-i*[*t*]*-ta-ru*: Forrer's supplement gives us an otherwise unknown verb, and so some may prefer to read *ki-ik-ki-i*[*š*]*-ta-ru*. Furthermore, a reduplicated present from *ki-* 'lie' would probably retain the static meaning of the primitive, and the context may be thought to favor the meaning 'become'. Nevertheless we follow Forrer in the belief that the remains of the character must point to *i*[*t*] rather than to *i*[*š*].

2.36–9 are translated by Götze, AOr. 2.158.

2.37. *ḫa-an-te-iz-zi-iš* must be interpreted to harmonize with *ta-a-an pí-e-da-aš*. — *ta-a-an pí-e-da-aš* DUMU-*RU*: no doubt a son of a secondary wife.

2.45. *ḫa-aš-ša-an-na-ša-an-za-kán* can scarcely be *hassanas-san-za-kan* (cf. Friedrich, ZA 2.282 f.), since the particle *-san* does not elsewhere appear with *-kan* or before *-za* (Götze, AOr. 5.30 f.). Hence we assume a derivative *hassannasas* with suffix *(a)sas* [178]. Another possibility is that the second *ša* is an erroneous repetition of the first; note *ša-an* in both places. — *Ú.UL* SIG$_5$-*in* = *natta lazzin* is very common in the omen texts, where it means 'not favorably'. Of course the phrase had no such trivial connotation as we are prone to feel in it.

2.49. Götze, AO 27.2.20, translates, 'und nun haben ihn die Götter der Königsfamilie genommen'. — *ḫa-aš-ša-an-na-i*: this metaplastic dat. should be added to the forms given in [216].

2.50. *ku-iš*: for the postponement of the substantive to the next clause, cf. on *kat-te-ir-ra-aḫ-ḫi-ir* (H 3.78). — ŠEŠ.MEŠ-*na* NIN.MEŠ-*na*: in spite of the Sumerian plural suffix, the phonetic complement shows that the underlying Hittite words are singular; see [182, 183]. They are probably datives of *a*-stems.

2.50 f. LUGAL-*wa-aš* . . . *šu-wa-a-i-e-iz-zi*: 'gives security with the king's head.'

2.51. *ḫal-zi-iš-tin*: see on *pa-an-ku-uš* (2.28). — *pa-iz-zi*: 'proceeds to'. Götze, AO 27.2.20: 'und wenn dann seine Sache zur Entscheidung kommt'.

2.53. [I]*Ta-ru-uḫ-šu-uš*: for the form, cf. [194].

2.54. *É-ri-iš-ši-iš-ši*: if this is not mere dittography, it is equivalent to Latin 'suo sibi'.

2.56 f. *ku-e-da-ni še-ir*: i.e. even if they are executed for an attempt upon the life of the king.

2.58. [KISL]AḪ.ḪI.A: the supplement is Götze's; see Friedrich, ZA NF 2.283.

2.59. *ma-a-an*: in early texts the word means 'when' rather than 'if'; so Götze.

2.60. *pí-ya-ni* = *piyanna*, infinitive of *pai-* 'give'. Cf. KBo.5.4.1.38 (Friedrich, Vert. 1.58): EGIR-*pa pí-ya-an-na Ú.UL a-a-ra*.

2.60 f. *ŠA* DUMU.MEŠ.LUGAL . . . [GIŠ]ŠUB: the interpretation is Götze's. One would expect ZI-*an* instead of UKÙ-*an*.

2.62. [LÚ.MEŠ]*A-BU BI-TUM*: carelessly written for *ABŪ BĪTI*.

2.63. [*nu ku-it*]: Götze suggests [*ták-ku*]. — *i-la-li-ya-an-zi*: KBo. 3.1.2.63 has the impossible *i-da-la-li-ya-an-zi*; KUB 11.6.10: *i-la-l*[.

2.64. So interpreted by Friedrich, ZA NF 2.288.

2.65. *ták-ki-iš-ki-iz-zi*: English idiom requires us to follow the number of the preceding verbs in the translation.

2.69. IZKIM-*iš*: perhaps the underlying Hittite word is *sagais*. Despite Cavaignac, RHA 1.10, the context forbids us to read the sign AGRIG (or ABRIG) 'vizier', even if that meaning were elsewhere attested.

2.73. *nu-uš-ma-ša-an* = *nu-smas-an*.

2.74–4.19. The surviving fragments indicate that these paragraphs contained various provisions for the reorganization of the government.

4.19 f. *e-eš-ḫa-na-aš iš-ḫa-a-aš* 'the master of the blood': cf. EN *DINI* (H 1.54, etc.). The duty of avenging murder rested upon the murdered man's heir.

4.21. *šar-ni-ik-du*: the rates of restitution are prescribed in the first six paragraphs of the code (below pp. 210 f.).

4.22. *na-aš-ta* usually stands at the head of its clause, as in H 2.55. — *pár-ku-nu-uš-kit₉-tin*: *parkunu-*, with personal object, often means 'acquit, forgive'; but such a meaning with the name of a crime as object is difficult. At any rate, the remainder of the paragraph forbids that interpretation here. The meaning must be 'clean out, eradicate'.

4.23. *ḫa-aš-ša-an-na*: so KBo.3.67.4.11. The final *an* of KUB 11.1.4. 23 is probably due to *ḫa-aš-ša-an-na-an-za* in the next line.

4.25. *nu ú-iz-zi*: in case of a change of subject a pronoun is normally employed. Since we have here *nu* instead of *na-aš*, Götze doubts the interpretation given in the translation.

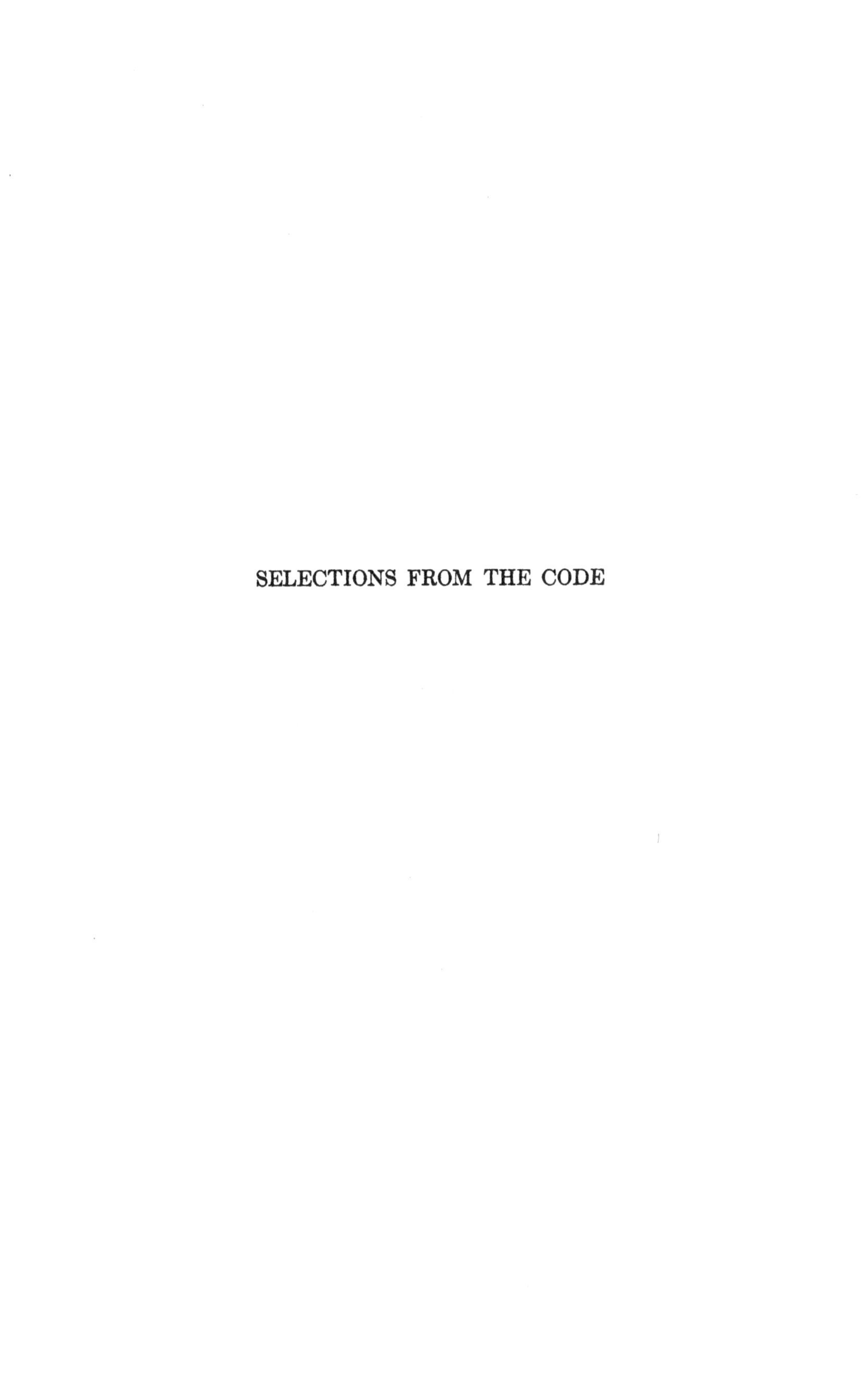

SELECTIONS FROM THE CODE

SELECTIONS FROM THE CODE

1.

2.

3.

4.

5.

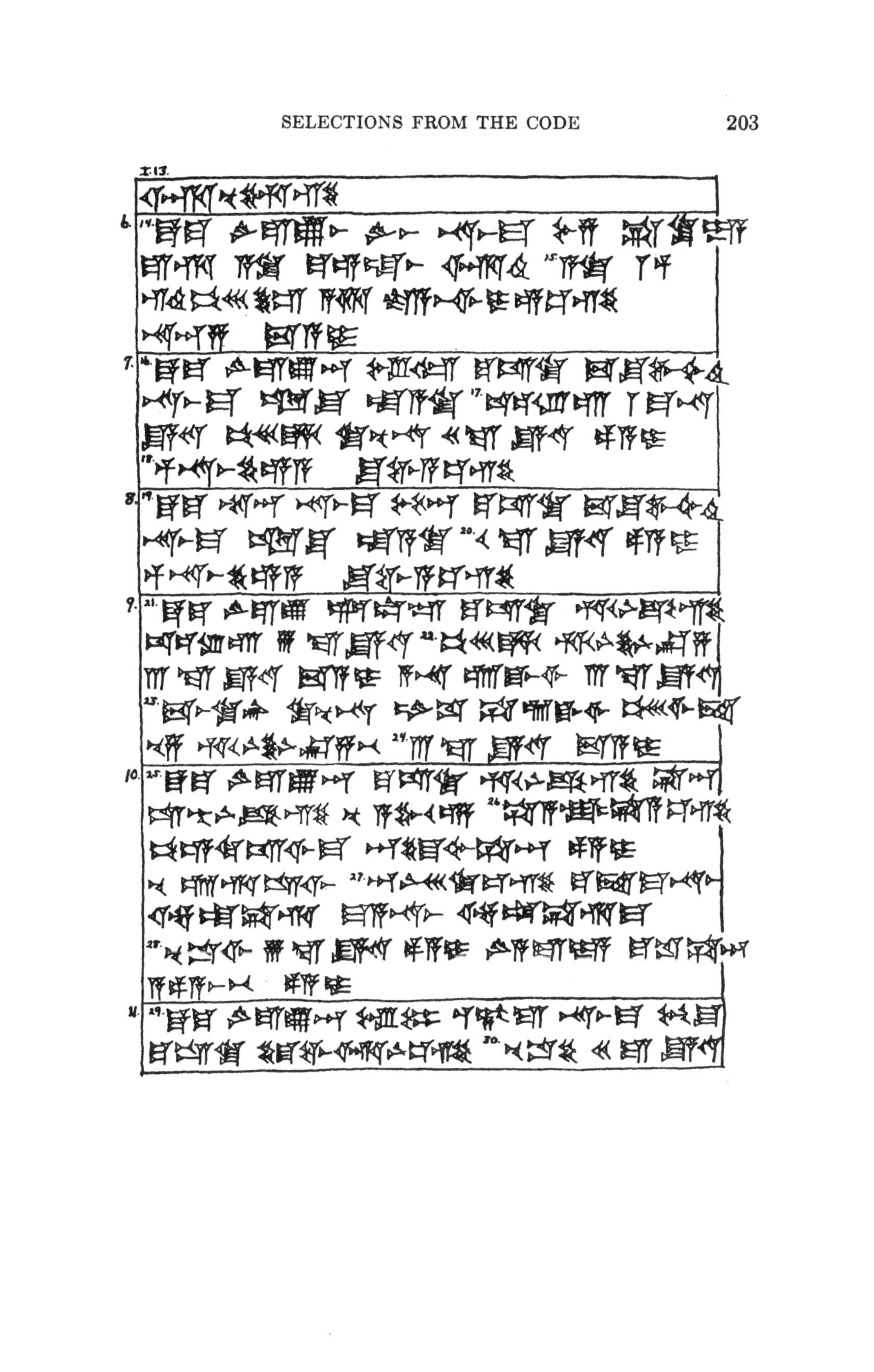

I. 13.

6.

7.

8.

9.

10.

11.

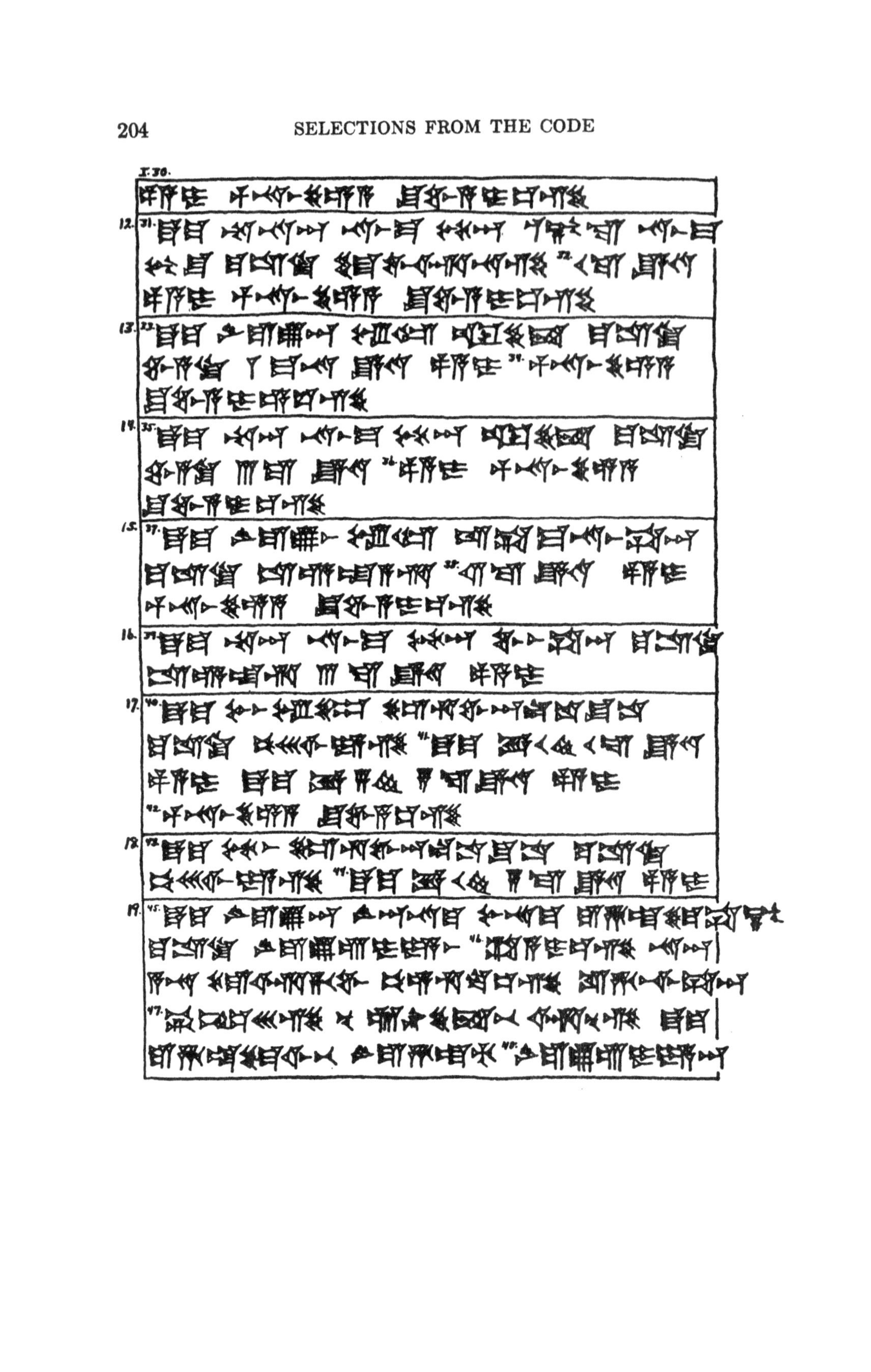

I. 30.

12.

13.

14.

15.

16.

17.

18.

19.

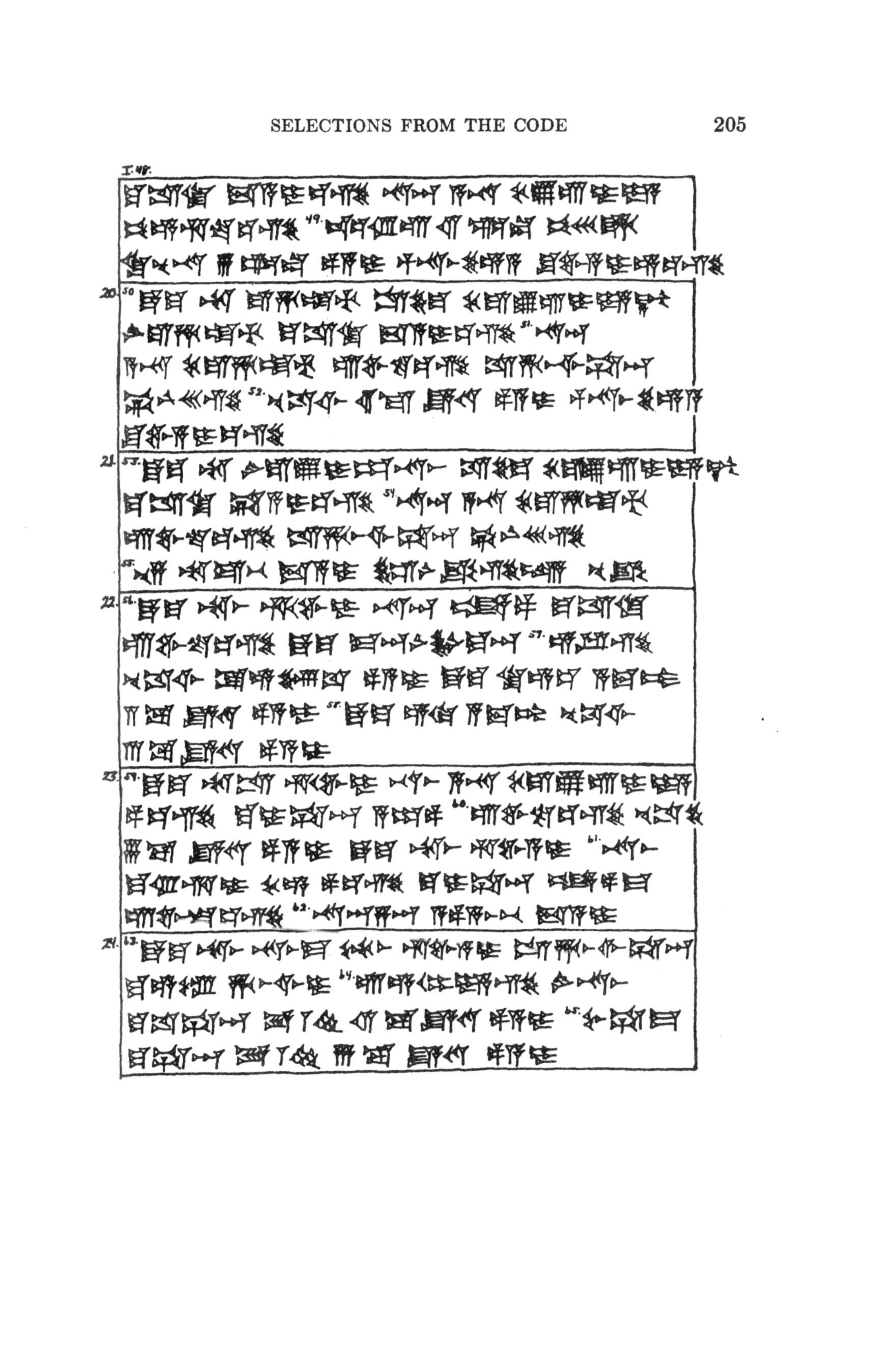

I. 48.

20.

21.

22.

23.

24.

I. 66.

25. 66. … 67. … 68. … 69. …

28. II. 5. … 6. … 7. … 8. … 9. … 10. …

29. 11. … 12. … 13. …

30. 14. … 15. …

31. 16. … 17. … 18. … 19. … 20. …

II. 21.

32. 21.

33. 22.

34. 23.
24.

35. 25.
26.

36. 27.
28.

37. 29.
30.

38. 31.
32.
33.

40. 37.
38.
39.
40.
41.
42.

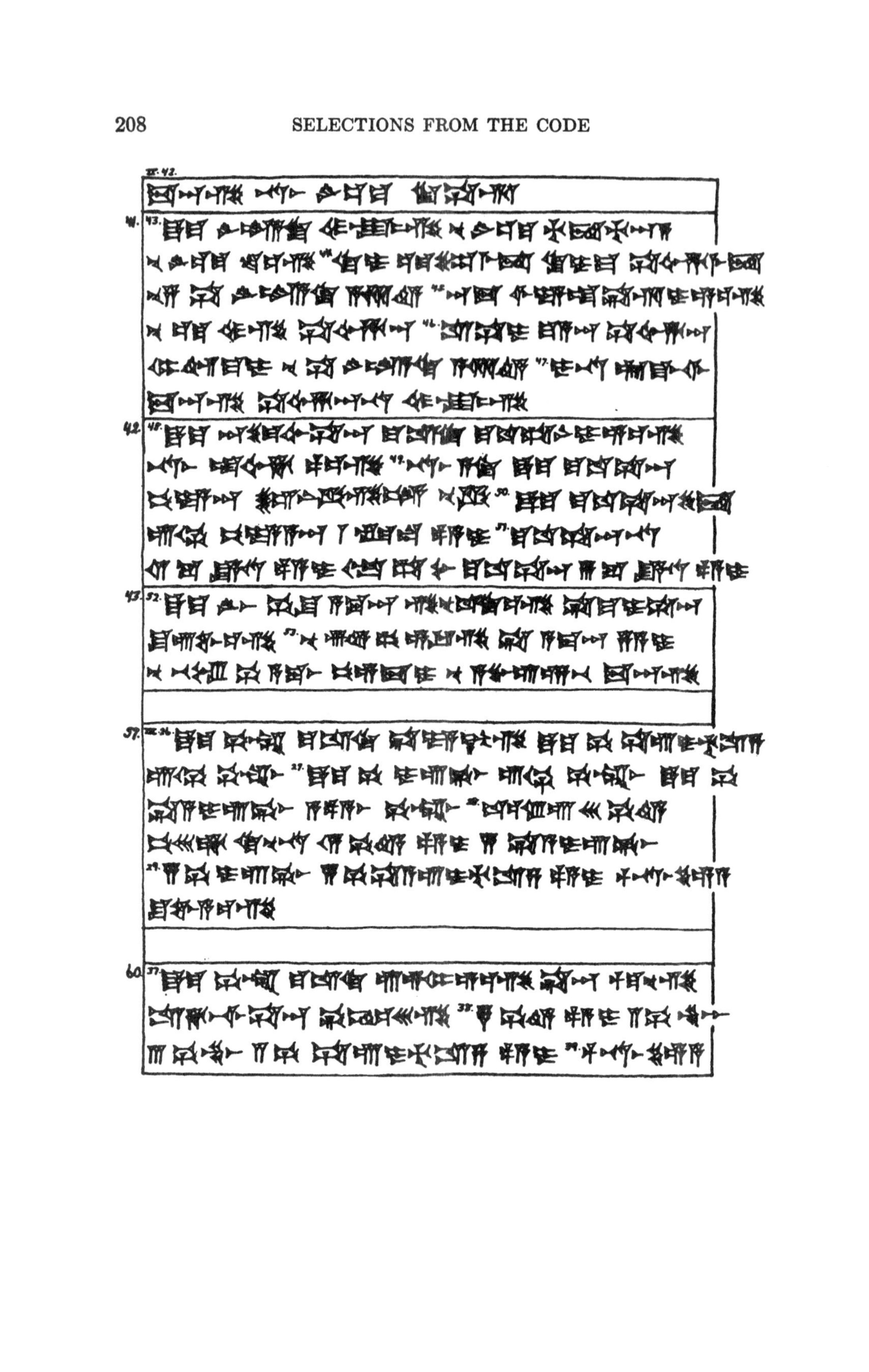

41.

42.

43.

57.

60.

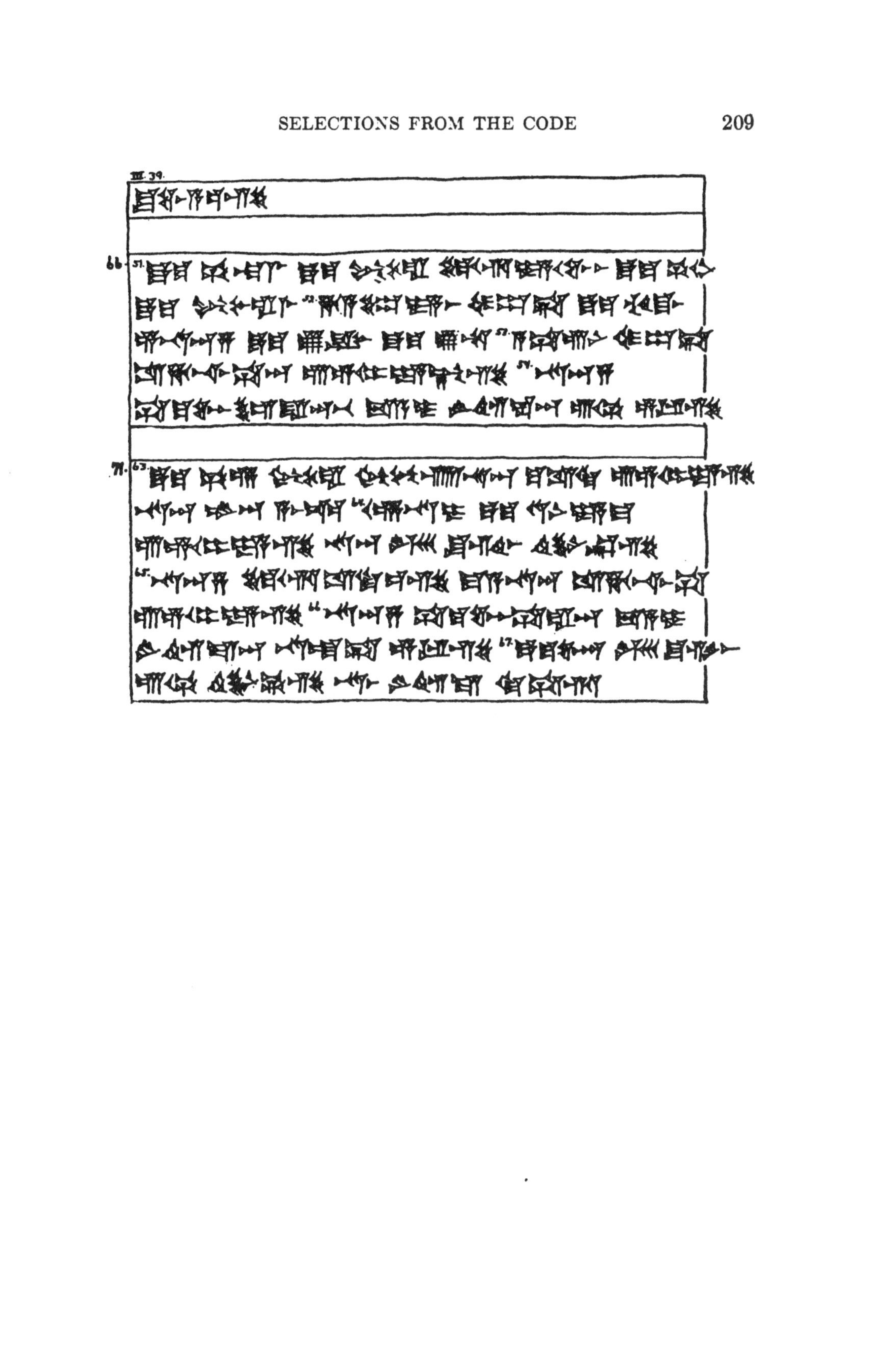

III. 39.

66.

71.

SELECTIONS FROM THE CODE

1

(1.1) *[ták-ku* LÚ*-an n]a-aš-ma* SAL*-an š[u-u]l-l[a-a]n-n[a-a]z ku-iš-ki ku-en-zi* (1.2) *[a-pu-u-un ar-nu-z]i Ú* 4 SAG.DU *pa-a-i* LÚ*-na-ku* SAL*-na-ku* (1.3) *[pár-na-aš-še-e-a] šu-wa-a-iz-zi*

2

(1.4) *[ták-ku* ERUM*-an] na-aš-ma* GÌM*-an šu-ul-la-an-na-az ku-iš-ki ku-en-zi a-pu-u-un ar-nu-zi* (1.5) [*Ú* 2 SA]G.[D]U *pa-a-i* LÚ*-na-ku* SAL*-na-ku pár-na-aš-še-e-a šu-wa-a-iz-zi*

3

(1.6) *[ták-ku* LÚ]*-an na-aš-ma* SAL*-an EL-LAM wa-al-aḫ-zi ku-iš-ki na-aš a-ki ki-eš-šar-ši-iš* (1.7) *[wa-aš-t]a-i a-pu-u-un ar-nu-zi Ú* 2 SAG.DU *pa-a-i pár-na-aš-še-e-a šu-wa-a-iz-zi*

4

(1.8) *[ták]-ku* ERUM*-an na-aš-ma* GÌM*-an ku-iš-ki wa-al-aḫ-zi na-aš a-ki QA-AZ-ZU wa-aš-ta-i* (1.9) *a-pu-u-un ar-nu-zi Ú* 1 SAG.DU*pa-a-i pár-na-aš-še-e-a šu-wa-a-iz-zi*

5

(1.10) *[ták]-ku* ^{LÚ}DAM.QAR ^{URU}*ḪA-AT-TI ku-iš-ki ku-en-zi* 1[$\frac{1}{2}$] *MA-NA* KUBABBAR *pa-a-i* (1.11) *pár-na-aš-še-e-a šu-wa-a-iz-zi ták-ku I-NA* KUR ^{URU}*LU-Ú-I-YA na-aš-ma I-NA* KUR ^{URU}*PA-LA-A* (1.12) 1[$\frac{1}{2}$] *MA-NA* KUBABBAR *pa-a-i a-aš-šu-se-it-ta šar-ni-ik-zi ma-a-an I-NA* KUR ^{URU}*ḪA-AT-TI* (1.13) *nu-za ú-na-at-tal-la-an-be ar-nu-uz-zi*

6

(1.14) *ták-ku* LÚ.GÀL.LU*-aš* LÚ*-aš na-aš-ma* SAL*-za ta-ki-ya* URU*-ri a-ki ku-e-la-aš ar-ḫi* (1.15) *a-ki* 1[$\frac{1}{2}$] ^{GI}*pí-eš-šar* A.ŠA(G) *kar-aš-ši-i-e-iz-zi na-an-za da-a-i*

7

(1.16) *ták-ku* LÚ.GÀL.LU*-an EL-LAM ku-iš-ki da-šu-wa-aḫ-ḫi na-aš-ma* KA×UD*-ŠU la-a-ki* (1.17) *ka-ru-ú* 1 *MA-NA* KUBABBAR *pí-eš-kir ki-nu-na* 20 *ZU* KUBABBAR *pa-a-i* (1.18) *pár-na-aš-še-e-a šu-wa-a-iz-zi*

SELECTIONS FROM THE CODE

1

(1) If anyone kills a man or a woman in a quarrel, he buries him and gives (as recompense) four persons, men or women (respectively); and he gives his farm buildings as security.

2

(4) If anyone kills a male or female slave in a quarrel, he buries him and gives (as recompense) two persons, men or women (respectively); and he gives his farm buildings as security.

3

(6) If anyone strikes a free man or woman and he dies, (if) his hand (alone) is at fault, he buries him and gives (as recompense) two persons; and he gives his farm buildings as security.

4

(8) If anyone strikes a male or female slave and he dies, (if) his hand (alone) is at fault, he buries him and gives (as recompense) one person; and he gives his farm buildings as security.

5

(10) If anyone kills a Hittite merchant, he pays one and a half pounds of silver, and gives his farm buildings as security; if in the country of Luwiyas or in the country of Palā, he pays a pound and a half of silver, and makes restitution for his goods; if in the country of Hatti, he buries the merchant himself.

6

(14) If a person, man or woman, dies in another (?) city, (the man) on whose farm he dies fences off one *pessar* and a half of a field, and buries him.

7

(16) If anyone blinds a free man or knocks out his teeth, formerly they paid one pound of silver, but now he pays twenty half-shekels of silver; and he gives his farm buildings as security.

8

(1.19) *ták-ku* ERUM-*an na-aš-ma* GÌM-*an ku-iš-ki da-šu-wa-aḫ-ḫi na-aš-ma* [KA×UD-Š]*U la-a-ki* (1.20) 10 *ZU* KUBABBAR *pa-a-i pár-na-aš-še-e-a šu-wa-a-iz-zi*

9

(1.21) *ták-ku* LÚ.GÀL.LU SAG.DU-*ZU ku-iš-ki ḫu-u-ni-ik-zi ka-ru-ú* 6 *ZU* KUBABBAR (1.22) *pí-eš-kir ḫu-u-ni-in-kán-za* 3 *ZU* KUBABBAR *da-a-i A-NA* É.GAL-*LIM* 3 *ZU* KUBABBAR (1.23) *da-aš-ki-ir ki-nu-na* LUGAL-*uš ŠA* É.GAL-*LIM pí-eš-ši-it nu-za ḫu-u-ni-*[*in*]*-kán-za-be* (1.24) 3 *ZU* KUBABBAR *da-a-i*

10

(1.25) [*t*]*ák-ku* LÚ.GÀL.LU-*an ku-iš-ki ḫu-u-ni-ik-zi ta-an iš-tar-ni-ik-zi nu a-pu-u-un* (1.26) *ša-a-ak-ta-a-iz-zi pí-e-di-iš-ši-ma an-tu-uḫ-ša-an pa-a-i nu* É-*ri-iš-ši* (1.27) *an-ni-eš-ki-iz-zi ku-it-ma-na-aš* SIG_5-*at-ta-ri ma-a-na-aš* SIG_5-*at-ta-ri-ma* (1.28) *nu-uš-ši* 6 *ZU* KUBABBAR *pa-a-i* [LÚ]A.ZU-*ya ku-uš-ša-an a-pa-a-aš-be pa-a-i*

11

(1.29) *ták-ku* LÚ.GÀL.LU-*an EL-LUM QA-AZ-ZU na-aš-ma* GÌR-*ŠU ku-iš-ki tu-wa-ar-ni-iz-zi* (1.30) *nu-uš-še* 20 *ZU* KUBABBAR *pa-a-i pár-na-aš-še-e-a šu-wa-a-i-iz-zi*

12

(1.31) *ták-ku* ERUM-*na-an na-aš-ma* GÌM-*an QA-AZ-ZU na-aš-ma* GÌR-*ŠU ku-iš-ki tu-wa-ar-na-zi* (1.32) 10 *ZU* KUBABBAR *pa-a-i pár-na-aš-še-e-a šu-wa-a-i-iz-zi*

13

(1.33) *ták-ku* LÚ.GÀL.LU-*an EL-LAM* KA×GAG-*še-it ku-iš-ki wa-a-ki* 1 *MA-NA* KUBABBAR *pa-a-i* (1.34) *pár-na-aš-še-e-a šu-wa-a-i-e-iz-zi*

14

(1.35) *ták-ku* ERUM-*an na-aš-ma* GÌM-*an* KA×GAG-*še-it ku-iš-ki wa-a-ki* 3 *ZU* KUBABBAR (1.36) *pa-a-i pár-na-aš-še-e-a šu-wa-a-i-iz-zi*

15

(1.37) *ták-ku* LÚ.GÀL.LU-*aš EL-LAM iš-ta-ma-na-aš-ša-an ku-iš-ki iš-kal-la-a-ri* (1.38) 12 *ZU* KUBABBAR *pa-a-i pár-na-aš-še-e-a šu-wa-a-i-iz-zi*

8

(19) If anyone blinds a male or female slave or knocks out his teeth, he pays ten half-shekels of silver; and he gives his farm buildings as security.

9

(21) If anyone has a man's head bewitched, formerly they paid six half-shekels of silver; the bewitched (man) gets three half-shekels of silver (and) they got three half-shekels of silver for the palace. (23) Now the king has remitted the (share) of the palace, and only the bewitched (man) gets three half-shekels of silver.

10

(25) If anyone has a man bewitched and he makes him ill, he takes care of (?) him, and in his place he furnishes a man, and he works in his house until he gets well. (27) But when he gets well, he pays him six half-shekels of silver, and the same man pays the physician his fee.

11

(29) If anyone breaks a free man's arm or leg, he pays him 20 half-shekels of silver; and he gives his farm buildings as security.

12

(31) If anyone breaks the arm or leg of a male or female slave, he pays ten half-shekels of silver; and he gives his farm buildings as security.

13

(33) If anyone bites a free man's nose, he pays a pound of silver; and he gives his farm buildings as security.

14

(35) If anyone bites the nose of a male or female slave, he pays three half-shekels of silver; and he gives his farm buildings as security.

15

(37) If anyone mutilates the ear of a free man, he pays twelve half-shekels of silver; and he gives his farm buildings as security.

16

(1.39) *ták-ku* ERUM-*an na-aš-ma* GÌM-*an* GEŠTUG-*aš-ša-an ku-iš-ki iš-kal-la-ri* 3 *ZU* KUBABBAR *pa-a-i*

17

(1.40) *ták-ku* SAL-*aš EL-LI šar-ḫu-wa-an-du-uš-šu-uš ku-iš-ki pí-eš-ši-ya-zi* (1.41) [*ták-k*]*u* ITU 10.KAM 10 *ZU* KUBABBAR *pa-a-i ták-ku* ITU 5.KAM 5 *ZU* KUB[ABBAR] *pa-a-i* (1.42) *pár-na-aš-še-e-a šu-wa-a-iz-zi*

18

(1.43) *ták-ku* GÌM-*aš šar-ḫu-wa-an-d*[*u-u*]*š-šu-uš ku-iš-ki pí-eš-ši-ya-zi* (1.44) *ták-ku* ITU 10.KAM 5 *ZU* KUBABBAR *pa-a-i*

19

(1.45) [*t*]*ák-ku* LÚ.GÀL.LU-*an* LÚ-*an-na-ku* SAL-*na-ku* URU*Ḫa-at-tu-ša-az ku-i*[*š-ki*] LÚ URU*Lu-ú-i-ya-*[*aš*] (1.46) *ta-a-i-iz-zi na-an A-NA* KUR URU*AR-ZA-U-WA pí-e-ḫu-te-iz-z*[*i i*]*š-ḫa-aš-ši-ša-an* (1.47) *ga-ne-eš-zi nu* É-*ir-še-it-be ar-nu-zi ták-ku* URU*Ḫa-at-*[*t*]*u-ši-be* LÚ URU*ḪA-AT-TI* (1.48) LÚ URU*Lu-ú-i-ya-an ku-iš-ki da-a-i-iz-zi na-an A-NA* KUR *LU-Ú-I-YA pí-e-ḫu-te-iz-zi* (1.49) *ka-ru-ú* 12 SAG.DU *pí-eš-kir ki-nu-na* 6 SAG.DU *pa-a-i pár-na-aš-še-e-a šu-wa-a-i-e-iz-zi*

20

(1.50) *ták-ku* ERUM URU*ḪA-AT-TI IŠ-TU* KUR URU*Lu-ú-i-ya-az* LÚ URU*ḪA-AT-TI ku-iš-ki da-a-i-iz-zi* (1.51) *na-an A-NA* KUR URU*ḪA-AT-TI ú-wa-te-iz-zi iš-ḫa-aš-ši-ša-an ga-ni-eš-zi* (1.52) *nu-uš-ši* 12 *ZU* KUBABBAR *pa-a-i pár-na-aš-še-e-a šu-wa-a-i-iz-zi*

21

(1.53) [*tá*]*k-ku* ERUM LÚ URU*Lu-i-um-na-aš IŠ-TU* KUR URU*Lu-ú-i-ya-az ku-iš-ki ta-a-i-iz-zi* (1.54) *na-an A-NA* KUR URU*ḪA-AT-TI ú-wa-te-iz-zi iš-ḫa-aš-ši-ša-an ga-ni-eš-zi* (1.55) *nu-za* ERUM-*ZU-be da-a-i šar-ni-ik-zi-il* NU.GÀL

22

(1.56) *ták-ku* ERUM-*aš ḫu-u-wa-i na-an* EGIR-*pa ku-iš-ki ú-wa-te-iz-zi ták-ku ma-an-ni-in-ku-an* (1.57) *e-ip-zi nu-uš-ši* KUŠE.SIR-*uš pa-a-i ták-ku ki-e-iz* ÍD-*az* 2 *ZU* KUBABBAR *pa-a-i* (1.58) *ták-ku e-di* ÍD-*az nu-uš-ši* 3 *ZU* KUBABBAR *pa-a-i*

16

(39) If anyone mutilates the ear of a male or female slave, he pays three half-shekels of silver.

17

(40) If anyone causes a free woman to miscarry, if (it is) the tenth month, he pays ten half-shekels of silver; if (it is) the fifth month, he pays five half-shekels of silver; and he gives his farm buildings as security.

18

(43) If anyone causes a slave woman to miscarry, if (it is) the tenth month, he pays five half-shekels of silver.

19

(45) If any Luwiyan man steals a person, whether man or woman, from Hattusas, and takes him to the country of Arzawa, (and) his master finds him, he brings (to Hattusas) his (i.e. the Luwiyan's) entire household. (47) If in Hattusas any Hittite man steals a Luwiyan man, and takes him to the country of Luwiyas, formerly they gave in recompense twelve persons, and now he gives six persons; and he gives his farm buildings as security.

20

(50) If any Hittite man steals a Hittite slave from the country of Luwiyas, and brings him to the country of Hatti, (and) his master finds him, he pays him twelve half-shekels of silver; and he gives his farm buildings as security.

21

(53) If anyone steals the slave of a Luwiyan man from the country of Luwiyas and brings him to the country of Hatti (and) his master finds him, he gets just his slave; (there is) no recompense.

22

(56) If a slave runs away and anyone brings him back, if he captures him nearby, he furnishes him (i.e. the captor) shoes; if on this side of the river, he pays two half-shekels of silver; if on the other side of the river, he pays him three half-shekels of silver.

23

(1.59) *ták-ku* ERUM-*iš ḫu-u-wa-i na-aš A-NA* KUR ^{URU}*LU-Ú-I-YA pa-iz-zi ku-i-ša-an a-ap-pa* (1.60) *ú-wa-te-iz-zi nu-uš-še* 6 *ZU* KUBABBAR *pa-a-i ták-ku* ERUM-*aš ḫu-wa-a-i* (1.61) *na-aš ku-ru-ri-i* KUR-*e pa-iz-zi ku-i-ša-an* EGIR-*pa-ma ú-wa-te-iz-zi* (1.62) *na-an-za-an a-pa-a-aš-be da-a-i*

24

(1.63) *ták-ku* ERUM-*aš na-aš-ma* GÌM-*aš ḫu-wa-a-i iš-ḫa-aš-ši-ša-an ku-e-el ḫa-aš-ši-i* (1.64) *ú-e-mi-ya-zi* LÚ-*na-aš ku-uš-ša-an* ITU 1.KAM 12 *ZU* KUBABBAR *pa-a-i* (1.65) SAL-*ša-ma ku-ša-an* ITU 1.KAM 6 *ZU* KU[BABBAR] *pa-a-i*

25

(1.66) [*ták-k*]*u* [L]Ú.GÀL.LU-*aš* ^{DUG}UTÚL-*i na-aš-ma lu-li-ya pa-ap-ri-iz-zi ka-ru-ú* (1.67) [6 *Z*]*U* KUBABBAR *pí-iš-kir pa-ap-ri-iz-zi ku-iš* 3 *ZU* KUBABBAR *pa-a-i* [É.GA]L-*an-na pár-na* (1.68) 3 *ZU* KUBABBAR *da-aš-ki-e-ir ki-nu-na* LUGAL-*uš ŠA* É.GAL-*LIM* [*pí-eš-ši*]-*it ku-iš pa-ap-ri-iz-zi* (1.69) *nu a-pa-a-aš-be* 3 *Z*[*U* KUBAB]BAR *pa-a-i pár-na-aš*-[*š*]*e-a šu-wa-i-iz-zi*

* * * * *

28

(2.5) *ták-ku* DUMU.SAL LÚ-*ni ta-ra-an-za ta-ma-i-ša-an pít-te-nu-zi ku*-[*i*]*š-ša*-[*a*]*n* (2.6) *pít-te-nu-uz-zi-ma nu ḫa-an-te-iz-zi-ya-aš* LÚ-*aš ku-it ku-i*[*t ku-uš-ša-ta*] (2.7) *ta-aš-še šar-ni-ik-zi at-ta-aš-ša an-na-aš Ú-UL šar-ni-in-kán*-[*z*]*i* (2.8) *ták-ku-wa-an at-ta-aš an-na-aš-ša ta-me-e-da-ni* LÚ-*ni pí-an-z*[*i*] (2.9) *nu at-ta-aš an-na-aš-ša šar-ni-in-kán-zi ták-ku at-ta-aš an-na-aš-ša* (2.10) *mi-im-ma-i na-an-ši-kán tu-uḫ-ša-an-ta*

29

(2.11) *ták-ku* DUMU.SAL-*aš* LÚ-*ni ḫa-me-in-kán-za nu-uš-ši ku-ú-ša-ta be-da-iz-zi* (2.12) *ap-pí-iz-zi-na-at at-ta-aš an-na-aš ḫu-ul-la-an-zi na-an-kán* LÚ-*ni* (2.13) *túḫ-ša-an-zi ku-ú-ša-ta-ma* 2-*ŠU šar-ni-in-kán-zi*

30

(2.14) *ták-ku* LÚ-*ša* DUMU.SAL *na-ú-i da-a-i na-an-za mi-im-ma-i ku-ú-ša-ta-ma* (2.15) *ku-it be-da-a-it na-aš-kán ša-me-en-zi*

23

(59) If a slave runs away and he goes to the country of Luwiyas, he pays whoever brings him back, six half-shekels of silver. (60) If a slave runs away, and he goes to a hostile country, whoever nevertheless brings him back, himself gets the slave.

24

(63) If a male or female slave runs away, (the man) at whose hearth his master finds him, pays as wages of a man for one month twelve half-shekels of silver, but he pays as wages of a woman for one month six half-shekels of silver.

25

(66) If a man puts filth into a pot or a cistern, formerly they paid six half-shekels of silver; he who puts the filth in pays three half-shekels of silver, and they used to take three half-shekels of silver for the palace court (?), and now the king has remitted (the share) of the palace. (69) The very one who puts the filth in (still) pays three half-shekels of silver; and he gives his farm buildings as security.

* * * * *

28

(5) If a girl is promised to a man, and another elopes with her, whatever the bride-price (paid) by the first man, (the one) who elopes with her, makes restitution to him; and (her) father (and) mother do not make restitution. (8) If (her) father and mother give her to the other man, (her) father and mother make restitution; if (her) father and mother refuse, they take her away from him.

29

(11) If a girl is betrothed to a man, and he pays the bride-price for her, (and) afterwards (her) father (and) mother violate it (i.e. the marriage contract), and take her away from the man, they return the bride-price in double the amount.

30

(14) If a man has not yet taken a girl, and he refuses her, he loses the bride-price which he has brought.

31

(2.16) *ták-ku* LÚ-*aš* *EL-LUM* GÌM-*aš-ša ši-e-li-eš na-at an-da a-ra-an-zi* (2.17) *na-an-za A-NA* DAM-*ŠU da-a-i nu-za* É-*ir Ù* DUMU.MEŠ *i-en-zi* (2.18) *ap-pí-iz-zi-an-na-at-kán na-aš-šu i-da-a-la-u-e-eš-ša-an-zi* (2.19) *na-aš-ma-at-kán ḫar-pa-an-ta-ri nu-za* É-*ir ták-ša-an šar-ra-an-zi* (2.20) DUMU.MEŠ-*az* LÚ-*aš da-a-i* 1 DUMU-*AM* SAL-*za da-a-i*

32

(2.21) *ták-ku-za* ERUM-*iš* SAL-*an* DA[M-*i*]*n da-a-i DI-IN-ŠU-NU QA-TAM-MA-be*

33

(2.22) *ták-ku-za* ERUM-*iš* GÌM-*an da-a-i DI-IN-ŠU-NU QA-TAM-MA-be*

34

(2.23) *ták-ku* ERUM-*iš* *A-NA* SAL-*TIM ku-ú-ša-ta be-da-a-iz-*[*z*]*i na-a*[*n-z*]*a* (2.24) *A-NA* DAM-*ŠU da-a-i na-an-kán pa-ra-a Ú-UL ku-iš-ki tar-na-i*

35

(2.25) *ták-ku* SAL-*an* *EL-LUM* ^{LÚ}AGRIG *na-aš-ma* ^{LÚ}SIPAD *pít-*[*t*]*e-n*[*u-z*]*i* (2.26) *ku-ú-ša-ta-aš-ši Ú-UL be-da-a-iz-zi na-aš I-*[*N*]*A* [M]U 3 [KAM GÌM]-*ša-ri-eš-zi*

36

(2.27) *ták-ku* ERUM-*iš* *A-NA* DUMU.NITA *EL-LIM ku-ú-ša-ta be-d*[*a-a-iz*]*-zi* (2.28) *na-an* ^{LÚ}*an-ti-ya-an-ta-an e-ip-zi na-an-kán pa-ra-a* [*Ú*]*-UL ku-*[*i*]*š-ki tar-na-i*

37

(2.29) *ták-ku* SAL-*an ku-*[*iš-k*]*i pít-te-nu-uz-zi* EGIR-*an-da-m*[*a*]*-a*[*š-m*]*a-aš-š*[*a š*]*ar-di-ya-aš pa-iz-zi* (2.30) *ták-ku* 2 LÚ.MEŠ *n*[*a*]*-a*[*š-m*]*a* 3 LÚ.MEŠ *ak-kán-zi šar-ni-ik-zi-i*[*l*] NU.GÁ[L *z*]*i-ik-wa* UR.BAR.RA *ki-ša-at*

38

(2.31) *ták-ku* LÚ.GÀL.LU.ME[Š *ḫa-a*]*n-ne-eš-ni ap-pa-an-te-eš nu-uš-m*[*a*]*-a*[*š*] *š*[*ar*]*-d*[*i-y*]*a-aš ku-iš-ki pa-iz-zi* (2.32) *na-aš-ta* [*ḫa-an-ni-i*]*t-tal-wa-aš kar-tim-mi-ya-an-ta-ri nu šar-di-ya-an* (2.33) *wa-al-aḫ-z*[*i n*]*a-aš a-ki šar-ni-ik-zi-il* NU.GÁL

* * * * *

31

(16) If a free man and a slave woman (are) in love (?) and come together (?), and he takes her for his wife, and they establish a household and have children, and afterwards they become incompatible or agree (to separate), and they divide the household, the man gets the children and the woman gets one child.

32

(21) If a slave takes a woman as his wife, their case is the same.

33

(22) If a slave takes a female slave, their case is the same.

34

(23) If a slave brings the bride-price for a woman, and (tries to) take her for his wife, no one surrenders (?) her.

35

(25) If an AGRIG or a shepherd elopes with a free woman, (and) does not bring the bride-price for her, she becomes a slave for three years.

36

(27) If a slave brings the marriage-price for a free young man, and (tries to) take him as husband (of his daughter?), no one surrenders him.

37

(29) If anyone elopes with a woman, and a rescuer goes after them, if two men or three men die, (there is) no recompense: 'You have become a wolf.'

38

(31) If men are arrested for trial, and anyone comes as a rescuer for them, and the opponents-at-law quarrel, and (someone) strikes the rescuer and he dies, (there is) no recompense.

* * * * *

40

(2.37) *ták-ku* LÚ ^{GIŠ}[TUKUL *ḫa*]*r-ak-zi* LÚ *IL-KI ti-it-ti-an-za nu* L[Ú] *I*[*L*]-*K*[*I*] *te-iz-zi* (2.38) *ki-i* ^{GIŠ}TUKUL-[*l*]*i-me-it ki-i-ma ša-aḫ-ḫa-mi-it nu-za ŠA* LÚ ^{GIŠ}TUKUL A.ŠA(G).ḪI.A (2.39) *an-da ši-y*[*a-at-t*]*a-ri-ya-zi* ^{GIŠ}TUKUL-*ya ḫar-zi ša-aḫ-ḫa-na iš-š*[*a-i*] (2.40) *ták-ku* ^{GIŠ}TUKUL [*mi-i*]*m-ma-i nu* A.ŠA(G).ḪI.A *ŠA* LÚ ^{GIŠ}TUKUL *ḫar-kán-ta-an š*[*a-me-en-zi*] (2.41) *na-an* LÚ.MEŠ URU-*r*[*i a*]*n-ni-eš-kán-zi ma-a-an* LUGAL-*uš* NAM.RA.ḪI.A *pa-a-i* (2.42) *nu-uš-ši* A.ŠA(G).ḪI.A *d*[*a-a*]*n-zi na-aš* <LÚ>^{GIŠ}TUKUL *ki-ša-ri*

41

(2.43) *ták-ku* LÚ *IL-KI ḫar-ak-zi nu* LÚ ^{GIŠ}TUKUL *ti-it-ti-an-za nu* LÚ ^{GIŠ}TUKUL *te-iz-zi* (2.44) *ki-i* ^{GIŠ}TUKUL-*li-me-it ki-i-ma ša-aḫ-ḫa-me-it nu-za ŠA* LÚ *IL-KI* A.ŠA(G).ḪI.A (2.45) *an-da ši-ya-at-ta-ri-i-e-iz-zi nu* ^{GIŠ}TUKUL *ḫar-zi ša-aḫ-ḫa-an* (2.46) *iš-ša-i ma-a-an ša-aḫ-ḫa-an mi-im-ma-i nu ŠA* LÚ *IL-KI* A.ŠA(G).ḪI.A (2.47) *I-NA* É.GAL-*LIM da-an-zi ša-aḫ-ḫa-an-na ḫar-ak-zi*

42

(2.48) *ták-ku an-tu-uḫ-ša-an ku-iš-ki ku-uš-ša-ni-i-e-iz-zi na-aš la-aḫ-ḫa pa-iz-zi* (2.49) *na-aš a-ki ták-ku ku-uš-ša-an pí-ya-an šar-ni-ik-zi-il* [NU.GÁL] (2.50) *ták-ku ku-uš-ša-an-še-it Ú-UL pí-ya-a-an* 1 SAG.DU *pa-a-i* (2.51) *ku-uš-ša-an-na* 12 *ZU* KUBABBAR *pa-a-i Ù ŠA* SAL *ku-uš-ša-an* 6 *ZU* KUBABBAR *pa-a-i*

43

(2.52) *ták-ku* LÚ-*aš* GUD-*ŠU* ÍD-*an zi-nu-uš-ki-iz-zi ta-ma-i-ša-an šu-ú-w*[*a*]-*iz-zi* (2.53) *nu* KUN GUD *e-ip-zi ta* ÍD-*an za-a-i nu BE-EL* GUD ÍD-*aš pí-e-da-i nu a-pu-ú-un-be da-an-zi*

* * * * *

57

(3.26) *ták-ku* GUD.MAḪ *ku-iš-ki ta-ya-az-zi ták-ku* GUD *ša-ú-i-ti-iš-za Ú-UL* GUD.M[A]Ḫ-*aš* (3.27) *ták-ku* GUD *i-ú-ga-aš Ú-UL* GUD.MAḪ-*aš ták-ku* GUD *ta-a-i-ú-ga-aš a-pa-a-aš* GUD.MAḪ-*aš* (3.28) *ka-ru-ú* 30 GUD.ḪI.A *pí-eš-kir ki-nu-na* 15 GUD.ḪI.A *pa-a-i* 5 *ta-a-i-ú-ga-aš* (3.29) 5 GUD *i-ú-ga-aš* 5 GUD *ša-a-ú-i-ti-iš-za pa-a-i pár-na-aš-še-e-a šu-wa-a-iz-zi*

* * * * *

40

(37) If a soldier disappears (and) a tenant farmer (is) assigned (to the soldier's farm), and the tenant farmer says: 'This (is) my military service, and this (is) my service to the landlord', and he takes over the soldier's farm, he both bears arms and performs service to the landlord. (40) If he refuses military service, he loses the vacated farm of the soldier, and the people in the village work it. (41) If the king sends a captive, they take the farm for him, and he becomes a soldier.

41

(43) If a tenant farmer disappears, and a soldier is assigned (to the tenant's farm), and the soldier says: 'This (is) my military service, and this (is) my service to the landlord', and he takes over the tenant farmer's farm, he bears arms (and) performs service to the landlord. (46) If he refuses service to the landlord, they take the tenant farmer's farm for the palace, and the service to the landlord ceases.

42

(48) If anyone hires a man and he goes to war and he dies, if the wages (have been) paid, there is no compensation. (50) If his wages (have) not (been) paid, he gives (in recompense) one person, and he pays twelve half-shekels of silver as wages, and as wages of a woman he pays six half-shekels of silver.

43

(52) If a man is driving his ox across a river, and another (man) pushes him (aside), and seizes the ox's tail and crosses the river, and the river carries the owner of the ox (away), they take him (i.e. the second man, as a slave?).

* * * * *

57

(26) If anyone steals a bull—if (it is) a calf of the same year (it is) not a bull, if (it is) a yearling (it is) not a bull, if (it is) a two-year-old, that (is) a bull—formerly they gave (in recompense) thirty cattle, and now he gives fifteen cattle—he gives five of two years, five cattle of one year, and five cattle of the same year; and he gives his farm buildings as security.

* * * * *

60

(3.37) *ták-ku* GUD.MAḪ *ku-iš-ki ú-e-mi-e-iz-zi ta-an pár-ku-nu-zi iš-ḫa-aš-ši-ša-an ga-n[e-eš-zi]* (3.38) 7 GUD.ḪI.A *pa-a-i* 2 GUD MU 2 3 GUD MU 1 2 GUD *ša-ú-i-ti-iš-za pa-a-i* (3.39) *pár-na-aš-še-e-a šu-wa-a-iz-zi*

* * * * *

66

(3.51) *ták-ku* GUD.APIN.LAL *ták-ku* ANŠU.KUR.RA *tu-u-ri-ya-u-wa-aš ták-ku* GUD.ÁB *ták-ku* EMÈ.AL.LAL (3.52) *ḫa-a-li-ya-aš ḫar-ap-ta ták-ku* MÁŠ.GA[L] *e-na-an-za ták-ku* UDU.SÍG+SAL *ták-ku* UDU.NITÁ (3.53) *a-ša-ú-ni ḫar-ap-ta iš-ḫa-aš-ši-ša-[an] ú-e-mi-ya-az-zi* (3.54) *na-an-za ša-ku-wa-aš-šar-ra-an-be d[a]-a-i* ^{LÚ}NÍ.ZU-*an* *Ú-UL e-ip-zi*

* * * * *

71

(3.63) *ták-ku* GUD-*un* ANŠU.KUR.RA ANŠU.GÌR.NUN.NA-*an ku-iš-ki ú-e-mi-ya-zi na-an* LUGAL-*an a-aš-ka* (3.64) *u-un-na-i ták-ku ut-ni-ya-ma ú-e-mi-ya-zi na-an* $^{LÚ.MEŠ}$ŠU.GI-*aš ḫi-in-kán-zi* (3.65) *na-an-za tu-u-ri-iš-ki-iz-zi ma-a-na-an iš-ḫa-aš-ši-ša ú-e-mi-ya-zi* (3.66) *na-an-za ša-ku-wa-aš-ša-ra-an da-a-i* ^{LÚ}NÍ.ZU-*an na-at-ta e-ip-zi* (3.67) *ták-ku-wa-an* $^{LÚ.MEŠ}$ŠU.GI-*aš* *Ú-UL ḫi-in-ga-zi na-aš* ^{LÚ}NÍ.ZU *ki-ša-ri*

60

(37) If anyone finds a bull and removes the mark of ownership (?), and its owner finds it, he gives (in recompense) seven cattle—he gives two cattle of two years, three cattle of one year, (and) two cattle of the same year; and he gives his farm buildings as security.

* * * * *

66

(51) If a plough ox or a harness horse or a cow or a female pack-ass gets into (someone's) corrals, if a large tame (?) goat or a ewe or a ram gets into (someone's) fold, and its owner finds it, he receives it in good condition; he does not seize him (as) guilty.

* * * * *

71

(63) If anyone finds an ox, a horse, (or) a mule, he takes it to the royal gate. (64) But if he finds it in the country, and the elders adjudge (?) it (to him), he has the use of it. (65) And if its owner finds it, he receives it in good condition; he does not seize him (as) guilty. (67) If the elders do not adjudge it (to him), he becomes guilty.

COMMENTARY

The Hittite code, like all other legal systems, was of gradual growth, and many evidences of development are to be observed in the documents themselves. In general the several provisions are ultimately based upon precedent, and so we need not be surprised to find that some of the offenses described cannot have been of frequent occurrence; a single case is enough to set a precedent (cf. paragraphs 13, 38, 43).

Although the selections here presented do not belong to the latest recension of the code (the one partially preserved in KBo.6.4), they certainly received their present form during the second empire (ca. 1450–1200 B.C.). They are based, however, upon a code that must have been drawn up during the first empire, as is shown by many linguistic archaisms (e.g. *tan* = *nan* — 1.25; *ta-se* 'et ei' — 2.7; *-aku* . . . *-aku* 'whether . . . or' — 1.2, 1.5; frequent asyndeton, as in 1.6, 1.10).

Our text generally follows that of Hrozný, CH 2–60, being based upon KBo.6.3; but we omit square brackets if any of the duplicate texts supply the gaps in the main text, and in two or three places we adopt the reading of another tablet in preference to KBo.6.3.

The Code has been translated by Hrozný, CH; Zimmern and Friedrich, AO 23.2; Walther, ap. J. M. P. Smith, The Origin and History of Hebrew Law 247–74. Friedrich presented an improved translation of several paragraphs in AO 24.3.27–30. There are important discussions of the code by Korošec, Zeitschrift der Savigny-Stiftung, Röm. Abt. 52.156–69, and by Götze, Kulturgeschichte 102–9.

1.2. [*ar-nu-z*]*i*: the meaning 'bury' is an inference from the use of the word in this and similar passages in the Code; cf. Gk. ἐκφέρω 'bury'. No doubt the courts compelled the murderer to pay the costs of the funeral. — LÚ-*na-ku* = *antuhsan-aku*; the noun agrees with the singular 4 SAG.DU, on which see [183].

1.3. [*pár-na-aš-še-e-a*]: see [201 fn. 88] and on H 1.33.

1.6 f. *ki-eš-šar-ši-iš* [*wa-aš-t*]*a-i*: i.e. he did not intend to kill.

1.8. *QA-AZ-ZU*: see [24d].

1.10. 1[1/2]: the tablet records 1 *ME* '100' both here and in 1.12; but that seems an unreasonably large sum. The signs for *ME* and for 1/2 differed so little that confusion was easy.

1.14. *ta-ki-ya*: the meaning is very uncertain. The corresponding paragraph of the later version of the Code (KBo.6.4.1.9–13) reads *da-me-*

e-da-ni, but the provisions there are certainly inconsistent with those of our paragraph, and so the words need not be equivalent. Walther, ap. J. M. P. Smith, The Origin and History of Hebrew Law 248, translates *ta-ki-ya* URU-*ri* 'in this or that village'. Götze suggests 'distant'. — *ar-ḫi*: the context requires the meaning 'on a farm'. For the etymology, see [74].

1.15. 1[1/2]: again (cf. on 1.10) the tablet reads 1 *ME*; but to judge by the measurements given in KUB 8.75, that would amount to a whole field. A very small space would suffice for burial purposes. — *da-a-i*: where it is a question of paying for burial we find *arnuzi*; but here the involuntary landlord must attend to the matter himself. Others interpret *da-a-i* as coming from *dā-* 'take'. Walther translates *na-an-za da-a-i* 'and he (the heir) may take it'. Götze suggests, 'and he (the deceased) gets it (for his burial)'. Some such interpretation as this would apparently harmonize better with the later version; cf. on *ta-ki-ya* (1.14).

1.24. *ZU*: Hrozný incorrectly read GÍN 'shekel'; see Sommer, BoSt. 10.35 f.

1.27. SIG_5-*at-ta-ri*: KBo.6.2.1.18 reads *la-a-az-zi-at-ta*.

1.31. *tu-wa-ar-na-zi*: contrast *twarnezi* (1.29), and see [297 and fn. 16].

1.33. *wa-ak-ki*: for the meaning, see Friedrich, AOr. 6.373–6. Of course it was never a common practice to bite an enemy's nose; and for that very reason the injury was the more humiliating on the one or two occasions when it was inflicted. Hence the unusually large fine. Since humiliation was of no consequence in the case of a slave, the next paragraph shows far more than the usual reduction of the fine.

1.36. Security is not usually required for the payment of so small a penalty; and the other recension of the first part of the Code (KBo. 6.4.1.35 f. = Hrozný, CH 84) lacks such a provision. Perhaps its inclusion here was an error.

1.37. LÚ.GÀL.LU-*aš* must be gen.; KBo.6.5.1.16 reads UKÙ-*an*, which corresponds to the acc. in the preceding paragraphs. — *iš-kal-la-a-ri*: see [111]. The middle voice here has no distinctive force.

1.40. Literally, 'if anyone throws away the entrails of a free woman'.

1.45. LÚ ^{URU}*Lu-ú-i-ya-*[*aš*]: the tablet reads *Lu-ú-i-ya-az*, doubtless with *az* from *Ḫa-at-tu-ša-az*. This is clearly the nominative corresponding to LÚ ^{URU}*Lu-ú-i-ya-an* (1.48).

1.46. KUR ^{URU}*AR-ZA-U-WA*: probably the Hittite form of the name was *Arzawas*; but it seems not to occur, and so we must use the Akkadian form. See on KUR ^{URU}*ḪA-AT-TI* (H 1.1).

1.47. É-*ir-še-it-be* 'his very house', i.e. all the slaves he has.

1.57. ÍD: no doubt, the Halys.

1.63–5. The two available texts do not agree. Hrozný restores as far as possible the fragmentary KBo.6.3.1.63–5; we have adopted instead the more nearly complete 6.2.1.54 f.

1.67. [É.GA]L-*an-na pár-na*: supplement, word-division, and meaning are all doubtful.

1.69. See on 1.36.

2.5. *ku-*[*i*]*š-ša-*[*a*]*n*: KBo.6.5.2.11 reads: *ku-uš-ša-*[*a*]*n*; Götze suggests the emendation, which involves only the addition of a vertical wedge to the sign for *uš*.

2.6. [*ku-uš-ša-ta*]: the supplement is Götze's.

2.7. *ta-aš-še* = *ta-se* 'et ei'.

2.9. The tablet reads: *ták-ku at-ta-aš-ša an-na-aš*.

2.10. *mi-im-ma-i*: the singular is very strange after the three plural verbs with the same subject.

2.11. *ḫa-me-in-kán-za* must mean something different from *taranza* (2.5), since the penalties differ in the two paragraphs. Either *hamenk-* denotes a legal betrothal (as against an informal promise) or it actually means 'marry'. — *be-da-iz-zi*: Güterbock, ZA NF 8.228 f., has shown that *beda*(*e*)- 'pay' must be distinguished from *pēdā-* 'bring'. It is probably a denominative verb from a noun related to *pēdā*.

2.12. *ap-pí-iz-zi-na-at* = *apezin-at*.

2.14. LÚ-*ša*: the conjunction -*a* is strange here, and the other recension lacks it; KBo.6.4.2.17: LÚ-*aš*. Perhaps we should assume an error.

2.18. *ap-pí-iz-zi-an*: cf. *apezin* (2.12).

2.19. *ḫar-pa-an-ta-ri*: Götze will demonstrate elsewhere that this verb means 'fasten together, join'; and in the middle, 'be associated, join (intrans.), agree'. Cf. below 3.52 f.

2.24. *pa-ra-ā . . . tar-na-i*: Götze, NBr. 73 f., interprets this phrase as 'enslave', partly because he feels that this paragraph and § 36 must deal with the same penalty as § 35. One might perhaps argue that the different wording points in just the opposite direction. Nevertheless, the interpretation adopted in the text is far from certain. Bechtel suggests, 'no one releases her (from the marriage)'.

2.25. LÚAGRIG: for a discussion of what little is known about the meaning of this word, see Deimel No. 452.

2.26. [GÌM]-*ša-ri-eš-zi*: cf. paragraph 175 (KBo.6.26.2.17 f.) which is a close parallel to paragraph 35, and reads: GÌM *e-eš-zi*. Probably our text contained the Hittite word spelled out in full.

2.27 f. The interpretation underlying our translation comes from Walther ap. J. M. P. Smith, The Origin and History of Hebrew Law 252. It is not altogether plausible, and so Bechtel suggests: 'If a slave provides the bride-price for a free son (i.e. the slave's son) and (the girl) takes him as her husband, no one releases her (from the contract)'. Perhaps the girl's parents tried to annul the marriage on the ground that the young man was the son of the slave. The difficulty is that the girl's father would have to accept the bride-price and the bride-groom, and it would be too violent a treatment of the text to understand that he is the subject of *epzi*. Götze thinks the paragraph may allude to homosexual marriage: 'If a slave brings the marriage price for a free young man, and takes him as mate, no one enslaves him'. But see Sommer, OLZ 38.281.

2.29 f. It is not clear which party suffers the casualties. Perhaps the rule is the same in either case, since both are using force to gain their objects.

2.29. *šar-di-ya-aš*: Götze now interprets this word as 'avenger', in spite of the vocabulary entry (KBo. 1.33.1); on which see Ungnad, OLZ 26.572 fn. 3; Friedrich, Vert. 1.167; Sommer, AU 180 fn. 3. He regards this paragraph and the next as survivals from a more primitive system, according to which the aggrieved party avenged his wrong with his own hand. The use of the verb *sartai-* (KBo.3.8.2.32), *sartiya-* (VBoT 120.3.10) does not harmonize with either interpretation of *sardiyas*.

2.32. [*ḫa-an-ni-i*]*t-tal-wa-aš*: Götze infers from *ḫa-an-ni-tal-wa-eš-šir* (KUB 21.17.1.3) 'they became opponents-at-law' that *hannittalwas* was synonymous with EN *DI-NI* (H 1.56, etc.).

2.37–47. See Götze, NBr. 54–9. Sommer, OLZ 38.280, cites a suggestion of Ungnad's that we read *IS-QU* 'share' rather than GIŠTUKUL in these paragraphs. I can get no satisfactory sense out of such a reading in the places where LÚ does not precede; for the word in question must correspond with *sahhan*.

2.39. *ša-aḫ-ḫa-an-na*: the translation 'service to the landlord' is not intended to imply that the landlord was a private person rather than a village or the king.

2.40. A.ŠA(G).ḪI.A: in spite of the Sumerian plural suffix the underlying Hittite word is singular, as is shown by the participle.

2.41. NAM.RA.ḪI.A: again the underlying Hittite word is singular; for KBo.6.2.2.22 reads NAM.RA.ḪI.A-*an*. For the use of the word, see on T 1.28.

2.42. *d*[*a-a*]*n-zi*: here and in 2.47 the word is virtually equivalent to its IE cognate, *dō-*.

3.37. *pár-ku-nu-zi* properly means 'cleanses'; Götze suggests the plausible interpretation given in the translation. Possibly *ši-ú-na-an* (T 2.32) is the name of such a mark of ownership; the nature of the mark is unknown.

3.38. MU 2, MU 1: the numerals in these phrases are written by horizontal wedges instead of the usual vertical wedges.

3.54. LÚNÍ.ZU: for the meaning, see Zimmern, ZA NF 2.319 f.

3.63. LUGAL-*an a-aš-ka*: see on I 2.56.

3.64. *na-an* LÚ.MEŠŠU.GI-*aš ḫi-in-kán-zi*: others translate 'they show (?) it to the elders', or the like. In favor of such an interpretation it may be urged (1) that it sharpens the contrast with the preceding sentence, and (2) that LÚ.MEŠŠU.GI-*aš* = LÚ.MEŠ*miyahuwantas* ought to be a dative, since *nt*-stems are more exact than other stems in the use of plural cases; cf. [182]. On the other hand, the meaning and the number of *henkanzi* favor our interpretation.

3.67. *ḫi-in-ga-zi*: probably for *henkanzi*; see [57].

ADDITIONS AND CORRECTIONS

P. 15, lines 15–6, for millenia, read millennia.

P. 27, under the sign *ḫar*, insert in the column of ideograms: ḪAR (GIŠ) *symbol, index, inventory.*

P. 32, under the sign KUŠ, add: 2. SU *omen from slaughtered animals.* Also in I 3.1 (p. 156) the reading should be changed to SU.

P. 34, under the sign NIN. This is a Sumerian reading for the sign, but not in the value 'sister', for which the correct Sumerian is unknown. Assyriologists generally call the sign SAL+KU, because in the standard Assyrian form it appears to be made up of these two signs. This would be misleading for Hittite, where the second element, by its four horizontal wedges, resembles TÚG rather than KU, which has only three. The signs KU and TÚG fell together in classical Assyrian. We might call the sign SAL+TÚG, but this would lead to more confusion, and so we have preferred to adopt the simpler reading NIN.

P. 39, line 7. The sign *tuḫ* should be read *túḫ*.

P. 54, line 66 beginning: for *nu-za* of autograph, read *nu-mu.*

P. 58, line 71 end: for 1-*aš e-ḫu,* read *nu-wa e-ḫu.*

P. 58, line 76 middle: for *ku-ru-ur,* read *ku-u-ru-ur.*

P. 58, line 78 beginning: for *ma-a-an,* read *ma-an.*

P. 59, line 9. Before LÚ*MU-DI-KA*, insert *A-NA*.

P. 60, line 30. There should be a space between the signs for *Ú-UL* and *ma-an-qa.*

P. 61, line 46 beginning: for *ku-i-e-eš,* read *ku-i-e-eš-ma.*

P. 86, line 9, insert: This verb primarily means 'fix, establish, determine'. The compound *parā handa(e)-* requires a god as its subject, and the verbal nouns *parā handātar* and *parā handandātar* clearly mean something like 'numen, divine power'. The preverb *parā* may have about the force of Lat. *prō* in *prōdūcere, prōferre,* etc., and suggest an emanation from the godhead. The phrase might be translated 'control by divine emanation'. The participle seems to me to carry some such meaning in H 1.47, and even more clearly in KUB 24.3.1.40: *pa-ra-a ḫa-an-da-an-za-ša-kán* (41) *an-[t]u-(uḫ)-wa-aḫ-ḫa-aš tu-uk-be A-NA* D*UTU* [URU]*A-RI-IN-NA aš-ši-ya-an-za* 'and the divinely controlled man is dear to thee, sun goddess of Arinna'. That the participle is sometimes used of a god is not strange; any human quality may be ascribed to a god. As to the two forms of the verbal noun, perhaps *parā handātar* emphasizes the subjective 'numen,' while *parā handātar,* being based upon the denominative from the participial stem, emphasizes rather the effect or manifestation of the power. Our texts, however, do not disclose any difference in meaning; see Götze, Hatt. 53 and fn. 2.

P. 97, line 15 from end: insert a *glossenkeil* before *ḫu-u-um-ma.*

P. 101, line 38 beginning: for *ap-pí-iz-zi-ya-az* of autograph, read *ḫa-an-te-iz-zi-ya-az.*

P. 102, line II.1: for *ki-e-iz-zi*, read *ki-e-iz-zi-ya*.
P. 102, line 2 beginning: for *nam-ma*, read *na-aš-ta*.
P. 103, A 3.4: see correction to p. 112.
P. 105, line 12: for *ša-ra*, read *ša-ra-a*.
P. 112, A 3.4: for *ú-i-ya-an-zi*, read *ú-i-ya-mi*. Cf. A 4.14: *ú-i-ya-iš-ki-mi*.
P. 114, line 7 from end. Read DA.KUR$_4$.RA.ḪIA-*ya*.
P. 120, line 14. After verb, insert: as also in 3.37. In both places *ehu* is accompanied by a preverb and the particle *-kan*. In KUB 24.1.1.13 = 24.2.1.11 it has the preverb *anda*, but not the particle.
P. 121, line 10 from end. Add: Güterbock would write *pád-da-an-zi*.
P. 122, line 20: see correction to p. 112.
P. 123, line 2. Add: The acc. *isnūran* 'dough' (KBo. 6.34.1.32) must be metaplastic if the proposed etymology is correct. There is, however, no recorded form of the word that cannot be derived from an *a*-stem.
P. 123. Insert after line 10: A 3.10 *ga-la-ak-tar*: this word is evidently a verbal noun in *-tar*; but here, as well as in 3.31, 4.19, and elsewhere, it denotes a concrete substance. KUB 17.10.2.12 f. suggests that it is from *galānk-* 'appease, propitiate'; in which case it should mean 'appeasement, means of appeasing'. See on *mu-ki-eš-šar* (A 4.17).
P. 132, line 10 beginning: Insert LÚ in the autograph before *a-ra-aḫ-zé-na-aš*.
P. 132, line 21 beginning: Insert crossed wedges in autograph to correspond to... in the transliteration.
P. 136, line 80 end, *ḫa-li-ya-aš*: The sign *ya* lacks a vertical wedge. See the Sign List for correct form.
P. 139, line 37 middle, *ku-iš-ki*: The sign *ki* should have a vertical wedge at the end.
P. 140, line 60 last word: for the sign *ga* in the autograph, substitute *ta*.
P. 145, line 44 middle: for *ḫu-u-da-ak* in the autograph, read *ḫu-u-da-a-ak*.
P. 146, line 61 end: for ŠA(G) *uš-ni*, read ŠA(G) KASKAL-*ni*.
P. 156, I 3.1: see correction to p. 32.
P. 173, line 9. Add: Bechtel prefers to translate 48–51 as follows: But if (there is) any flame here and there and dry wood, and he who quenches it (i.e. whose duty it is to quench it) (and) to whom subsequently error befalls (i.e. he fails to put the fire entirely out) within the temple of his god, and nevertheless only the temple is destroyed, while Hattusas and the king's estate are not destroyed—(then) he who commits the error is likewise destroyed along with his descendants.

www.ingramcontent.com/pod-product-compliance
Lightning Source LLC
Chambersburg PA
CBHW060623250426
43670CB00056B/1943

* 9 7 8 1 7 2 5 2 8 0 1 5 1 *